A

PRACTICAL GRAMMAR

OF THE

ENGLISH LANGUAGE

BY

THOS. W. HARVEY, A. M.

Originally published by
Van Antwerp, Bragg & Co.

This edition published by

**MOTT
MEDIA**

PRESENT PUBLISHER'S PREFACE

Thomas W. Harvey's *English Grammar* has been a classic for over a century. It was first published by the same company which produced the McGuffey Readers, and it had great influence on several generations of American students. It is a complete grammar, and thus is appropriate for advanced study, beginning in about seventh grade, and for a lifetime of reference use after that.

In updating this textbook, we revised the punctuation section and punctuation usage throughout the book to conform to contemporary usage. In grammar, a few rules were dropped and a few added, but grammatical rules change slowly over time, so not much of this revising was necessary. Usage changes somewhat more rapidly, so we had some updatings in verb forms, phraseology, hyphenations, and forms of friendly and business letters. Many of Harvey's examples are from the Bible and other literature, so they are left as they were, but some of the everyday examples are updated. A sentence about a horse and buggy, for instance, may be rewritten to one about a car.

All revisions conform to the authority of *Webster's New International Dictionary, Second Edition*. Other standard references were consulted as needed during the work. Several comments from *The Elements of Style* by Strunk and White have been quoted herein to bring insight to difficult language problems. For the masterful job of updating this textbook, credit belongs to Eric C. Wiggin.

Through all the revisions, we have left the content as close to the original as possible. The famous Harvey grammar is here for modern users. We proudly present this classic to students and their teachers everywhere.

George M. Mott, President
MOTT MEDIA, INC.

PREFACE

Accuracy and facility in the use of language, both spoken and written, are the chief ends to be secured by the study of grammar. To secure these ends, a thorough acquaintance with the elements, forms, structure, and laws of our mother tongue, is indispensable; and a practical knowledge of these can be acquired only by patient, persistent exercise in he analysis and synthesis of syllables, words, and sentences.

The plan of this treatise is in strict accordance with this educational doctrine. The author has endeavored to present the subject in a simple, concise, and perspicuous manner, and to furnish such "models" for necessary routine work as the student may use to the best advantage. He would call special attention to these "models," and suggest that more attention be paid to those relating to synthesis than most teachers have heretofore thought advisable. He has purposely avoided the discussion of mere theories; preferring, rather, a plain didactic statement or clear indication of his own views, especially on those points that annoy and perplex both pupil and teacher. Experience has taught him that such discussions serve only to confuse and discourage the beginner, and are of questionable utility to the advanced student. Neither the erudition of the teacher nor the exhaustive completenes of the text book used, can compensate for the lack of intelligent, systematic *drill* in the classroom.

Actuated by a desire to render the labor of the classroom more pleasant and effective, by furnishing an attractive means for instruction in a useful branch of study, the author ventures the hope that this revision will commend itself to the favorable notice and consideration of his fellow teachers.

October, 1878

CONTENTS

PROSODY

DIAGRAMS

ENGLISH GRAMMAR

1. DEFINITIONS

1. A **word** is the sign of an idea.

2. **Language** is the expression of thought by means of words. It may be either *spoken* or *written*.

Spoken language is the expression of ideas by the *voice*.

Written language is the expression of ideas by the use of *written or printed characters* representing sounds.

3. **Grammar** treats of the principles and usages of language.

4. **English grammar** teaches how to speak and write the English language correctly.

5. English grammar is divided into four parts: *orthography*, *etymology*, *syntax*, and *prosody*.

6. **Orthography** treats of elementary sounds, letters, syllables, and spelling.

7. **Etymology** treats of the classification, derivation, and properties of words.

8. **Syntax** treats of the construction of sentences.

9. **Prosody** treats of the quantity of syllables, of accent, and of the laws of versification.

PART I

ORTHOGRAPHY

2. DEFINITIONS

1. **Orthography** treats of elementary sounds, letters, syllables, and spelling.

2. An **elementary sound** is one which cannot be separated into two or more distinct sounds.

3. A **letter** is a character used to represent either an elementary sound or a combination of elementary sounds; as, *a, x.*

Letters are divided into *vowels* and *consonants.* Vowels are used to represent *vocals*; consonants, to represent *subvocals* and *aspirates.*

4. A **syllable** is a sound or a combination of sounds uttered with one impulse of the voice, and may be represented by a letter or a group of letters; as, *man, man-ner, man-u-mit.*

5. A **word** is either a syllable or a combination of syllables; as, *hat, men-tion, phi-los-o-phy.*

3. ELEMENTARY SOUNDS

1. There are forty-two elementary sounds in the English language.

2. They are divided into *vocals*, *subvocals*, and *aspirates.*

3. **Vocals** are those sounds which are made with the vocal organs open, and consist of pure tone only. They are also called *tonics.*

4. **Subvocals** are those sounds which are obstructed by the vocal organs in the process of articulation. They are sometimes called *subtonics.*

5. **Aspirates** are mere emissions of breath, articulated by the lips, tongue, teeth, and palate. They are sometimes called *atonics.*

TABLE OF ELEMENTARY SOUNDS

4. VOCALS

ā	long, as in lāte	ī	long, as in tīme
ă	short, as in hăt	ĭ	short, as in tĭn
å	middle, as in tålk	ō	long, as in cōld
ä	Italian, as in ärm	ŏ	short, as in hŏt
a̤	broad, as in a̤ll	o͞o	long, as in o͞oze
â	double, as in câre	o͝o	short, as in bo͝ok
ē	long, as in ēve	ū	long, as in lūte
ĕ	short, as in ĕll	ŭ	short, as in cŭp
ẽ	as in ẽrr		

5. SUBVOCALS AND ASPIRATES

1. **Subvocals and aspirates** may be divided into six classes, viz.:

Labials, or *lip sounds*, which are made by the lips;

Linguals, or *tongue sounds*, made by the tongue;

Linguo-dentals, or *tongue-teeth sounds*, made by the tongue and teeth;

Linguo-nasals, or *tongue-nose sounds*, articulated by the tongue, the sound passing through the nose;

Palato-nasals, or *palate-nose sounds*, made by the palate, the sound passing through the nose;

Palatals, or *palate sounds*, made by the palate.

2. The *subvocals* are arranged on the left of the page, and the corresponding *aspirates* on the right.

LABIALS

b, as in bib	**p**, as in lip
v, as in save	**f**, as in life
w, as in way	**wh**, as in when
m, as in am	

LINGUO-DENTALS

d, as in lid	**t**, as in tat
th, as in this	**th**, as in thin
j, as in jar	**ch**, as in rich
z, as in size	**s**, as in hiss
z, as in azure (azh ′ur)	**sh**, as in hush

LINGUALS

l, as in lull
r, as in roar
(Have no corresponding aspirates.)

LINGUO-NASAL

n, as in man
(Has no corresponding aspirate.)

PALATO-NASAL

ng, as in song
(Has no corresponding aspirate.)

PALATALS

$\overline{g}$, as in nag
y, as in yes

k, as in kick
(Has no corresponding aspirate.)
h, as in how

Rem.—The sounds respresented by *l*, *m*, *n*, and *r*, are sometimes called *liquids*, because they easily unite with other subvocals or aspirates.

6. LETTERS

There are twenty-six **letters** in the English alphabet. As there are more elementary sounds than letters, it becomes necessary that some letters represent more than one sound. Letters also combine to represent sounds for which there are no single representatives, and the same sound is frequently common to a number of letters. Letters and combinations of letters are often used as substitutes for other letters.

7. DIPHTHONGS, DIGRAPHS, AND TRIGRAPHS

1. A **diphthong** consists of two vocals sounded together in the same syllable.

Rem.—There are two diphthongal sounds, represented by four diphthongs, viz.: *ou*, *ow*, *oi*, *oy*, as in *foul*, *now*, *boil*, *cloy*.

2. A **digraph** consists of two vowels written together in the same syllable, one only being pronounced, or both representing a single elementary sound.

Rem.—There are twenty-four digraphs, viz.: *aa*, Canaan; *ae*, Gaelic; *ai*, gain; *au*, maul; *aw*, maw; *ay*, may; *ea*, meat; *ee*, need; *ei*, ceiling; *eo*, people; *eu*, feud; *ew*, new; *ey*, they; *ie*, thief; *oa*, coat; *oe*, foe; *oi*, avoirdupois; *oo*, moon; *ou*, tour; *ow*, flow; *ua*, guard; *ue*, sue; *ui*, guise; *uy*, buy.

3. A **trigraph** consists of three vowels written together in the same syllable, one only being pronounced, or the three together representing a single vocal sound, or diphthong.

Rem. 1—There are eight trigraphs, viz.: *aye*, aye; *awe*, awe; *eau*, beau, beauty; *eou*, gorgeous; *eye*, eye; *ieu*, lieu; *iew*, view, *owe*, owe.

Rem. 2—In such words as *Christian*, *alien*, *union*, *i* does not form a digraph with the following vowel, but is a substitute for *y*. In the unaccented terminations *cean*, *cial*, *sion*, *tion*, the combinations *ce*, *ci*, *si*, *ti*, are substitutes for *sh*.

Rem. 3—In such words as *herbaceous*, *gracious*, *precious*, *e* and *i* do not form trigraphs with the following vowels, but the combinations *ce*, *ci* are substitutes for *sh*.

8. DOUBLE CONSONANTS

Double consonants consist of two consonants written together in the same syllable, representing a single elementary sound.

Rem.—They are *ch*, chaise, chord; *gh*, laugh; *ph*, physic; *sh*, hush; *th*, thin, this; *wh*, when; *ng*, sing.

9. SUBSTITUTES

A **substitute** represents a sound usually represented by another letter or combination of letters.

A *long* has three substitutes: *ê*, tête; *ei*, feint; *ey*, they.

A as in *air* has two substitutes: *e*, there; *ei*, heir.

A *broad* has two substitutes: *o*, cord; *ou*, sought.

E *long* has three substitutes: *i*, marine; *ie*, fiend; *ay*, quay.

E *short* has three substitutes: *ay*, says; *u*, bury; *ie*, friend.

E as in *er* has three substitutes: *i*, sir; *y*, myrrh; *o*, work.

I *long* has three substitutes: *y*, thyme; *ei*, Steinway; *oi*, choir.

I *short* has six substitutes: *y*, hymn; *e*, England; *u*, busy; *o*, women; *ee*, been; *ai*, captain.

O *long* has three substitutes: *eau*, beau; *ew*, sew; *oa*, goal.

O *short* has two substitutes: *a*, what; *ow*, knowledge.

U *long* has five substitutes: *eau*, beauty; *ieu*, lieu; *iew*, view; *ew*, new; *ui*, suit.

U *short* has one substitute: *o*, son.

F has two substitutes: *gh*, laugh; *ph*, philosophy.

J has two substitutes: *g*, rage; *di*, soldier.

K has four substitutes: *c*, can; *ch*, chord; *ck*, black; *qu*, pique.

S has two substitutes: *c* before *e*, *i*, and *y*, center, cistern, cyst; *z*, quartz.

T has one substitute; *ed* final, after any aspirate except *t*.

V has two substitutes: *f*, of; *ph*, Stephen.

W has one substitute: *u*, quick. It is understood before *o* in *one*, *once*.

X is used as a substitute for *ks*, as in *wax*; *gz*, as in *exact*; *ksh*, as in *noxious*; *z*, as in *xenon*.

Y has one substitute: *i*, alien. It is frequently understood before *u*, as in *verdure*.

Z has three substitutes: *c*, sacrifice (sometimes); *s*, his; *x*, Xenia.

CH has one substitute: *ti*, question.

SH has six substitutes: *ce*, ocean; *ci*, facial; *si*, pension; *ti*, motion; *ch*, chaise; *s*, sugar.

ZH has four substitutes: *si*, fusion; *zi*, brazier; *z*, azure; *s*, measure.

NG has one substitute: *n*, generally before palatal sounds; as in *ink*, *uncle*, *conquer*.

10. FORMS OF THE LETTERS

1. **Letters** are of different styles; as, Roman, *Italic*, *Script*, Old English.

2. **Types** for printing are of various sizes:

Great Primer,
English,
Pica,

Small Pica,
Long Primer,
Bourgeois,
Brevier,

Minion,
Nonpareil,
Agate,
Pearl,
Diamond.

3. Letters are used either as capital letters or as small letters.

Rem.—Printers call small letters *lower case*.

11. CAPITAL LETTERS

1. The first word of every sentence, or the first word after a full pause, should begin with a capital letter.

Ex.—Winds blow. Snow falls. The heavens are aflame.

2. The first word after a formal introductory word or clause may begin with a capital letter.

Ex.—"*Resolved*, That the sum of three thousand dollars be appropriated," etc.

"Be it enacted by the General Assembly of the State of Ohio, That section fourteen," etc.

3. Each item of an enumeration of particulars, arranged in paragraphs, should begin with a capital letter.

Ex.—"These expenditures are in proportion to the whole expenditures of government:

>   In Austria, as thirty-three percent;
>   In France, as thirty-eight percent;
>   In Great Britain, as seventy-four percent."

4. The first word of a direct quotation, or of an important statement, a distinct speech, etc., should begin with a capital letter.

Ex.—"When thou saidst, Seek ye my face; my heart said unto thee, Thy face, Lord, will I seek." "Dora said, 'My uncle took the boy.'" "One truth is clear: Whatever is, is right."

5. The first word in every line of poetry usually begins with a capital letter.

Ex.—"Put your best foot foremost, or I fear
That we shall miss the mail: and here it comes
With five at top; as quaint a four in hand
As you shall see—three piebalds and a roan."

Rem.—In humorous poetry, when a word is divided at the end of a line, the first letter of the next line may be a capital or a small letter.

Ex.—"Faith, he's got the Knicker-
  Bocker Magazine."

>   "Here doomed to starve on water gru-
>   el, never shall I see the U-
>   niversity of Gottingen."

6. Proper names of persons, places, months, days, etc., should begin with capital letters.

Ex.—James, Emma, Boston, July, Wednesday, James Monroe, O. W. Holmes.

7. Titles of honor or distinction, used alone or accompanied by nouns, should begin with capital letters.

Ex.—*Earl* Russell; the *Duke* of York; *Mr.* Wilson; *Mrs.* Smith; *Dr.* Johnson; *General* Harrison; *Sir* Robert Peel; George the *Third*; Charles the *Bold.*

8. Names of things personified should usually begin with capital letters.

Ex.—"Come, gentle *Spring*! ethereal *Mildness*! come."

"In *Misery's* darkest cavern known,
His useful care was nigh,
When hopeless *Anguish* poured his groan,
And lonely *Want* retired to die."

9. The first and last words and all other words in headings and titles should begin with capital letters, except *a, an, the*, short conjunctions, and short prepositions.

Ex.—*A Practical Grammar of the English Language*; Directions to the Student; "I have read *The Tent on the Beach*."

10. All appelations of the Deity should begin with capital letters.

Ex.—God; the Most High; the Supreme; the Infinite One; Divine Providence; the Father, the Son, and the Holy Ghost; our Lord Jesus Christ.

Rem. 1—A word referring to the Deity, but not used as an appellation, should sometimes begin with a capital letter.

Ex.—"The *Hand* that made us is divine."
"The spangled heavens, a shining frame,
Their great *Original* proclaim."

Rem. 2—A pronoun, whose expressed antecedent is the name of the Diety, usually requires no capitals; as, "O *thou* merciful God!" "God provides for all *his* creatures."

Rem. 3—The pronouns *he, his, him, thy*, and *thee*, referring to names of the Deity, in sentences where their antecedents are understood, may sometimes begin with capital letters; as, "The hope of my spirit turns trembling to *Thee*"; "Trust in *Him*, for *He* will sustain thee."

11. Nouns denoting the race or nation of individuals should begin with capital letters.

Ex.—The French; the Spaniards; the English; the Anglo-Saxons.

12. Words derived from proper names should begin with capital letters.

Ex.—American, Spaniard, Danish, Johnsonian, Icelandic.

Rem.—When such words become common nouns by losing their reference to their original proper nouns, they should not begin with capital letters; as, a louis d'or; a guinea; chinaware.

13. Words of special importance may begin with capital letters.

Ex.—The Tariff, the Sub-Treasury Bill, the Commissioner of Common Schools, "Be prepared for the Great Day," "Angler's Companion: a Complete and Superior Treatise on the Art of Angling."

Ex.—Congress; the President; the Legislature. "Be prepared for the Judgment Day."

14. In natural history, *generic* names, or names of genera, should commence with capital letters. *Specific* names, or names of species, if derived from proper nouns, should also commence with capitals; otherwise, with small letters. Scientific terms are usually printed in italics.

Ex.—*Rosa Gallica, Rosa alba*; *Anomma Burneisteri, Anomma rubella*; *Spongites Townsendi, Spongites flexuosus.*

15. The pronoun I and the interjection O should be capitals.

Ex.—   "Sleep, O gentle Sleep,
Nature's soft nurse, how have I frighted thee."

Rem.—*O* and *oh* are both interjections. *O* is used in a formal or poetic direct address; as, "O Lord, how long?" *Oh* is informal or other than direct address; as, "Oh, Tom, look at the sunset!" "Oh boy!" *Oh* is capitalized only when it begins a sentence or quotation. *O* is always capitalized.

GENERAL REMARKS

1. Indirect quotations, or words quoted as the peculiar language of authors, should not begin with capital letters; as, "A man is an 'individual,' or a 'person,' or a 'party,' " "A fine house is always a 'palatial residence.' "

2. In writing many compound names of places, usage is not uniform. When the parts remain separate, or are connected by a hyphen, each should begin with a capital letter: when the parts are consolidated, but one capital letter should be used; as, New Castle, New-Castle, Newcastle.

3. In advertisements, posters, etc., different styles and sizes of type are used, and quite frequently the rules for the use of capitals are not observed.

4. Names, signs, titles, and mottoes, designed to attract attention, are printed in various styles: frequently in capitals.

12. EXERCISES TO BE CORRECTED

1. it is a pleasant thing to see the sun. man is mortal. flowers bloom in summer.

2. *Resolved*, that the framers of the constitution, etc.

3. The town has expended, the past year:
   for grading streets, $15,000
   for public buildings,   15,000

4. He said "you are too impulsive." Remember the maxim, "a penny saved is a penny earned."

5. "The day is past and gone;
   the evening shades appear;
   o may we all remember well
   the night of death draws near."

6.—James and samuel went to baltimore last august; The general assembly meets on the first monday in february.

7. The bill was vetoed by the president; John Jones, esq.; Richard the third; "The opposition was led by lord Brougham."

8. "When music, heavenly maid, was young,
   While yet, in early Greece, she sung,
   The passions, oft, to hear her shell,
   Throng'd around her magic cell."

9. central park; the Ohio river; I have read *great expectations*; the atlas mountains are in Africa.

10. The lord shall endure forever; Remember thy creator; divine love and wisdom; "The ways of providence."

11. "I know that my redeemer liveth"; "I am the way, the truth, and the life"; "The word was made flesh."

12. Those are chinese; the turkomans are a wandering race; the gypsies of Spain; the indians are fast disappearing.

13. The swiss family Robinson; a russian serf; "The rank is but the Guinea's stamp"; a Cashmere shawl; a Damask rose.

14. The emancipation proclamation; the art of cookery (a title); the Missouri compromise; the whisky insurrection; "A treatise on the science of education and the art of teaching."

15. i don't like to study grammar. i write correctly enough, now. oh, how i wish school was out.

13. ITALICS, SMALL CAPITALS, ETC.

1. Emphatic words, phrases, and clauses are frequently printed in italics.

Ex.—"Do not you *grieve* at this?" "The truth is, his lordship *weeps for the press, and wipes his eyes with the public.*"—*Curran.*

2. Words borrowed from foreign languages should be printed in italics.

Ex.—"Each word stood quite *per se.*"—*Lamb.* This odd *quid pro quo* surprised me into vehement laughter."—*Walpole.*

3. The names of authors, annexed to selections from their writings, are usually printed in italics.

Ex.—"His coward lips did from their color fly."—*Shakespeare.*

4. Parenthetical words and phrases are frequently printed in italics.

Ex.—Old gentleman (*looking quite unconcerned*), "Run away, has she?"

5. Names of ships, books, newspapers, and periodicals are frequently printed in italics or small capitals.

Ex.—"The *Quaker City* has arrived." "The *Journal of Science* is committed to no such policy as that."

6. Words requiring special emphasis are occasionally printed in small capitals or capitals.

Ex.—"I brand him as a *rogue*, a THIEF, a COWARD."—*Placard.*

Rem. 1—Italicized words in the King James Bible are those supplied by translators to explain the original.

Rem. 2—In manuscripts, <u>one line</u> drawn under a word indicates *italics*; <u>two lines</u> , SMALL CAPITALS; <u>three lines</u> , CAPITALS.

Rem. 3—In this work, **full-faced types** are also used for distinction.

14. SYLLABLES

1. A **syllable** may be composed:

Of a vowel, diphthong, digraph, or trigraph; as, *o*-men, *au*-thor, *eau*-de-cologne.

Of a vowel or diphthong, with one or more consonants prefixed or affixed; as, l-*o*, b-*oy*, *a*-m, *a*-nd.

Of a vowel or diphthong, with one or more consonants prefixed and affixed; as, *b*-a-*d*, *fr*-a-*nk*.

2. A **vocal sound** is an essential part of a syllable.

3. **Synthesis** is the process of combining elementary sounds.

4. **Analysis** is the process of separating a syllable or word into its elementary sounds.

15. MODELS FOR ANALYZING SYLLABLES

MODEL I

Lo . . . . . Give both sounds in quick succession, **L-o**, and pronounce the word.

MODEL II

Lo . . . . . is a syllable, containing two elementary sounds.

L . . . . . . is a consonant-subvocal-lingual. (*Give its sound.*)

o . . . . is a vowel-vocal, long sound. (*Give its sound.*)

MODEL III

Clank . . . Give the five sounds in quick succession, **c-l-a-n-k**, and pronounce the word.

MODEL IV

Clank . . . is a syllable, containing five elementary sounds.

C . . . . . . is a consonant-aspirate-palatal, substitute for *k*. (*Give its sound.*)

l . . . . is a consonant-subvocal-lingual. (*Give its sound.*)

a . . . . is a vowel-vocal, short sound. (*Give its sound.*)

n . . . . is a consonant-subvocal-palatal-nasal, substitute for *ng*. (*Give its sound.*)

k . . . . is a consonant-aspirate-palatal. (*Give its sound.*)

MODEL V

Boy . . . . Give the three sounds in quick succession, **b-a-i**, and pronounce the word.

MODEL VI

Boy . . . . is a syllable, containing three elementary sounds.

B . . . . . . is a consonant-subvocal-labial. (*Give its sound.*)

oy . . . . . . is a diphthong, representing *a* broad, and *i* short. (*Give the sound of each in quick succession.*)

MODEL VII

View . . . Give the two sounds in quick succession, **v-u**, and pronounce the word.

MODEL VIII

View . . . is a syllable, containing two elementary sounds.
V . . . . . . is a consonant-subvocal-labial. (*Give its sound.*)
iew . . . . . is a trigraph, equivalent to *u* long. (*Give its sound.*)

Note—Either set of models may be used in analyzing syllables. The models for complete analysis need not be used after the classification of elementary sounds shall have been thoroughly learned.

Analyze the following words, omitting all silent letters:

And, fly, warm, elm, fin, sing, wax, when, sue, light, pot, home, zinc, valve, kid, ask, sun, goat, jolt.

Form syllables by prefixing a consonant to **a, ay, eau, oy**;

By prefixing two or more consonants to **e, oo, ow, i**;

By affixing one, two, or more consonants to any of the vowels or diphthongs.

16. WORDS

1. **A word** may consist of one or more syllables.

A word of *one* syllable is called a **monosyllable**; as, *care, man.*

A word of *two* syllables is called a **dissyllable**; as, *care-ful, man-ly.*

A word of *three* syllables is called a **trisyllable**; as, *care-ful-ness, man-li-ness.*

A word of *four or more* syllables is called a **polysyllable**; as, *com-mu-ni-ty, ec-cen-tric-i-ty.*

2. **Accent** is a stress of voice placed upon a particular syllable. It may be either *primary* or *secondary*, the primary being the more forcible.

3. Every word of more than one syllable has one of its syllables accented.

4. In words having both a primary and a secondary accent, the secondary occurs nearest the beginning; as, *in'compatibil'ity, in'comprehen'sible.*

Rem.—Some polysyllables have two subordinate accents; as, *con'stitu'-tional'ity, incom'prehen'sibil'ity.*

17. MODELS FOR ANALYZING WORDS

Tree . . . . is a word of one syllable: therefore a *monosyllable*.

Nature . . . . is a word of two syllables: therefore a *dissyllable*. It is accented on the first syllable.

Commotion . . . is a word of three syllables: therefore a *trisyllable*. It is accented on the second syllable.

Indefatigable . . is a word of six syllables: therefore a *polysyllable*. Its secondary accent is on the first syllable, and its primary accent on the third.

Note—After a word is analyzed according to one of these models, analyze each syllable according to the preceding models. In separating a word into syllables, divide it as it is pronounced. In writing, never divide a syllable at the end of a line. Each line should end with a word or an entire syllable.

Analyze the following words.

Sand, lead sack; unction, famous, greatly; endeavor, infamous, candidly; unpopular, information, gratuitous; domestication, interrogation, incredulity; incomprehensible, indefensibleness; incompatibility, incompassionately.

Write each of the above words in your notebooks, and divide them into syllables, marking the accented syllables.

Correct the accent in the following words.

Advertise 'ment, prima 'ry, contra 'ry, legis 'lature, lament 'able, seconda 'ry, infa 'mous, armis 'tice, admi 'rable, interest 'ing.

Change the accent of the following words to the second syllable, and give the meaning of each word before and after the change.

In 'sult, fer 'ment, reb 'el, rec 'ord, pre 'lude, con 'jure, en 'trance, es 'cort, in 'crease, in 'valid, ob 'ject, in 'cense, es 'say.

18. CLASSES

1. **Words** are either *primitive* or *derivative*.

2. A **primitive** or **radical** word is one in no way derived from another in the same language; as, *mind*, *faith*.

3. A **derivative** word is one formed by joining to a primitive some letter or syllable to modify its meaning; as, *re*-mind, faith-*ful*.

4. A **compound** word is one formed by uniting two or more primitive or derivative words; as, *bookkeeper, Anglo-Saxon*.

5. A **prefix** is that part of a derivative word which is placed before the radical; as, *re*-call, *re*-mind.

6. A **suffix** is that part of a derivative word which is placed after the radical; as, faith-*ful*, change-*able*.

7. Prefixes and suffixes are called **affixes**.

PART II

ETYMOLOGY

19. PARTS OF SPEECH

1. **Etymology** treats of the classification, derivation, and properties of words.

2. With reference to meaning and use, words are divided into nine classes, called **parts of speech**.

In the sentence, "The man gave the boy a book, a sled, and a knife," the words *man*, *boy*, *book*, *sled*, and *knife* are names of objects. They are called *nouns*, which means *names*. All words used as the names of objects are *nouns*. A *noun* may name a person, place, thing, or idea.

3. A **noun** is a name; as, *bird, Mary, light.*

Point out the nouns in the following sentences.

1. The horses are in the pasture. 2. A needle has a sharp point. 3. The clouds rested on the summit of the mountain. 4. The boys got into the boat and rowed into the middle of the stream. 5. The king was overtaken by a shower a short distance from the avenue that surrounded the city. 6. Henry and Oliver are living with Mr. Fields, their uncle. 7. Cease from anger and forsake wrath.

In the sentence, "There are two sweet apples on that plate," *sweet* denotes that the apples possess a certain quality, that of being sweet; *two* denotes the number of apples; and *that* is used to designate, or point out, the plate on which the apples are. These words are called **adjectives**, and they are said to describe or define the nouns which follow them.

4. An **adjective** is a word used to describe or define a noun; as, *small* birds, *four* boys, *that* fox.

Point out the nouns and adjectives in the following sentences.

1. A poor cripple lives in that cottage. 2. Those pupils are very studious. 3. Each soldier drew his battle blade. 4. Furious storms sweep over these lovely isles. 5. Seven vessels were wrecked in the late storm. 6. There are twenty dimes in two dollars. 7. The dry, hot air was still and oppressive.

In the sentence, "I gave him my book, and he studied his lesson," *I* and *my* are used instead of the name of the person speaking, and *him*, *his*, and *he*, instead of the name of the one to whom the book was given. In the sentence, "Who has the book which you were reading?" *who* is used instead of the name of the person inquired for; *which*, instead of the word *book*; and *you*, instead of the name of the person addressed. Each of these words is called a *pronoun*, which means *instead of a noun*.

5. A **pronoun** is a word used instead of a noun; as, "He is *my* uncle," "*Who* came with *you*?"

Point out the nouns, adjectives, and pronouns in the following sentences.

1. I do not know where you live. 2. Who gave her that pencil? 3. She came from home an hour ago. 4. What have you there, my son? 5. Their house is much larger than our uncle's. 6. Your father is her mother's brother. 7. Whose farm is for sale in your neighborhood?

In the sentence, "Horses run," *run* expresses *action*. In the sentence, "I am," *am* expresses *being*. In the sentence, "The boy sleeps," *sleeps* expresses *state* or *condition*. These words are used to affirm action, being, or state of their subjects. They are called *verbs*. Verbs may also express action, being, or state without affirming it; as, *to run*, *to be*, *to sleep*.

6. A **verb** is a word which expresses action, being, or state; as, Mary *plays*, I *am*, the house *stands*.

Point out the nouns, pronouns, and verbs in the following sentences.

1. The farmer plows in the spring and fall. 2. Their father gave them money. 3. Great tears sprang to their eyes. 4. They followed the cattle home. 5. The landlord answered his question. 6. He ordered him to go. 7. The pupils who had passed a good examination went home with joyful hearts.

In the sentence, "I saw a boy writing with a pencil," *writing* denotes what the boy was doing, but it does not affirm anything of the boy. It modifies *boy*, like an adjective. In the sentence, "I saw a letter written by a boy," *written* is used as a modifier of *letter*. Both of these words are derived from the verb *to write*, and each of them modifies a noun. They partake, therefore, of the properties of the verb and the adjective; *i.e.*, they express action, and they modify nouns. Such words are called *participles*, which means *partaking of*. Some participles partake of the properties of the verb and the noun.

Rem.—It helps to identify the subject and verb of the sentence before looking for the participles. In both these sentences, *I* is the subject and *saw* is the verb. *Boy* and *letter* are therefore objects of the verb *saw*; they cannot also be subjects, of course. *Writing* and *written*, therefore, cannot be verbs in these sentences—for verbs must have subjects. So they are *participles*.

7. A **participle** is a word derived from a verb, and partakes of the properties of a verb and of an adjective or a noun; as, "I saw a bird *flying*," "A letter *written* in haste may be regretted."

Point out the participles in the following sentences.

1. A light was seen, shining from afar. 2. He sent me a shell picked up on the seashore. 3. A deer, running at full speed, was killed by a man. 4. The house struck by lightning belonged to Mr. Ellis. 5. The letter, folded neatly, was put into an envelope. 6. My photograph, taken twenty years ago, has been lost. 7. The enemy, driven from the field, rallied at the fort.

In the sentence, "The man then drove very rapidly over the bridge," *then* and *rapidly* modify drove—*then* denoting the *time*, and *rapidly* the *manner* of driving. *Very* modifies *rapidly* by denoting the *degree of rapidity* with which the man drove. These words, and all words used in a similar manner, are called *adverbs*. Adverbs may also modify adjectives and participles.

8. An **adverb** is a word used to modify a verb, an adjective, a participle, or an adverb; as, "He runs *swiftly*," "You are *very* kind," "The letter was written *hastily*," "He came *too* slowly."

Point out the adverbs, verbs, and adjectives in the following sentences.

1. He who gives cheerfully gives twice. 2. His affairs were managed imprudently. 3. Proceed slowly and cautiously. 4. We shall never see his like again. 5. You have not acted wisely. 6. We must study diligently. 7. Our dinner, cooked hastily, was eaten greedily.

In the sentence, "Vessels sail on the ocean," the group of words, *on the ocean*, modifies *sail* by telling where the vessels sail. The word *on* connects *ocean* and *sail*, and shows the relation between them. In the sentence, "We reached the summit of the mountain," *of* shows the relation between *mountain* and *summit*. Words used in this manner are called *prepositions*. *Ocean* is called the object of *on*; *mountain*, the object of *of*.

9. A **preposition** is a word used to show the relation between its object and some other word; as, "He came *from* Troy."

Point out the prepositions in these sentences.

1. The boy fell over a chair into a tub of water. 2. I came from Boston to Cincinnati in 1985. 3. We rested by the roadside. 4. He walked up the valley towards the house of his friend. 5. Walk with me in the garden. 6. I went to the doctor for advice, but he was not at home.

In the sentence, "John and Henry study algebra," *and* joins, or connects, the two nouns *John* and *Henry*. In the sentence, "I will go if you will stay," *if* connects the two sentences, *I will go* and *you will stay*. Words used in this manner are called *conjunctions*. They may connect words, groups of words, or sentences.

10. A **conjunction** is a word used to connect words, sentences, or parts of sentences; as, "John *and* Elisha are brothers," "I must go, *but* you may stay."

Point out the conjunctions and prepositions in these sentences.

1. He is wise and prudent. 2. James or John will call upon you. 3. I study because I wish to learn. 4. Neither Jane nor Sarah was in the room. 5. I shall not go, if it rains. 6. He is rich but is very unhappy. 7. Worship the Lord, for he is our God.

In the sentence, "Oh, how tired I am!" the word *oh* denotes feeling or emotion. It is not used in the statement of a fact or in asking a question. Many words denoting grief, joy, pity, pain, etc., are used in a similar manner. They are called *interjections*.

11. An **interjection** is a word used to denote feeling or emotion; as *ah, alas, phooey.*

Point out the interjections in the following exercises.

1. Hurrah! We have won! 2. Phooey! That is nonsense. 3. Ha, ha, ha! I am glad of it. 4. "Oh," said John. 5. What! Tired so soon?

THE NOUN

20. ORAL LESSON

Write in your notebooks the names of five objects in the schoolroom. These words, as you perceive, are not the objects themselves, but their *names*. Now write the names of five objects not in the schoolroom. What are these words called? *Ans.*— Nouns. Why? *Ans.*—Because they are names. Write the names of five of your schoolmates. What are these words called? *Ans.*—Nouns. Why? *Ans.*—Because they are names.

Are there not other names by which your schoolmates are called? *Ans.*—Yes; they may be called *girls* and *boys*. Can the name "girl" be applied to all the girls in the room? *Ans.*—Yes. Can the name "Sarah" be applied to all the girls in the room? *Ans.*—It cannot. Why? *Ans.*—All the girls are not named "Sarah." There are Mary, and Charlotte, and Jane, and Susan, and many other names for girls.

We have, then, two kinds of nouns, or names. One kind can be applied to each one of a class, and the other kind can be applied to a particular one only. The first kind are called *common nouns*— they are names *common* to all the individuals of a class; the second are called *proper nouns*—they are names of *particular* objects, and are used to distinguish their objects from the classes to which they belong. What kind are the names *horse, book, boy, girl, map, blackboard*? *Ans.*—Common nouns. Why? *Ans.*— Because they can be applied to each one of a class. What kind are the names *John, Charles, Washington, Boston, Europe*? *Ans.*—Proper nouns. Why? *Ans.*—Because they can be applied to particular persons, or particular places only and distinguish them from the classes to which they belong.

21. DEFINITION

A **noun** is a name; as, *desk, Richard, goodness, army.*

22. CLASSES

1. There are two classes of nouns: *common* and *proper.*

2. A **common noun** is a name which may be applied to any one of a kind or class of objects; as, *boy, child, book, radiation.*

3. A **proper noun** is the name of some particular person, place, people, or thing; as, *Charles, Cincinnati, France,* the *Titanic.*

Rem. 1—A *proper noun* is used to distinguish an object from the class to which it belongs. A word not used for that purpose is not a proper noun.

Rem. 2—Whenever a *proper noun* is used in such a manner as to admit of its application to each individual of a class, it becomes a *common noun*; as, "He is the *Cicero* of our age," "Bolivar was the *Washington* of South America," "He piled *Ossa* upon *Pelion* to accomplish his purpose."

Rem. 3—When two or more words form but one name, they are taken together as one noun; as, *New York*; *Niagara Falls*; *John Milton*; *Lord Bacon*; *Chief Justice Chase.*

Rem. 4—Common nouns may be divided into four classes: *class nouns, abstract nouns, collective nouns,* and *participial nouns.*

Class nouns are names which can be applied to each individual of a class or group of objects; as, *horse, apple, man.*

An **abstract noun** is the name of a quality considered apart from the object in which it is found; as, *brightness, cohesion.*

Collective noun is a name singular in form, though denoting more than one; as, *herd, jury, swarm, school, assembly.*

A **participial noun** is the name of an action or a state of being; as, *singing, standing, seeming.*

Rem. 6—Words, phrases, and clauses used as nouns, or in the relations in which nouns occur, are called **substantives**, and when thus used have all the properties of nouns.

Rem. 7—Such words as *mass, heap, furniture,* names of collections of objects without life, are *class* nouns, not *collective* nouns. They are sometimes called **mass nouns**.

23. PROPERTIES

The **properties** of the noun are *gender, person, number,* and *case.*

24. GENDER

1. **Gender** is a distinction of nouns and pronouns with regard to sex.

Rem.—*Sex* is a natural distinction of objects—*gender* is a grammatical distinction of words used to represent objects.

2. There are four genders: *masculine, feminine, common,* and *neuter.*

3. The **masculine gender** denotes males; as, *father, uncle, king, governor.*

4. The **feminine gender** denotes females; as, *mother, aunt, queen, governess.*

5. The **common gender** denotes either males or females, or both; as, *parent, children, bird, cattle.*

6. The **neuter gender** denotes neither males nor females; as, *stove, city, pen, ink, tree, house.*

Rem. 1—By a figure of speech, called *personification,* sex is sometimes ascribed to inanimate objects. The nouns denoting them are then regarded as either masculine or feminine.

Ex.—"The *ship* has lost *her* rudder." "The meek-eyed *morn* appears, *mother* of dews." "The *sun* in *his* glory; the *moon* in *her* wane."

Rem. 2—Names of animals are regarded as either masculine or feminine according to the qualities ascribed.

Ex.—"The *nightingale* sings *her* song." "The *lion* meets *his* foe boldly." "The *fox* made *his* escape."

Rem. 3—Nouns used to denote both genders, though strictly applicable to males only, or females only, are usually regarded as masculine.

Ex.—"*Heirs* are often disappointed." "The *English* are a proud people." "The *poets* of America."

Rem. 4—The distinction of gender is not observed in speaking of inferior animals, and sometimes even of children.

Ex.—"The *bee* on *its* wing." "The *child* in *its* cradle."

7. There are three ways of distinguishing the masculine and feminine genders:

1. By using different words:

Ex.—Bachelor, maid, spinster; bridegroom, bride; brother, sister; boy, girl; cock, hen; drake, duck; earl, countess; father, mother; gentleman, lady; hart, roe; male, female; man, woman; Mr., Mrs.; Sir, Madam; nephew, niece; son, daughter; uncle, aunt; Charles, Caroline; Augustus, Augusta.

2. By different terminations:

Ex.—Abbot, abbess; baron, baroness; host, hostess; actor, actress; prior, prioress; benefactor, benefactress; executor, executrix; murderer, murderess; sorcerer, sorceress.

3. By prefixes and suffixes:

Ex.—Manservant, maidservant; Mr. Smith, Mrs. Smith, Miss Smith; peacock, peahen; workman, housewife.

25. PERSON

1. **Person** is that property of a noun or pronoun which distinguishes the speaker, the person spoken to, and the person or object spoken of.

2. There are three persons: *first*, *second*, and *third*.

3. The **first person** denotes the speaker; as, "*I, John*, was in the isle that is called Patmos," "Many evils beset *us* mortals."

4. The **second person** denotes the person addressed; as, "*James*, be more careful," "*Fellow Citizens*, the crisis demands the utmost vigilance."

5. The **third person** denotes the person or object spoken of; as, "*Milton* was a *poet*," "*Rome* was an *ocean of flame*," "I am reading *Tennyson's Poems*."

Rem. 1—The writer or speaker often speaks of himself, or the person he addresses, in the third person; as, "*Mr. Johnson* has the pleasure of informing *Mr. Mason* that he has been elected Honorary Member of the Oriental Society."

Rem. 2—A noun in the predicate is of the third person, though the subject may be of the first or second.

Ex.—"*You* are the *man* wanted." "*We* are *strangers*." "*I* am *he* whom you saw."

26. NUMBER

1. **Number** is that property of a noun which distinguishes one from more than one.

2. There are two numbers: *singular* and *plural*.

3. The **singular number** denotes but one; as, *apple, flower, boy, girl*.

4. The **plural number** denotes more than one; as, *apples, flowers, boys, girls*.

27. FORMATION OF THE PLURAL

1. Nouns whose last sound will unite with the sound represented by *s*, form their plurals by adding *s* only to the singular; as, book, *books*; boy, *boys*; desk, *desks*.

2. Nouns whose last sound will not unite with the sound represented by *s*, form their plurals by adding *es* to the singular; as, church, *churches*; box, *boxes*; witness, *witnesses*.

3. Nouns ending in *y* preceded by a consonant, change *y* into *i*, and add *es*; as, glory, *glories*; mercy, *mercies*.

4. Most nouns ending in *f* change *f* to *v*, and add *es*; those ending in *fe* change *f* to *v*, and add *s*; as, beef, *beeves*; wife, *wives*.

5. Most nouns ending in *o* preceded by a consonant, add *es*; as, cargo, *cargoes*. Nouns ending in *o* preceded by a vowel, add *s*; as, folio, *folios*.

6. Some nouns form their plurals irregularly; as, man, *men*; ox, *oxen*; tooth, *teeth*; mouse, *mice*.

7. Letters, figures, marks, and signs add *'s*; as, "Mind your *p's* and *q's*;" the 9's and 11's; the − 's; the + 's; the &'s and *'s.

8. In compound words, the part which is described by the rest is generally pluralized; as, *brothers*-in-law, *courts*-martial; wagon-*loads*, ox-*carts*.

9. Compound words from foreign languages form their plurals according to (1) and (2); as, *tete-a-tetes*, *piano-fortes*, *ipse-dixits*, *scir-faciases*.

10. Some compound words have both parts made plural; as, knight-templar, *knights-templars*; ignis-fatuus, *ignes-fatui*.

11. Compound terms composed of a proper noun and a title, may be pluralized by adding a plural termination to either the name or the title, but not to both; as, the Miss *Browns*, the *Misses* Brown; the *Messrs*. Thompson; "May there be *Sir Isaac Newtons* in every science."

12. When the title is preceded by a numeral, the name is always pluralized; as, the three Miss *Johnsons*; the two Dr. *Bensons*; the two Mrs. *Kendricks*.

13. Some nouns have two plurals, but with a difference in meaning; as, brother, *brothers* (of the same family), *brethren* (of the same society); die, *dies* (stamps for coining), *dice* (for gambling); fish, *fishes* (individuals), *fish* (quantity, or the species); genius, *geniuses* (men of genius), *genii* (spirits); index, *indexes* (tables of contents), *indices* (algebraic signs).

14. Proper nouns, and words generally used as other parts of speech, are changed as little as possible, and usually add *s* only in forming their plurals; as, Mary, *Marys*; Sarah, *Sarahs*; Nero, *Neros*; "The novel is full of *ohs*, *bys*, *whys*, *alsos*, and *nos*."

15. Many nouns from foreign languages retain their original plurals, changing *us* to *i*; *um* and *on* to *a*; *is* to *es* or *ides*; *a* to *ae* or *ata*; and *x* or *ex* to *ces* or *ices*; as, calculus, *calculi*; arcanum, *arcana*; criterion, *criteria*; thesis, *theses*; ephemeris, *ephemerides*; nebula, *nebulae*; calix, *calices*; index, *indices*.

28. GENERAL REMARKS ON NUMBER

1. Abstract nouns, and names of material substances, have no plural forms; as, *silver, vinegar, hemp, tar, frankness, darkness*. When different kinds of the same substance are referred to, a plural form may be used; as, *sugars, vinegars, wines, oils*.

2. Some nouns have no singular forms; as, *ashes, bellows, billiards, compasses, clothes, lees, pants, scissors, shears, tongs. News* and *molasses* have the plural form, but are regarded as singular. *Lungs, bowels*, and a few others, have a singular form denoting a part of the whole; as, "The left *lung*."

3. Some nouns have no singular forms, but are singular or plural in meaning; as, *alms, amends, corps, mumps, measels, nuptials, odds, riches, series, suds, tidings*, and some others.

4. The names of some of the sciences are either singular or plural in meaning, according as they denote the science or the objects of which the science treats; as, *ethics, mechanics, mathematics, optics, pedagogies, physics, etc.*

5. Some nouns are alike in both numbers; as, *sheep, deer, vermin, salmon, trout, dozen, gross, hose, yoke.*

29. CASE

Case is the relation of a noun or pronoun to other words. Nouns have four cases: *nominative, possessive, objective,* and *absolute,* or *nominative absolute.*

Rem.—The term *case* is also applied to the *form* of a noun or pronoun when used independently, or as a part of a sentence.

30. NOMINATIVE CASE

The **nominative case** is the use of a noun or pronoun as the subject or the predicate of a proposition.

Ex.—"The *sun* is shining." "That man is a *sailor.*" In the first sentence, "sun" is in the nominative case, because it is used as the *subject* of the proposition; in the second, "sailor" is in the nominative case, because it is used as the *predicate* of the proposition.

31. POSSESSIVE CASE

1. The **possessive case** is the use of a noun or pronoun to denote ownership, authorship, origin, or kind.

Ex.—*Susan's* book; *Gray's* Botany; the *sun's* rays; *boys'* hats; *men's* clothing.

2. The possessive case *singular* is formed by annexing *'s* to the nominative; as, *John's, Clarence's.*

3. The possessive case *plural* is formed by annexing the apostrophe only, when the nominative plural ends with *s*; as, *boys'*, "The Ohio State *Teachers'* Association."

Rem. 1—Plural nouns not ending with *s*, form their possessive case by annexing *'s*; as, *men's* hats; *children's* shoes.

Rem. 2—In *compound names*, the possessive sign is annexed to the last word; as, "*Daniel Webster's* speeches." In *complex names* it is annexed to the last word; as, "The *Bishop of Dublin's* palace." In a *series of terms*, and *common* possession, it is annexed to the last term; as, "*Day & Martin's* Garage." In a *series of terms*, and *separate* possession, it is annexed to each term; as, "*Webster's* and *Worcester's* Dictionaries."

Rem. 3—When a noun in the possessive case is limited by a noun in apposition with it, or by a descriptive phrase, the possessive sign is annexed to the noun immediately preceding the object possessed, though not always to the name of the possessor; as, "Her Majesty, *Queen Elizabeth II's* government," "The captain of the *Fulton's* wife died yesterday." Here "captain" is in the possessive case, and "Fulton" in the objective, governed by the preposition "of."

Rem. 4—In compound words, the sign of possession is placed at the end; as, "The *knight-templar's* costume," "My *brother-in-law's* residence."

Rem. 5—"For *conscience'* sake," "For goodness' sake," etc., are idiomatic exceptions to the general rule for forming the possessive case singular.

Rem. 6—The sign ['s] is a contraction of *is* or *his*; as, *John's*, *King's*; anciently written, *Johnis*, *Kingis*, *Johnes*, *Kinges*, or *Moses* his laws.

32. OBJECTIVE CASE

The **objective case** is the use of a noun or pronoun as the object of a transitive verb in the active voice, or of a preposition.

Ex.—"John studies *grammar*." "The book is on the *table*." In the first sentence, "grammar" is the object of the transitive verb "studies" in the second, "table" is the object of the preposition "on."

Rem.—A noun or pronoun used to complete the meaning of a transitive verb is called a **direct object**; as, "I bought a *book*." When added to a verb to denote that *to* or *for* which anything is or is done, or that *from* which anything proceeds, it is called an **indirect object**; as, "I bought *him* a book." In this sentence, "book" is the *direct* and "him" the *indirect* object of "bought." When an indirect object precedes the direct, the preposition should be omitted; when it follows, it should be expressed; as, "I gave *him* an apple," "I gave an apple *to him*."

33. ABSOLUTE CASE

The **absolute** or **nominative absolute case** is the use of a noun independent of any governing word.

Ex.—"*John*, bring me a book." "Your *fathers*, where are they?" "*Honor* being lost, all is lost."

Rem. 1—A noun or pronoun in this case has the same form that it would have were it in the nominative case. Hence, the case may, with propriety, be called *nominative absolute*—this term indicating both the *form* and the *use* of the word.

Rem. 2—A noun may be in the **nominative absolute case**:

1. *By direct address*; as, "*Charles*, come to me." This use is sometimes called the **vocative case**.

2. *By mere exclamation*; as, "Oh, Popular *Applause!*"

3. *By pleonasm*, or by placing the noun before the sentence in which an affirmation is made concerning it; as, "*Gad*, a troop shall overcome him."

4. *With a participle*; as, "The *sun* being risen, we pursued our journey."

5. *By position: i.e.,* by using it as the heading of a chapter, as the superscription to a letter, etc.; as, "A Flood," "Louis Agassiz."

34. NOUNS IN APPOSITION

A noun limiting the meaning of another noun, denoting the same person, place, or thing, is, by **apposition**, in the same case.

Ex.—"Washington the *general* became Washington the *statesman*." "We visited New York, the *metropolis* of the United States." "In her brother *Abraham's* house."

35. DECLENSION

The **declension** of a noun is its variation to denote *number* and *case*.

EXAMPLES

	Singular	Plural		Singular	Plural
Nom.	Boy	Boys	*Nom.*	Fly	Flies
Poss.	Boy's	Boys'	*Poss.*	Fly's	Flies'
Obj.	Boy	Boys	*Obj.*	Fly	Flies
Nom.	Charles	_____	*Nom.*	Goodness	_____
Poss.	Charles's	_____	*Poss.*	Goodness'	_____
Obj.	Charles	_____	*Obj.*	Goodness	_____

36. PARSING

Parsing consists, (1) in naming the part of speech; (2) in telling its properties; (3) in pointing out its relation to other words; (4) in giving the rule for its construction.

37. ORDER OF PARSING

1. A noun, and why?
2. Common or proper, and why?
3. Gender, and why?
4. Person, and why?
5. Number, and why?
6. Case, and why?
7. Rule for construction.

38. MODELS FOR PARSING

I. *"Mary* sings."

Mary . . . . . is a *noun*; it is a name; *proper*, it is the name of a particular person; *feminine gender*, it denotes a female; *third person*, it denotes the person spoken of; *singular number*, it denotes but one; *nominative case*, it is used as the *subject* of the proposition, "Mary sings." Rule I. "The subject of a proposition is in the nominative case."

II. "Horses are *animals.*"

Animals . . . is a *noun*; *common*, it can be applied to any one of a class or kind; *common gender*, it denotes either males or females; *third person*; *plural number*, it denotes more than one; *nominative case*, it is used as the *predicate* of the proposition, "Horses are animals." Rule II. "A noun or pronoun used as the predicate of a proposition, is in the nominative case."

III. "The poet *Milton* was blind."

Milton . . . . is a *noun*; *proper*; *masculine gender*, it denotes a male; *third person*; *singular number*; *nominative case*, in apposition with 'poet." Rule IV. "A noun or pronoun used to limit the meaning of a noun or pronoun, by denoting the same person, place, or thing, is in the same case."

IV. *"Henry's* lesson is learned."

Henry's . . . is a *noun*; *proper*; *masculine gender*; *third person*; *singular* *number*; *possessive case*, it denotes possession, and modifies "lesson." Rule III. "A noun or pronoun used to limit the meaning of a noun denoting a different thing, is in the possessive case."

V. "John studies *grammar*."

Grammar..is a *noun*; *common*; *neuter gender*; *third person*; *singular number*; *objective case*, it is used as the object of the transitive verb "studies." Rule VI. "The object of a transitive verb in the active voice, or of its participles, is in the objective case."

VI. "The book lies on the *table*."

Table .....is a *noun, common*; *neuter gender*; *third person*; *singular number*; *objective case*, it is used as the object of the preposition "on." Rule VII. "The object of a preposition is in the objective case."

VII. "*William*, open the door."

William ...is a *noun*; *proper*; *masculine gender*; *second person*; *singular number*; *absolute case*, it is the name of a person addressed. Rule V. "A noun or pronoun used independently, is in the absolute case."

Note......For models for parsing participial nouns, see Section 90.

39. EXERCISES

Parse all the nouns in the following sentences. This may be done as an oral exercise.

1. The wind blows. 2. The sun shines. 3. Horses run. 4. The vessel sails. 5. Scholars study. 6. Grass grows. 7. Fire burns. 8. Liberty is sweet. 9. St. Helena is an island. 10. Lead is a metal. 11. Cicero was an orator. 12. Grammar is a science. 13. The storm's fury is past. 14. Henry's health is good. 15. The king's palace is on fire. 16. Jane borrowed Sarah's book. 17. Mr. Johnson sells boys' hats. 18. The defeat of Xerxes' army was the downfall of Persia. 19. John struck James. 20. Joseph bought the book. 21. Peter studies algebra. 22. The horse kicked the boy. 23. The man wrote a letter. 24. Samuel lives over the river. 25. Martha went with Susan. 26. James is going to Cincinnati. 27. The boy ran by the mill. 28. "Friends, Romans, Countrymen! Lend me your ears!" 29. "To arms! They come! The Greek! The Greek!" 30. "My daughter! Oh, my daughter!" 31. "Your fathers, where are they?" 32. "My son—have you seen him?"

Parse all the nouns in the following sentences.

1. Johnson the doctor is a brother of Johnson the lawyer. 2. Shakespeare

lived in Queen Elizabeth I's reign. 3. "Ah, Warwick! Warwick! Wert thou as we are!" 4. Temperance is a virtue. 5. "King Agrippa, believest thou the prophets?" 6. The inferior animals are divided into five classes: quadrupeds, fowls, fishes, reptiles, and insects. 7. The little army fought bravely on that day. 8. Where are the Platos and Aristotles of modern times? 9. I have seen Mr. Squires, the bookseller and stationer.

Correct all errors in the following sentences.

1. I have two brother-in-laws. 2. There were three knight-templars in the procession. 3. Nebulas are sometimes called stardust. 4. I saw the two Mrs. Jackson. 5. He called at Steele's the banker's. 6. The Jones' were all there. 7. The boys slate was broken. 8. The mens' wages should be paid promptly. 9. She is reading in her sister's Susan's book. 10. He studied O. B. Pierce' Grammar. 11. He has octavoes, quartoes, and folioes, among his books. 12. There are three chimnies on that house. 13. We regard them as singular phenomenons.

THE ADJECTIVE

40. ORAL LESSON

Here are some apples, nice for eating: what shall we call them? *Ans.— Ripe* apples. I have just eaten one, and it tasted sweet: what else can we call them? *Ans.—Sweet* apples. They are quite soft: what else can we call them? *Ans.—Mellow* apples. Write on your papers, *"Ripe, sweet, mellow* apples." All these words denote some quality of the apple: what shall we call them? *Ans.—Quality words.* A very good name.

Let us count the apples: *one* apple, *two* apples, *three* apples, *four* apples. Let's also number them: the *first* apple, the *second* apple, the *third* apple, the *fourth* apple. Write these numbers on your papers, as I write them on the blackboard—*one, two, three, four; first, second, third, fourth.* What shall we call these words? *Ans.—Number words.*

When I speak of the apple nearest me, I say, *"This* apple"; when, of one farther from me, *"That* apple." Do the words *this* and *that* denote any *quality* of the apples? *Ans.—*They do not. What do they do, then? *Ans.—* They point them out. Very well: what shall we call them? *Ans.—*Pointing-out words.

You see that all the words we have used, in some manner describe "apples." Some denote quality; some, number; some merely point out. What is the word "apple?" *Ans.—*A noun. Then they all describe a noun. What are all of these words? *Ans.—Adjectives.*

The "quality words" we will call *descriptive adjectives*, because they describe by denoting some quality. The "number words" and "pointing-out words" do not denote quality. We will call them *definitive adjectives.* Write, "This is a good book." What is "good?" *Ans.*—An adjective. Why? *Ans.*—It describes the word "book." What kind? *Ans.*—Descriptive. Why? *Ans.*—It denotes a quality belonging to the book. Write, "These two books are mine." What are "these" and "two"? *Ans.*—Adjectives. Why? *Ans.*—They describe "books." What kind? *Ans.*—Definitive. Why? *Ans.*— They define without denoting any quality.

Write, "Every man can do some good." What are "every" and "some"? *Ans.*—Adjectives. Why? *Ans.*—They limit nouns. What kind? *Ans.*— Definitive. Why? *Ans.*—They define without denoting any quality.

41. DEFINITION

An **adjective** is a word used to describe or define a noun; as, *wise* men, *that* book, *three* steamships, the *fourth* stanza.

42. CLASSES

Adjectives may be divided into two general classes: *descriptive* and *definitive.*

43. DESCRIPTIVE ADJECTIVES

1. A **descriptive adjective** limits or describes a noun by denoting some quality belonging to it.

Ex.—A *round* table, a *square* table, a *sour* apple, a *sweet* apple, a *good* boy, a *bad* boy, an *Italian* sunset, *twinkling* stars.

Rem. 1—Words commonly used as other parts of speech, sometimes perform the office of descriptive adjectives, and should be parsed as such.

Ex.—A *gold* ring, a *silver* cord, the *California* pine, a *make-believe* patriot, *double-distilled* nonsense. "The West is as truly *American*, as genuinely *Jonathan*, as any other part of our country."

Rem. 2—An adjective is frequently limited by a word joined to it by a hyphen. The compound term thus formed is called a *compound adjective*, and should be parsed as a single word.

Ex.—A *high-sounding* title, an *ill-matched* pair.

Rem. 3—Adjectives derived from verbs are called *participial adjectives.* They are usually placed before the nouns which they modify.

Ex.—We walked across a *plowed* field and soon came to the *flowing* spring.

Rem. 4—When a descriptive adjective represents a noun understood, or not expressed, the article must be prefixed; as, "The *wise* are provident," "The *good* are happy." Adjectives thus used should be parsed as *adjectives used as nouns*.

Tell which of the adjectives in the following sentences are descriptive, and which are compound and participial.

1. The unfortunate man was a hard-working mechanic. 2. The fields looked beautiful. 3. English books are costly. 4. The howling storm is passed. 5. The soil is very productive. 6. The water falls into a marble basin. 7. I prefer a New England winter to an Australian summer.

44. DEFINITIVE ADJECTIVES

1. A **definitive adjective** limits or defines the application of a noun without expressing any of its qualities.

Ex.—*The* Ohio, *that* man, *three* dollars, the *third* seal, a *two-fold* reference. "*All* men are mortal." "*Each* soldier received his pay."

2. Definitive adjectives are divided into three classes: *articles*, *pronominal adjectives*, and *numeral adjectives*.

45. ARTICLES

1. "The" is called the **definite article**, because it definitely points out the object which it defines or restricts; as, "*The* book is on *the* table," "*The* horse ran over *the* bridge."

2. "A" or "an" is called the **indefinite article**, because it defines or restricts in an indefinite or general manner; as, "A book is on *a* table," "*A* horse ran over *a* bridge."

"**An**" should be used before words beginning with a vowel sound; "**a**," before words beginning with a consonant sound. They are spoken of as *one* article, because they are merely an earlier and a later form of the same word.

Rem.—An article sometimes limits not a noun alone, but a noun as limited by other words; as, "*The old men* retired early; *the young men* remained until midnight." The article here limits the complex ideas "old men" and "young men." "*An early spring* is no sign of *a fruitful season*." The article here limits the complex ideas "early spring" and "fruitful season."

46. PRONOMINAL ADJECTIVES

1. **Pronominal adjectives** are definitives, most of which can, without an article prefixed, represent a noun understood; as, *all* are Adam's race, *each* is ready for battle, *yonder* is the highest hill in the state; or, *all* men, *each* soldier, *yonder* mountain. When pronominal adjectives replace nouns, they function as pronouns, as in the first three examples. But when they point to a noun, pronominal adjectives function as adjectives, as in the second three examples.

2. They may be divided into three classes: *demonstratives*, *distributives*, and *indefinites*.

3. In the examples that follow, some pronominal adjectives function as pronouns, others as adjectives.

47. DEMONSTRATIVES

Demonstratives point out objects definitely. They are: *this*, *that*, *these*, *those*, *former*, *latter*, *both*, *same*, *yon*, *yonder*.

1. **This** (plural **these**) distinctly points out an object as near in place or time; as, "*This* desk and *these* books."

2. **That** (plural **those**) distinctly points out an object as not near, or not so near as some other object; as, "*That* desk and *those* books."

3. In speaking of two objects, *that* should refer to the former, and *this* to the latter; as, "*These* horses are larger than *those*."

4. **Former** and **latter** are used to designate which of two objects previously mentioned is referred to; as, "The cry of danger to the *Union* was raised to divert their assaults upon the *Constitution*. It was the *latter*, and not the *former*, which was in danger."

5. **Both** implies *the one and the other*; as, "*Both* forts were taken," "James and Silas were *both* tardy."

6. **Same** denotes an identical object or one of like kind; as, "That is the *same* man we saw yesterday," "Both tables are made of the *same* wood."

7. **Yon** and **yonder** denote in view, but at a distance; as, "*Yon* house on the hill," "*Yonder* mountain is a volcano."

48. DISTRIBUTIVES

Distributives represent objects as taken separately. There are four distributives: *each*, *every*, *either*, *neither*.

1. **Each** can be applied to one of two or any greater number; as, "*Each* warrior drew his battle blade," "*Each* part is useless without the other."

2. **Every** denotes each without exception or all taken separately; as, "His *every* word was true," "They received *every* man a penny," "*Every* person in the room was astonished."

3. **Either** should be applied to one of two objects only; as, "*Either* road leads to town," "You may have *either* house."

4. **Neither** means *not either*; as, "Which of the two shall I take? Both? One? Or *neither* one?"

49. INDEFINITES

Indefinites refer to objects in a general way, without pointing out any one in particular. The principal indefinites are: *all, any, another, certain, divers, enough, few, little, many, much, no, none, one, own, other, several, some, sundry, which, whichever, whichsoever, what, whatever, whatsoever.*

1. **All** describes *objects taken together*; as, "*All* the men were at work in the fields," "*All* men are mortal."

2. **Any** denotes *a single one of many*, or *some*; as, "Have you *any* wheat to sell?" "Neither go into the town, nor tell it to *any* in the town."

3. **Another**, or **other**, means *not the same*; as, "He took *another* road," "He will let out his vineyard to *other* husbandmen."

4. **Certain** denotes *one* or *some*; as, "And there came a *certain* poor widow, and she threw in two mites," "And I, Daniel, was sick *certain* days."

5. **Divers** means *unlike, numerous*; as, "A scarf of *divers* colors of needlework," "*Divers* miracles."

6. **Enough** denotes a *sufficiency*; as, "I have *enough* for my brother," "*Enough* has been said already."

7. **Few** denotes *a small number*; as, "Many shall be called, but *few* chosen," "I have a *few* old books."

8. **Little** means *small in quantity, amount, or duration*; as, "A *little* learning is a dangerous thing."—*Pope.* "A *little* sleep, a *little* slumber, a *little* folding of the hands to sleep."

9. **Many** denotes *a large number*; as, "*Many* men of *many* minds," "The mutable, rank-scented *many*."—*Shakespeare.*

10. **Much** denotes *a large quantity*; as, "There is *much* wealth in this town," "Thou shalt carry *much* seed out into the field, and shalt gather but little in."

11. **No** means *not any*, *none*. When used as a noun in the plural number, it means those who vote in the negative; as, "The *noes* have it."

12. **None** means *not one*, or *not any*; as, "Ye shall flee when *none* pursueth you," "Thou shalt have *none* assurance of thy life." Use "no one" when *one* only is meant; "none" when *more than one* are referred to.

13. **One** corresponds to *another*; as, "They love *one another*," *i.e.*, each person loves the other.

14. **Own** implies *possession*; as, "My *own* home," "Our *own* dear mother."

15. **Several** denotes *any small number more than two*; as, "*Several* victories." Also, *single*, *individual*; as, "I'll kiss each *several* paper for amends."

16. **Some** denotes *an indeterminate number* or *quantity*; as, "*Some* money," "I have brought *some* books."

17. **Sundry** means *various*, *divers*; as, "*Sundry* foes," "For *sundry* weighty reasons."—*Shakespeare.*

Rem.—**Whichsoever** and **whatsoever** differ from **whichever** and **whatever** only in intensity; as, I want none *whatsoever* (absolutely none at all).

50. NUMERAL ADJECTIVES

1. **Numeral adjectives** are those which express number and order definitely; as, *four*, *fourth*, *fourfold*.

2. They are divided into three classes: *cardinal*, *ordinal*, and *multiplicative*.

3. **Cardinal numerals** denote simply the number of objects; as, *two*, *thirteen*, *fifty*, *a thousand*.

4. **Ordinal numerals** mark the position of an object in a series; as, *second*, *thirteenth*, *fiftieth*, *the thousandth*.

5. **Multiplicative numerals** denote how many fold; as, *twofold*, *fourfold*.

GENERAL REMARKS

1. When *such*, *many*, *only*, *but*, and *not* are followed by the indefinite article *a* or *an*, the phrases *such a*, *many a*, etc., limit singular nouns; as, "If you repay me not on *such a* day," "*Many a* time," "He is *but a* man," "*Not a* drum was heard." These phrases may be parsed as single words.

2. When definitive adjectives are used in connection with descriptive adjectives, the former should be placed first; as, "*That* valuable property," "*Ten* small houses."

3. A *cardinal* numeral used as a noun, requires no article: an *ordinal* should have the article prefixed; as, "Were not *ten* cleansed?" "The *tenth* was rescued."

4. *Each other* and *one another* are sometimes called **reciprocals**, because they are reciprocally related; as, "They mutually assist *each other*," "They help *one another*." Parse "each" and "one" as *adjectives used as nouns*, as representing a number of individuals taken separately. Use "each other" in referring to two individuals, and "one another" in referring to more than two. Parse "other" and "another" as *adjectives used as nouns* in the objective case after the verbs that precede them.

5. Adjectives which vary in form to denote number, should agree in number with the nouns they limit. Say, "*this* sort," but "*these* sorts."

51. COMPARISON

1. **Comparison** is a variation of the adjective to express different degrees of quality; as, *wise, wiser, wisest; good, better, best.*

2. There are three **degrees of comparison**: the *positive*, the *comparative*, the *superlative*.

3. The **positive** degree ascribes to an object the simple quality, or an equal degree of the quality; as, "A *mild* winter," "She is as *good* as she is *beautiful*."

4. The **comparative** degree ascribes to one of two objects a higher or lower degree of the quality than that ascribed to the other; as, "A *milder* winter than usual," "Mary is *less studious* than Emma."

5. The **superlative** degree ascribes the highest or lowest degree of the quality to one of more than two objects; as, "The *mildest* winter ever known," "The *least skillful* rider could do no worse."

Rem. 1—The suffix *ish*, and the words *rather, somewhat*, etc. denote the possession of a small amount of the quality; as, *bluish, rather* young, *somewhat* uncomfortable.

Rem. 2—The words *altogether, far, by far, vastly, much, very, exceedingly, a most, a little, too, very, slightly, greatly*, etc., denote a high degree of the quality without implying comparison as, *very* useful, *exceedingly* welcome, a *most* valuable invention.

Rem 3—Adjectives denoting qualities which cannot exist in different degrees, cannot, with propriety, be compared, but when not taken in their full sense, they may be used in the comparative and superlative degrees.

Ex.—Blind, deaf, perfect, right, level, square, straight, perpendicular, equal, naked, honest, sincere, hollow, empty, dead. "My *sincerest* regards." "Our sight is the *most perfect* of our senses."

52. COMPARATIVES AND SUPERLATIVES

1. In **ascending** comparison, the comparative and superlative degrees are regularly formed—

1st. By adding to the positive of monosyllables, *r* or *er* for the comparative, and *st* or *est* for the superlative; as, *wise, wiser, wisest; hard, harder, hardest.*

2d. By prefixing to the positive of adjectives of more than one syllable, *more* for the comparative, and *most* for the superlative; as, *honorable, more honorable, most honorable.*

Rem. 1—Most adjectives of two syllables ending in *y* or *le*, after a consonant, or accented on the second syllable, form their comparative and superlative degrees like monosyllables; as, *holy, holier, holiest; gentle, gentler, gentlest.*

Rem. 2—Some adjectives of two syllables, ending in a vowel or liquid sound, form their comparative and superlative degrees like monosyllables; as, *handsome, handsomer, handsomest; narrow, narrower, narrowest.*

Rem. 3—Some words are expressed in the superlative degree by adding the suffix *most*; as, *hindmost, innermost.*

2. In **descending** comparison, the comparative is formed by prefixing *less*, and the superlative by prefixing *least*, to the positive; as, *wise, less wise, least wise.*

3. Some adjectives are compared *irregularly*; as, *good, better, best; bad, worse, worst.*

Rem. 1—Monosyllables are sometimes compared by prefixing *more* and *most*; as, "A foot *more light*, a step *more true.*"—*Scott.*

Rem. 2—Two or more adjectives modifying the same word, may be compared by prefixing *more* and *most* to the first; as, "The *more nice* and *elegant* parts"; "*Most potent, grave*, and *reverend* seigniors."—*Shakespeare.*

53. ORDER OF PARSING

1. An adjective, and why?
2. Descriptive or definitive, and why?

3. Compare it, if it admits of comparison.
4. Degree of comparison, and why?
5. What does it describe or define?
6. Rule.

54. MODELS FOR PARSING

I. *"Every diligent* boy received *merited* praise."

Every ..... is an *adjective*, it is a word used to describe or define the meaning of a noun; *definitive*, it defines without expressing any quality; *distributive pronominal*, it represents objects taken separately; it cannot be compared, and belongs to "boy." Rule XII. "An adjective or participle belongs to some noun or pronoun."

Diligent ... is an *adjective*; *descriptive*; it describes a noun by denoting some quality; *compared*, *pos.* diligent, *comp.* more diligent, *sup.* most diligent: *positive degree*, and belongs to "boy." Rule XII.

Merited ... is an *adjective*; *descriptive*; *compared*, *pos.* merited, *comp.* more merited, *sup.* most merited: *positive degree*, and belongs to "praise." Rule XII.

II. *"Many a fine* intellect is buried in poverty."

Many a ... is an *adjective*; *definitive*; *indefinite pronominal*; it refers to objects in a general way: it cannot be compared, and belongs to "intellect." Rule XII.

Fine ...... is an *adjective*; *descriptive*; *compared*, *pos.* fine, *comp.* finer, *sup.* finest; *positive degree*, and belongs to "intellect." Rule XII.

III. "The *first two* engravings are *American harvest* scenes."

The .... is an *adjective*; *definitive*; *definite article*; it cannot be compared, and belongs to "engravings." Rule XII.

First ...... is an *adjective*; *definitive*; *numeral*; it denotes number: *ordinal*; it marks the position of an object in a series: it cannot be compared, and belongs to "engravings." Rule XII.

Two ...... is an *adjective*; *definitive*; *numeral*; *cardinal*; it denotes the number of objects: it cannot be compared, and belongs to "engravings." Rule XII.

American . is an *adjective*; *descriptive*; it cannot be compared, and belongs to "scenes." Rule XII.

Harvest . . . is an *adjective*; *descriptive*; it cannot be compared, and belongs to "scenes." Rule XII.

IV. "The weather is *pleasant*."

Pleasant . . . is an *adjective*; *descriptive*; *compared*, *pos*. pleasant, *comp*. more pleasant; *sup*. most pleasant: *positive degree*, and belongs to "weather." Rule XII.

55. EXERCISES

Parse the nouns and adjectives in the following sentences.

1. A loud report was heard. 2. Fearful storms sweep over these beautiful islands. 3. Life is but a vapor. 4. These walks are quiet and secluded. 5. I feel sad and lonely. 6. The fields look green. 7. He took a twofold view of the subject. 8. Either road leads to town. 9. Each soldier was a host in himself. 10. Both horses are lame. 11. Such a law is a disgrace to any state. 12. Repeat the first four lines in concert. 13. "My drowsy powers, why sleep ye so?" 14. "One story is good until another is told." 15. The Australian gold fields are very extensive. 16. The floor was formed of six-inch boards.

17. None think the great unhappy but the great.—*Young.* 18. To make a long story short, the company broke up and returned to the more important concerns of the election.—*Irving.* 19. Grim-visaged war hath smoothed his wrinkled front.—*Shakespeare.* 20. For nine long years, session after session, we have been lashed round and round this miserable circle of occasional arguments and miserable expedients.—*Burke.* 21. Dim with the mist of years, gray flits the shade of power.—*Byron.*

22. Can storied urn, or animated bust
Back to its mansion call the fleeting breath?—*Gray.*

23. With secret course, which no loud storms annoy,
Glides the smooth current of domestic joy.—*Johnson.*

24. My opening eyes with rapture see
The dawn of this returning day.

25. With many a weary step, and many a groan,
Up the high hill he heaves a huge round stone.—*Pope.*

56. CAUTIONS

Caution I—Always use *an* before *vowel sounds*; always use *a* before *consonant sounds*.

Ex.—1. An hour; an oak. 2. A woman; a year; a eulogy; such a one; a history; a historian.

Caution II—Observe that *the* denotes a *particular one*, or is used to distinguish one class or species from another, and that *a* or *an* denotes *one*, but not a particular one.

Ex.—1. A dime is the tenth part of a dollar. 2. An eagle is a bird of prey. 3. The robot is a modern invention. 4. The subject of his lecture was the steam engine. 5. The lion is the king of beasts. 6. The horse which you saw belongs to me.

Caution III—Do not use *them* for *those*, *this here* for *this*, or *that there* for *there*.

Ex.—1. He bought ten of *those* (not them) horses. 2. I do not like *this* (not this here) weather. 3. What have you done with *that* (not that there) umbrella? 4. Did you put *those* (not them) books on *that* (not that there) table? 5. I wish you would write *those* (not them) rules on the blackboard.

Caution IV—Avoid double comparatives and superlatives, such as these bad examples.

Ex.—1. He seems more cheerfuller today. 2. He is the most miserablest man I ever saw. 3. More sharper than a serpent's tooth is vile ingratitude. 4. Worser evils than poverty can be imagined.

Caution V—In most constructions, place ordinal adjectives before cardinals.

Ex.—Sing the first two and the last three verses, (not, sing the two first and the three last verses).

Caution VI—Do not use adverbs as adjectives.

Ex.—1. I feel bad (not badly) this morning. 2. The country looks beautiful (not beautifully) in June. 3. Things now look more favorable (not more favorably). 4. This rose smells sweet (not sweetly).

Caution VII—Use such adjectives as express the exact meaning intended.

Ex.—1. I will sell any (not either) of the four radios for ten dollars. 2. None (not neither) of my three brothers went to college. 3. He paid each (not all) of the laborers forty dollars a day. 4. There are fewer (not less) boys in school now than formerly.

THE PRONOUN

57. ORAL LESSON

Notice what I write: "John took John's hat, and put John's hat on John's desk." Do you think this is a correct sentence? *Ans.*—No, sir, we do not.

What words are unnecessarily repeated? *Ans.*—"John" and "hat." Write the sentence on your paper as you think it should be written. Sarah, you may read what you have written. (Sarah reads "John took his hat, and put it on his desk." The teacher writes it on the blackboard.) Now, the words used in the place of "John" and "hat" are called *pronouns*, which means "instead of nouns." What shall we call all words used instead of nouns? *Ans.*—Pronouns.

I will write again: "*I* write, *you* read, but *he* whispers." What are the words "I," "you," and "he"? *Ans.*—Pronouns. Why? *Ans.*—Because they are used instead of nouns. What *person* is "I"? *Ans.*—*First person*, because it stands for the person speaking. What *person* is "you"? *Ans.*—*Second person*, because it stands for the person spoken to. What *person* is "he?" *Ans.*—*Third person*, because it stands for the person spoken of. Those words which show by their form the *person* of the nouns they represent are called *personal pronouns*. What kind of pronouns are these words? *Ans.*—Personal pronouns.

Write this sentence: "The man who was with me is a lawyer." What is "me"? *Ans.*—A pronoun. What other pronoun is there in the sentence? *Ans.*—"Who." That is right—and what word does "who" stand for? *Ans.*—Man. But "who" can be used to represent the *first*, *second*, or *third person*; as, "I *who* speak to you," "You *who* listen," "He *who* whispers." It does not change its form to denote person, but *relates* to some noun, and must be of the same person and number as the noun to which it relates. It is therefore called a *relative pronoun*. What shall we call all similar words? *Ans.*—Relative pronouns.

Write this sentence: "Who has lost a pencil?" The word "who" is here used in asking a question. We will call it an *interrogative pronoun*. What shall we call those pronouns which are used in a similar manner? *Ans.*—Interrogative pronouns.

Write this sentence: "That book is mine." What two words can I use instead of "mine?" *Ans.*—"My book." "Mine," then, stands for both the possessor and the thing possessed. We will call it a *possessive pronoun*. What shall we call all words used in a similar manner? *Ans.*—Possessive pronouns.

58. DEFINITION

1. A **pronoun** is a word used instead of a noun: as, *his* book, *my* house; "*Whom* did *you* see?"

2. The **antecedent** of a pronoun is the noun, or equivalent expression, instead of which the pronoun is used. It usually precedes, but sometimes follows, the pronoun.

Ex.—"The poor *widow* lost *her* only son." Here "widow" is the antecedent of "her." "True to *his* flag, the *soldier* braved even death." "Soldier" is the antecedent of "his."

3. The antecedent may be a noun, a different pronoun, a phrase, or a clause.

Ex.—"A *pupil that* is studious will learn." "Pupil" is the antecedent of "that." "*He who* runs may read." "He" is the antecedent of "who." "He desired *to pray*, but *it* was denied him." "To pray" is the antecedent of "it." "*He has squandered his money*, and he now regrets *it*." "He has squandered his money" is the antecedent of "it."

4. The antecedent may be omitted: in which case it is said to be understood.

Ex.—"*Who* steals my purse steals trash." "The person," or "he," understood, is the antecedent of "who."

59. PROPERTIES

1. The **properties** of a pronoun are *gender, person, number*, and *case*.

2. The *gender, person*, and *number* of a pronoun are always the same as those of its antecedent, but its *case* depends upon the construction of the clause in which it is found.

60. CLASSES

Pronouns are divided into four classes: *personal, possessive, relative*, and *interrogative*.

61. PERSONAL PRONOUNS

1. **Personal pronouns** both represent nouns and show by their form whether they are of the first, second, or third person. They are either *simple* or *compound*.

2. The **simple personal pronouns** are *I, you, he, she*, and *it*, with their declined forms, *we, our, us, my, mine, you, your, his, him, her, its, they, their, them*, (also *thou, ye, thy, thine, thee*).

Note—The older forms are included in these pronoun sections because of their value to students of the King James Bible, Shakespeare, and other English literature.

3. The **compound personal pronouns** are formed by adding *self* or *selves* to some form of the simple personals; as, *myself*, *yourselves*, *himself*, *themselves*.

62. DECLENSION

1. The simple personal pronouns are declined as follows:

FIRST PERSON

	Singular			Plural
Nom.	I		*Nom.*	We
Poss.	My or mine		*Poss.*	Our
Obj.	Me		*Obj.*	Us

SECOND PERSON

	Ancient				Modern	
	Singular	Plural			Singular	Plural
Nom.	Thou	Ye		*Nom.*	You	You
Poss.	Thy or thine	Your		*Poss.*	Your	Your
Obj.	Thee	You		*Obj.*	You	You

THIRD PERSON

	Singular				Plural
	MASC.	FEM.	NEUT.		NEUT. OR COM.
Nom.	He	She	It	*Nom.*	They
Poss.	His	Her	Its	*Poss.*	Their
Obj.	Him	Her	It	*Obj.*	Them

2. The compound personal pronouns are declined as follows:

FIRST PERSON

	Singular			Plural
Nom. and Obj.	Myself		*Nom. and Obj.*	Ourselves

SECOND PERSON

	Singular			Plural
Nom. and Obj.	Thyself or Yourself		*Nom. and Obj.*	Yourselves

THIRD PERSON

	Singular			Plural
	MASC., FEM., and NEUT.			
Nom. and Obj.	Himself / Herself / Itself		*Nom. and Obj.*	Themselves

GENERAL REMARKS

1. *Mine* and *thine* were formerly used before words commencing with a vowel sound, in preference to *my* and *thy*, as in the King James Bible and Shakespeare. They are still used thus in poetry; as, "*Thine* eyes I see thee raise."

2. *Thou*, *thy*, *thine*, *thee*, *thyself*, and *ye*, though used in the King James Bible and other sacred writings, are now seldom used except in poetry and in solemn style. They may be regarded as antiquated forms. *You*, *your*, *yours*, and *yourself* are now preferred.

Thou, *thee*, and *thy* in the King James Bible are familiar and singular (cf. Psa. 23:4-5). *Thou* is nominative, and *thee* is in the objective case. *Ye* and *you* are less familiar and generally plural (compare I Ki. 9:6, KJV, with the same verse in the NIV. Cf. *The Sermon on the Mount*, Matt. 5:11, 13, etc. wherein Jesus addresses the whole group as "ye." Cf. also Matt. 10:22-23). Caution: In phrases like "Ye Old Curiosity Shop," *Y* is the runic letter *thorn*. It is a substitution for *th*, so the first word is here the article *the*, NOT the pronoun *Ye*.

3. *You*, originally plural, and still requiring a verb in the plural number, is used to represent singular as well as plural nouns.

4. *We* is often used in place of *I*, in royal proclamations, editorials, and when the speaker or writer wishes to avoid the appearance of egotism; as, "*We*, George III, King of Great Britain and Ireland, do proclaim," etc. "*We* formerly thought differently, but have changed *our* mind."

5. *It* is sometimes used in the nominative without referring to any particular antecedent; and in the objective for euphony alone; as, "*It* thunders," "*It* seems to me," "*It* is a true saying," "Come and trip *it* on the green."

6. The compound personal pronouns are used in the nominative and objective cases only. To express emphatic distinction in the possessive case, the word *own* is used instead of *self* or *selves*; as, "Let every pupil use his *own* book," "Successful merchants mind their *own* business, not that of their neighbors."

7. Since the English language has no pronoun of the third person singular and common gender, usage has sanctioned the employment of the masculine forms *he*, *his*, *him*, for that purpose; as, in speaking of scholars generally, we say, "A thorough scholar studies *his* (never their) lesson carefully."

8. When reference is made to a group containing males only, or females only, the masculine or feminine forms should be used, as the case may require.

9. When pronouns of different *persons* are used, the *second* should precede the *third*, and the *third* the *first*; as, "*You* and *he* and *I* were boys together."

63. ORDER OF PARSING

1. A pronoun, and why?
2. Personal, and why?
3. Simple or compound.
4. What is its antecedent?
5. Gender, person, and number? Rule.
6. Decline it.
7. Case, and why?
8. Rule.

64. MODELS FOR PARSING

I. "*I* have seen *him*."

I . . . . is a *pronoun*; *personal*; it shows by its form whether it is of the first, second, or third person: *simple*; its antecedent is the name, understood, of the person speaking:—*gender, first person, singular number*, to agree with its antecedent: Rule IX. "Pronouns must agree with their antecedents in gender, person, and number;" declined, *singular, nom.* I, *poss.* my, *obj.* me; *plural, nom.* we, *poss.* our, *obj.* us: *nominative case.* Rule I.

Him . . . . is a *pronoun*; *personal*; *simple*; its antecedent is the name, understood, of the person spoken of: *masculine gender, third person, singular number*, to agree with its antecedent: Rule IX: declined, *sing., nom.* he, *poss.* his, *obj.* him; *plural, nom.* they, *poss.* their, *obj.* them: *objective case.* Rule VI.

II. "James, lend *me* your book."

Me . . . . is a *pronoun*; *personal*; *simple*; its antecedent is the name, understood, of the speaker:—*gender, first person, singular number*, to agree with its antecedent: Rule IX. *decline it*; *objective case*, it is the *indirect object* of the transitive verb "lend." Rule VI.

III. "The soldiers helped *themselves*."

Themselves . is a *pronoun*; *compound personal*; it is formed by adding *selves* to one of the declined forms of a simple personal; its antecedent is "soldiers": *masculine gender*, *third person*, *plural number*, to agree with its antecedent: Rule IX: *decline it: objective case*, it is the object of the transitive verb "helped." Rule VI.

IV. "I *myself* heard him say so."

Myself...... is a *pronoun*; *compound personal*; its antecedent is the name, understood, of the speaker:—*gender*, *first person*, *singular number*, to agree with its antecedent: Rule IX: *decline it*: *nominative case*, in apposition with "I." Rule IV.

65. EXERCISES

Parse the nouns, personal pronouns, and adjectives in the following sentences.

1. He and I attend the same school. 2. She gave her sister a new book. 3. Have you seen him today? 4. I saw it with my own eyes. 5. You yourself told me so. 6. The wicked is snared in the work of his own hands. 7. I bought the book and read it. 8. They live in our house. 9. I see them winding on their way. 10. For we dare not make ourselves of the number, or compare ourselves with some that commend themselves; but they, measuring themselves by themselves, and comparing themselves among themselves, are not wise.

11. My country, 'tis of thee,
      Sweet land of liberty,
            Of thee, I sing.

12. Thou great Instructor, lest I stray,
      Teach thou my erring feet thy way.

66. POSSESSIVE PRONOUNS

1. **Possessive pronouns** are words used to represent both the possessor and the thing possessed. They are: *mine, thine, his, hers, ours, yours, theirs.*

2. To denote emphatic distinction, *my own* is used for *mine, his own* for *his, thy own* for *thine, our own* for *ours, your own* for *yours, their own* for *theirs.*

Ex.—"This book is *my own*." "Stand, the ground's *your own*, my braves!" "Do not borrow nor lend pencils: each scholar should have one of *his own*."

67. ORDER OF PARSING

1. A pronoun, and why?
2. Possessive, and why?
3. What is its antecedent?
4. Gender, person, and number, and why? Rule.
5. Case, and why? Rule.

68. MODELS FOR PARSING

I. "That book is *hers*, not *yours*."

Hers ...... is a *pronoun*; *possessive*; it represents both the possessor and the thing possessed; its antecedent is "book"; *neuter gender*, *third person*, *singular number*, to agree with its antecedent: Rule IX: *nominative case*, it is used as the predicate of the proposition, "That book is hers": Rule II.

Yours ..... is parsed in a similar manner; equivalent to "your book."

II. "The ground's *your own*."

Your own . is a *pronoun*; *possessive*; its antecedent is "ground": *neuter gender*, *third person*, singular number; *nominative case*; it is used as the predicate of the proposition, "The ground's your own." Rule II.

69. EXERCISES

Parse the possessive pronouns in the following sentences.

1. The farm is neither his nor theirs. 2. Is that horse of yours still lame? 3. I did not hear that lecture of yours last evening. 4. He is an old friend of ours. 5. This book is not mine; it must be his or hers. 6. That carriage of theirs is a very fine one. 7. Friend of mine, why so sad?

70. RELATIVE PRONOUNS

1. A **relative pronoun** is used to represent a preceding word or phrase, called its antecedent, to which it joins a limiting clause; as, "The man *whom* you saw is my father."

Rem. 1—The **antecedent** is a word or phrase on which the relative clause depends. It may be either a *definite* or an *indefinite* object. When the object is indefinite, the relative clause stands alone; as, "*Who* steals my purse steals trash."

Rem. 2—The difference between personal and relative pronouns is shown by the following distinctions: 1. Personal pronouns have a distinct form for each grammatical person; as, first person, *I*; second person, *thou* or *you*; third person, *he*, *she*, or *it*: the relatives do not change their form for person. 2. A personal pronoun may be the subject of an independent sentence; as, *"He* is well.'' A relative can never be thus used; it is always found in a dependent clause; as, "Laws *which* are unjust should be repealed.''

Rem. 3—Relatives serve two purposes in a sentence; one, to represent nouns in any relation; the other, to join a limiting clause to the antecedent. The first is a *pronominal*, the second, a *conjunctive* use.

2. Relative pronouns are either *simple* or *compound*.

3. The **simple relatives** are *who*, used to represent persons; *which* and *what*, to represent things; *that*, to represent both persons and things; and *as*, to take the place of *who*, *which*, or *that*, after *such*, *many*, and *same*.

Rem. 1—*What* is sometimes used as a definitive adjective as well as a relative, in the same sentences. In such a case it is placed before the noun it limits; as, "I send you *what* money I have,'' *i.e.*, "I send you *the* money *which* I have.'' When the noun it limits is understood, *what* takes its place, and should be parsed, first as a pronominal adjective, and secondly as a relative.

Rem. 2—*That* is a *relative* when *who*, *whom*, or *which* can be substituted for it; as, "He *that* [*who*] is slow to wrath, is of great understanding.'' It is a *pronominal adjective* when it immediately precedes a noun, expressed or understood; as, *"That* book is yours,'' "I did not say *that*.'' It is a *conjunction* when it joins a dependent clause to its principal; as, "I know *that* my Redeemer liveth.''

Rem. 3—*What*, when a relative, can be changed into *that which*, or *the thing which*, and is called a *double relative*; as, "Tell me *what* [*that which*] you know,'' "I got *what* [*the thing which*] I desired.'' *That*, or *the thing*, should be parsed as the antecedent part of *what*, and *which* as the relative. The antecedent part, *that*, is usually a pronominal adjective, either limiting a noun expressed, or representing it understood.

Rem. 4—Besides being a *relative*, *what* may be an *interrogative pronoun*; as, *"What* did you say?''—a *pronominal adjective*; as, *"What* book have you?''—an *interjection*; as, *"What*! Is thy servant a dog, that he should do this?''—an *adverb*; as, *"What* [*partly*] by force, and *what* by fraud, he secures his ends.''

71. DECLENSION

Singular and Plural			*Singular and Plural*	
Nom.	Who		*Nom.*	Which
Poss.	Whose		*Poss.*	Whose
Obj.	Whom		*Obj.*	Which

The **compound relatives** are formed by adding *ever*, *so*, and *soever* to the simple relatives. They are: *whoever, whoso, whosoever, whichever, whichsoever, whatever,* and *whatsoever.*

Rem.—*Whoever, whoso,* and *whosoever,* are equivalent to *he who,* or *anyone who;* as, "*Whoever* studies will learn," *i.e., "Anyone who* studies will learn." *Whichever* and *whichsoever* are equivalent to *any which;* as, "*Whichever* way you may take will lead to the city," *i.e., "Any* way *which* you may take," etc. *Whatever* and *whatsoever* are equivalent to *anything which;* as, "I am pleased with *whatever* you may do," *i.e.,* "I am pleased with *anything which* you may do." Compound relatives are indeclinable, and should be parsed like the simple relative *what.*

72. ORDER OF PARSING

1. A pronoun, and why?
2. Relative, and why?
3. Name its antecedent.
4. Simple or compound?
5. Gender, person, and number, and why? Rule.
6. Decline it.
7. Case, and rule.

73. MODELS FOR PARSING

I. "A man *who* is industrious will prosper."

Who ......is a *pronoun; relative;* it represents a preceding word or phrase, to which it joins a limiting clause: its antecedent is "man": *simple: masculine gender, third person, singular number,* to agree with its antecedent: Rule IX: *nominative case;* it is used as the subject of the subordinate proposition "who is industrious": Rule I.

II. "I am he *whom* ye seek."

Whom ....is a *pronoun; relative;* its antecedent is "he": *simple: masculine gender, third person, singular number:* Rule IX: *objective case;* it is the object of the transitive verb "seek": Rule VI.

III. "Happy is the man *that* findeth wisdom."

That ...... is a *pronoun*; *relative*; its antecedent is "man": *simple*: *masculine gender, third person, singular number*: Rule IX: *nominative case*; it is the subject of the subordinate proposition "that findeth wisdom": Rule I.

IV. "The horse *which* you sold me is lame."

Which .... is a *pronoun*; *relative*; its antecedent is "horse": *simple*: *neuter gender, third person, singular number*; Rule IX: *objective case*; it is the object of the transitive verb "sold": Rule VI.

V. "I remember *what* you said."

What ..... is a *pronoun*; *relative*; it is a *double relative*, equivalent to *that which—"that"* being the *antecedent* part, and *"which,"* the *relative*. Parse *"that"* as a "pronominal adjective used as a noun," in the objective case after "remember."

Which .... is a *pronoun*; *relative*; its antecedent is "that": *neuter gender, third person, singular number*; *objective case*; object of the transitive verb "said": Rule VI.

VI. "That is the man *whose* house we occupy."

Whose .... is a *pronoun*; *relative*; its antecedent is "man": *masculine gender, third person, singular number*; Rule IX: *possessive case*; modifies "house": Rule III.

VII. *"Whoever* studies will learn."

Whoever .. is a *pronoun*; *relative*; *compound*; it is equivalent to *he who*, or *anyone who—"he"* being the *antecedent* part, and *"who"* the *relative*. Parse *"he"* as a personal pronoun, subject of "will learn," or *"one"* as a "pronominal adjective used as a noun," subject of "will learn," and *"who"* as a relative, by preceding models.

VIII. *"Whatever* purifies, sanctifies."

Whatever .. is a *pronoun*; *relative*; *compound*; it is equivalent to *that which*. Parse *"that"* and *"which"* according to Model V—*"that"* being the subject of "sanctifies"; *"which,"* of "purifies."

IX. *"Whoso* keepeth the law is a wise son."

Whoso .... is a *pronoun*; *relative*; *compound*; it is equivalent to *he who*, or *anyone who*. Parse according to Model VII.

X. "As many *as* came were baptized."

As .... is a *pronoun*; *relative*; its antecedent is "many": *simple*: *common gender, third person, plural number*; Rule IX: *nominative case*; it is used as the subject of the subordinate proposition "as came," *i.e.*, "who came": Rule I.

74. EXERCISES

Parse the relative pronouns in the following sentences.

1. Those who sow will reap. 2. He that hateth, dissembleth with his lips. 3. They that forsake the law, praise the wicked; but such as keep the law, contend with them. 4. There is no class of persons that I dislike so much as those who slander their neighbors. 5. The house which you admire so much belongs to the man whom we see yonder. 6. Whatever is, is right. 7. Whatsoever ye shall ask in my name, that will I do. 8. He will do what is right. 9. This is the dog that worried the cat that killed the rat that ate the malt that lay in the house that Jack built. 10. A kind person avoids doing whatever injures others.

75. INTERROGATIVE PRONOUNS

1. The **interrogative pronouns** are *who*, *which*, and *what*, when used in asking questions; as, "*Who* goes there?" "*Which* is yours?" "*What* did you say?"

2. The **subsequent** of an interrogative pronoun is that part of the answer which is represented by it. An interrogative must agree with its subsequent in gender, person, and number.

Rem. 1—When a definite object is referred to, *which* and *what* are pronominal adjectives, limiting the name of the object inquired for; as, "*Which* lesson shall we learn?" "*What* book shall we study?" When an indefinite object is referred to, the interrogative takes its place; as, "*Which* is mine?" "*What* say you?"

Rem. 2—The interrogatives *who* and *which* are declined like relative pronouns.

Rem. 3—Apply Rule IX in parsing interrogatives, changing "antecedents" to "subsequents."

76. ORDER OF PARSING

1. A pronoun, and why?
2. Interrogative, and why?
3. Name its subsequent, if expressed.
4. Gender, person, and number. Rule.
5. Decline it.
6. Case, and why? Rule.

77. MODELS FOR PARSING

I. *"Who* goes there?"

Who . . . is a *pronoun*; *interrogative*; it is used in asking a question: its subsequent is indefinite: *gender* and *person* indeterminate: *singular number*, to agree with its subsequent: Rule IX: *nominative case*; it is used as the subject of the sentence "Who goes there?" Rule I.

II. *"Which* is yours?"—The large one.

Which. . is a *pronoun*; *interrogative*; its subsequent is "one": *neuter gender, third person, singular number*; Rule IX: *nominative case*; it is used as the subject of the sentence "Which is yours?" Rule I.

III. *"What* is that man?"—A blacksmith.

What . . is a *pronoun*; *interrogative*; its subsequent is "blacksmith": *masculine gender, third person, singular number*; Rule IX; *nominative case*; it is used as the predicate of the sentence "What is that man?" Rule II.

78. EXERCISES

Parse the interrogative pronouns in the following sentences.

1. Who saw the horse run? 2. Whose house is that on the hill yonder? 3. Whom did he call? James. 4. For whom did he inquire? 5. Which will you have, the large or the small book?

6. Whom did you take me to be? 7. What shall I do? Wait. 8. What can be more beautiful than that landscape? 9. Which is the lesson? 10. Who told you how to parse "what"?

Parse the relative and interrogative pronouns in the following sentences.

1. Who is in the garden? My father. 2. I do not know who is in the garden. 3. Tell me what I should do. 4. What vessel is that? 5. Always seek for what you need the most. 6. Whose house was burned last night? Mr. Hubbard's. 7. The boy closed the shutters which darkened the room. 8. What is his name? 9. Whoever enters here should have a pure heart. 10. I gave all that I had.

Parse the nouns, pronouns, and adjectives in the following sentences.

1. Virtue is the condition of happiness. 2. Ye are the light of the world. 3. That garment is not well made. 4. One ounce of gold is worth sixteen ounces of silver. 5. The prayers of David, the son of Jesse, are ended. 6. Every man went to his own house. 7. The army is loaded with the spoils of many nations. 8. Be of the same mind one toward another.

9. He sacrificed everything he had in the world: what could we ask more?
10. Who's here so base that would be a bondman? 11. I speak as to wise men: judge ye what I say. 12. Liberty was theirs as men: without it they did not esteem themselves men. 13. The death of Socrates, peacefully philosophizing with his friends, is the most pleasant that could be desired.

14. O Popular applause! what heart of man
    Is proof against thy sweet, seducing charms?

15. What black, what ceaseless cares besiege our state:
    What strokes we feel from fancy and from fate.

16. Unveil thy bosom, faithful tomb;
    Take this new treasure to thy trust;
    And give these sacred relics room
    To slumber in the silent dust.

17. Thy spirit, Independence, let me share,
    Lord of the lion heart and eagle eye:
    Thy steps I'll follow with my bosom bare;
    Nor heed the storm that howls along the sky.—*Smollett*

18.   The glad will laugh
    When thou art gone; the solemn brood of care
    Plod on, and each one as before will chase
    His favorite phantom: yet all these shall leave
    Their mirth and their employment, and shall come
    And make their bed with thee.—*Bryant.*

79. CAUTIONS

Suggestion: as an oral exercise, the students may correct these examples.

Caution I—Do not omit the subjects of declarative and interrogative sentences, as in these examples of incorrect usage.

Ex.—1. Am sorry you cannot go with me. 2. Hope you are well. 3. Came home late last night. 4. What say? 5. Why stay here? 6. Going home late, found the door locked. 7. Read "Snow Bound": like it very much.

Caution II—Do not omit the sign of possession in forming the possessive case of nouns, nor use it in forming the possessive case of pronouns.

Ex.—1. Mr. Arter sells boys hats. 2. The girls bonnets were blown into the lake. 3. That house is her's. 4. Frances' mother is an actress. 5. Have you seen Mr. Pierce' new house. 6. Who's horse ran away?

Caution III—Do not use the objective-case forms of pronouns as subjects or predicates.

Ex.—1. Him and me study arithmetic. 2. It is me, and not her, who wishes to see you. 3. You and him and me were boys together. 4. Me and the doctor were there. 5. Did you say it was me who broke the window?

Caution IV—Do not use "who" as the object of a transitive verb or preposition.

Ex.—1. Who are you talking to? 2. Tell me who you work for. 3. He is a man who I do not like. 4. Who did your sister marry?

Caution V—Do not use "which" as a relative to represent persons, or "who" to represent animals, or objects without life.

Ex.—1. Those which are rich should not be proud. 2. The dog whom you bought, was stolen. 3. It was old dog Hero who was killed. 4. They which study will learn.

Caution VI—Do not use improper forms of possessive pronouns.

Ex.—1. Is that book your'n or her'n? 2. I think it is her'n. 3. That book is his'n. 4. He had no car, so he borrowed our'n. 5. You did not see his horses or our'n, did you?

Caution VII—Do not use a pronoun and its antecedents as subjects of the same sentence.

Ex.—1. The girls they all screamed. 2. Mr. Snell he has gone to Paris. 3. The dogs they barked, and the horses they ran. 4. Many words they darken speech. 5. Ella Jones she is my classmate.

Note—The teacher may wish to use the examples above as an oral exercise, having the students supply the correct usage for each.

THE VERB

80. ORAL LESSON

The teacher writes on the blackboard, "A horse runs," and asks, "What does the horse do?" *Ans.*—A horse *runs*. What else may a horse do? *Ans.*— A horse *trots*, *walks*, *gallops*, *eats*, *drinks*, etc. Write these words on your papers. Are they the names of things? *Ans.*—They are not: they are the names of actions. What shall we call them? *Ans.*—*Action words.* A very good name, but grammarians call them *verbs*.

Write on your papers, "John studies." What is the subject of the sentence? *Ans.*—"John." What is the predicate? *Ans.*—"Studies." Does the sentence tell what John studies? *Ans.*—It does not. Write "grammar" after the verb "studies." The sentence now reads, "John studies *grammar*." In this sentence, the meaning of "studies" is *completed* by the word "grammar." What element is that word? *Ans.*—An objective element.

A verb which requires an object to complete its meaning, is called a *transitive* verb; a verb which does not require an object to complete its meaning, is called an *intransitive* verb. What is "studies" in the sentence "John studies grammar?" *Ans.*—A transitive verb. Why? *Ans.*—Because its meaning is completed by an object. What is "run," in the sentence "John runs?" *Ans.*—An intransitive verb. Why? *Ans.*—Because its meaning is not completed by an object.

Write this sentence. "The fields look green." What is the subject of this sentence? *Ans.*—"Fields." What is the predicate? *Ans.*—"Green." What is the office of the word "look"? *Ans.*—It asserts the predicate "green" of the subject "fields." Correctly answered. Its use is *copulative*; and such copulative words are called *copulative* or *linking verbs* because they couple or link the subject with the predicate adjective. What is "look" in this sentence? *Ans.*—A copulative verb. What is "seems" in the sentence "He seems afraid?" *Ans.*—A copulative verb. Why? *Ans.*—Because it asserts the predicate of the subject.

Rem.—Verbs which can be replaced by *are* or *is* are *copulative* verbs. Others are *transitive* or *intransitive*.

81. DEFINITION

A **verb** is a word which expresses being, action, or state; as I *am*; George *writes*; The house *stands*.

Rem.—The *being*, *action*, or *state*, may be stated abstractly or represented as belonging to a subject; as, "To *write*," "Boys *write*," "*To seem*," "He *seems* discouraged."

82. CLASSES WITH RESPECT TO USE

1. With respect to their *use*, verbs may be divided into *copulative*, *transitive*, and *intransitive*.

2. A **copulative verb** is used to join a predicate to a subject, and to make an assertion; as, "Sugar *is* sweet," "He *seems* honest."

Rem.—The copula *to be* is the only *pure* copulative. The verbs *become*, *seem*, *appear*, *stand*, *walk*, and other verbs of *motion*, *position*, and *condition*, together with the passive verbs *is named*, *is called*, *is styled*, *is elected*, *is appointed*, *is constituted*, *is made*, *is chosen*, *is esteemed*, and some others, are frequently used as copulatives.

Ex.—"The road *became* rough." "The men *appeared* cheerful." "He *was styled* the Czar of all the Russias." "Sir Walter Scott *was called* the Wizard of the North." "General Washington *was elected* first President of the United States."

3. A **transitive verb** requires an object to complete its meaning; as, "The hunter *killed* a bear," "The scholar *learned* his lesson," "That house *has* seven gables."

4. An **intransitive verb** does not require an object to complete its meaning; as, "Flowers *bloom*," "Grass *grows*," "The wind *blows* furiously."

Rem. 1—The action expressed by a *transitive* verb has reference to some object external to the subject, upon which it acts: the action expressed by an *intransitive* verb has no such reference, but affects the subject only. If an object is required to complete its meaning, a verb is transitive, otherwise intransitive. A verb in the passive form is transitive if its subject in the passive voice can be made its object in the active.

Ex.—"That boy *studies* algebra." The verb "studies" is transitive, because its meaning is completed by the object "algebra." "That boy *studies*." The verb "studies" is transitive, because some word, as *lesson, grammar*, etc., is required to complete its meaning. "The winds *blow*." The verb "blow" is intransitive, because the action expressed by it affects the subject only, and does not require the addition of an object to complete its meaning. "The letter *was written* by me," *i.e.,* I *wrote* the letter. The verb "was written" is transitive, because its subject in the passive voice becomes its object in the active.

Rem. 2—A verb which represents its subject as *causing to do* what the verb expresses, is said to be used in a *causative* sense.

Ex.—"The farmer *burns* wood," *i.e.,* "The farmer *causes wood to burn*." "The pirate *sank* the ship," *i.e.,* "The pirate *caused the sinking* of the ship." The verbs "burns" and "sank" are used in a causative sense.

Rem. 3—Some verbs are transitive in one signification, and intransitive in another.

Ex.—"It *breaks* my chain." "Glass *breaks* easily." "He *returned* the book." "I *returned* home." "The vessel *ran* the blockade." "The horses *ran*."

Rem. 4—An intransitive verb becomes transitive when it is followed by an object like itself in meaning.

Ex.—"He *lives* a noble *life*." "And he *dreamed* yet another *dream*." "Those men *are playing a game* of chess." "*Grinned* horribly a ghastly *smile*."

83. CLASSES WITH RESPECT TO FORM

1. With respect to their *form*, verbs are either *regular* or *irregular*.

2. A **regular verb** forms its past indicative and perfect participle by adding *d* or *ed* to the present indicative, or simplest form of the verb; as, love, *love-d*, *love-d*; count, *count-ed*, *count-ed*.

3. An **irregular verb** does not form its past indicative and perfect participle by adding *d* or *ed* to the present indicative; as, see, *saw*, *seen*; go, *went*, *gone*.

84. PROPERTIES

The **properties** of verbs are *voice, mode, tense, number,* and *person.*

85. VOICE

1. **Voice** is that form of the *transitive* verb which shows whether the subject acts or is acted upon.

2. **Transitive verbs** have two voices: an *active* and a *passive voice.*

3. The **active voice** represents the subject as acting upon an object; as, "John *struck* James," "The boy *was studying,*" "The cat *caught* the mouse."

4. The **passive voice** represents the subject as being acted upon; as, "James *was struck* by John," "The mouse *was caught,*" "The lesson *was studied.*"

5. The passive voice is formed by prefixing some form of the neuter verb *to be* to the perfect participle of a transitive verb.

Rem. 1—The direct object of a verb in the active voice becomes its subject in the passive.

Ex.—"The boy *shut* the door" (*active*). "The door *was shut* by the boy" (*passive*). "He *saw* the comet." "The comet *was seen* by the astronomer."

Rem. 2—Certain verbs are sometimes used, with a passive signification, in the active voice.

Ex.—"This stick *splits* easily." "Butter *sells* for forty cents." "This ground *plows* well." "The stone *breaks* readily." "I have nothing *to wear.*" "He has some ax *to grind.*" "He has no money *to spend* foolishly." "Wheat *sells* for one dollar a bushel."

Rem. 3—A few verbs sometimes assume the passive form, though used in an active sense.

Ex.—"The melancholy days *are come*," *i.e.*, *have* come. "Babylon *is fallen*," *i.e.*, *has* fallen. "She *is gone*," *i.e.*, *has* gone. "The hour *is arrived*," *i.e.*, *has* arrived." "He *was come* now," he said, "to the end of his journey."

Rem. 4—The passive voice is used when the agent is unknown, or when we wish to conceal it and call attention to the act and its *object* alone; as, "The robbery *was committed* (by some person unknown, or known but not mentioned) in broad daylight," "This wall *was built* to protect the banks of the river." When we wish to make the agent prominent, the active voice should be used; as, "The escaped convict *committed* the robbery in broad daylight."

86. EXERCISES

Tell which of the verbs, in the following sentences, are in the active voice, and which in the passive.

1. Sarah loves flowers. 2. John was astonished at the news. 3. William saw a meteor. 4. A meteor was seen. 5. I have written a letter. 6. That poem was written by Saxe. 7. He should have waited longer. 8. The heavens declare the glory of God. 9. He found the money.

87. THE PARTICIPLE

1. A **participle** is a word derived from a verb, partaking of the properties of a verb and of an adjective or a noun.

Rem.—The participle is so called from its partaking of the properties of a verb and of an adjective or a noun. It is the attributive part of the verb, used without assertion. It is not a verb, consequently neither *mode* nor *tense* belongs to it. It simply denotes *continuance* or *completion* of action, being, or state, relatively to the time denoted by the principal verb of the sentence in which it is found.

2. There are three participles: the *present*, the *perfect*, and the *compound*. The present and the compound have both an active and a passive form and use. The perfect has an active and a passive use.

3. The **present participle** denotes the continuance of action, being, or state; as, *loving, being loved*.

Rem.—The *present participle* always ends in *ing*. It may be used as an assumed attribute, or be affirmed of a subject. In the sentence, "*Leaning* my head upon my hand, I began to picture to myself the miseries of imprisonment," "leaning" depends upon or modifies "I." It is an assumed attribute. "In the sentence, "I was **leaning** my head upon my hand," "leaning" is affirmed of the subject "I." The present participle may also be used:

1st. As an adjective; as, "*Twinkling* stars." When thus used, it is called a *participial adjective*; and when it denotes a *quality* rather than an *act*, it usually admits of comparison; as, "A *most loving* companion."

2d. As a noun; as, "I am fond of *reading*." "Reading," in this sentence, is a *participial noun*, and is the object of the preposition "of." By some grammarians, a participial noun is called an "infinitive ending in ing," or a *"gerund."*

3d. As a noun, with the modifications of a verb; as, *"Describing* a past *event* as present, has a fine effect in language." In this sentence, the participial noun "describing" is modified by "event," its object. Participial nouns may also be modified by adverbs; as, "I am fond of *traveling rapidly*." Here, "traveling" is modified by the adverb "rapidly."

4. The **perfect participle** denotes the *completion* of action, being, or state; as, *seen, appointed*.

Rem.—This participle generally ends in *d, ed, t, n*, or *en*. It is frequently used as an adjective, but never as a noun, and is usually, but not always, found in compound forms of the verb.

Ex.—"He died, *loved* by all." "Her promise, *made* cheerfully, was kept faithfully." "I have *written* a letter." "You should have *known* better." "That house was *built* in 1780."

5. The **compound participle** denotes the *completion* of action, being, or state, at or before the time represented by the principal verb; as, *"Having written* the letter, he mailed it."

Rem.—This participle is formed by placing *having* or *having been* before the perfect participle; as, *"Having bought* the horse, he went home," "The lessons *having been recited*, the school was dismissed." It may be used as a noun; as, "I am accused of *having plotted* treason," "He is charged with *having been engaged* in the slave trade." It is also formed by placing *having been* before the present participle; as, *"Having been loving."*

88. EXERCISES

Give the present, perfect, and compound participles of the following verbs.

Rely, find, help, study, recite, inquire, answer, plow, cultivate, join, emulate, spell, grow, paint, resemble, hope, suffer, sit, see, go, come, lay, arrive, exhaust, enjoy, write, read, learn, ventilate.

Write five sentences, each containing a present participle.

Model—"Mary is *studying* her lesson."

Write five sentences, each containing a perfect participle.

Models—"I have *learned* my lesson." "The army, *flushed* with victory, marched onward."

Write five sentences, each containing a present and a perfect participle.

Model—"A boy *playing* on the seashore, found an oar *lost* from a boat."

Write five sentences, each containing a compound participle.

Model—"The notes *having been paid*, the mortgage was canceled."

Write five sentences, each containing a participial adjective.

Model—"*Rolling* stones gather no moss."

Write five sentences, each containing a participial noun.

Models—"*Skating* is good exercise." "Much depends upon his *observing* the rule."

89. ORDER OF PARSING

1. A participle, and why?
2. From what verb is it derived?
3. Present, perfect, or compound, and why?
4. To what does it belong?
5. Rule.

90. MODELS FOR PARSING

I. "I heard the wolves *howling* in the forest."

Howling . . . . is a *participle*: it partakes of the properties of a verb and of an adjective: it is derived from the verb "howl": *present participle*; it denotes *continuance*: it belongs to "wolves." Rule XII.

II. "Take this letter, *written* by myself."

Written . . . . is a *participle*: it is derived from the verb "write": *perfect participle*; it denotes *completion*: it belongs to "letter." Rule XII.

III. "The train *having left*, we returned home."

Having left . . . . is a *participle*: it is derived from the verb "leave": *compound participle*; it denotes the completion of an act before the time represented by the principal verb: it belongs to "train." Rule XII.

IV. "Their leader *having been killed*, the robbers fled."

Having been killed . . is a *participle*: it is derived from the verb "kill": *compound participle*: it belongs to "leader." Rule XII.

V. "*Whispering* is forbidden."

Whispering . . . . is a *noun*; *participial*; it is derived from the verb "whisper": *neuter gender*; *third person*; *singular number*; *nominative case*. Rule I.

91. EXERCISES

Parse the nouns, pronouns, adjectives, and participles in the following sentences.

1. I have heard the bells tolling. 2. He saw the letter opened. 3. Gambling is a vice. 4. Boys like running, jumping, and skating. 5. The vessel anchored in the bay has lost her sails. 6. Having sold my farm, I shall move to Iowa. 7. The burning of the capitol was a wanton outrage. 8. Have you not seen strong men weeping? 9. The general having been captured, the army was defeated. 10. Your remaining here would ruin us all.

11. Said but once, said but softly, not marked at all, words revive before me in darkness and solitude.—*DeQuincey.* 12. A man hardened in depravity would have been perfectly contented with an acquittal so complete, announced in language so gracious.—*Macaulay.*

13. I heard the ripple washing in the reeds,
    And the wild water lapping on the crags.—*Tennyson.*

14. Toiling, rejoicing, sorrowing,
    Onward through life he goes,
    Something attempted, something done,
    Has earned a night's repose.—*Longfellow.*

92. AUXILIARIES

1. **Auxiliary verbs** are those which are used in the conjugation of other verbs. They are often called *helping verbs.*

2. They are: *do, be, have, shall, will, may, can, must.*

Rem. 1—*Do, be, have,* and *will* are often used as principal verbs; as, "He *does* well," "I *am*," "We *have* salvation in Christ," "He *willed* me a thousand dollars."

Rem. 2—The auxiliaries were originally used as principal verbs, followed by the infinitives of what are now called the principal verbs; as, "I *can* [to] read," "You *may* [to] go," "He *has* [to] come." The sign *to* is now dropped, and the infinitive is regarded as the principal verb; the auxiliaries being used merely to show the relations of *mode* and *tense*.

Rem. 3—The auxiliaries, when used as such, except *must*, which is used in the present tense only, have two tenses: the *present* and the *past*.

93. CONJUGATION OF THE AUXILIARIES
PRESENT TENSE

	Singular			*Plural*	
1st Person	2d Person	3d Person	1st Person	2d Person	3d Person
I	*You*	*He*	*We*	*You, Ye*	*They*
am	are	is	are	are	are
do	do	does	do	do	do
have	have	has	have	have	have
will	will	will	will	will	will
shall	shall	shall	shall	shall	shall
may	may	may	may	may	may
can	can	can	can	can	can
must	must	must	must	must	must

PAST TENSE

was	were	was	were	were	were
did	did	did	did	did	did
had	had	had	had	had	had
would	would	would	would	would	would
should	should	should	should	should	should
might	might	might	might	might	might
could	could	could	could	could	could

Note—In the King James Bible and other writings of that time, present tense of second person singular is: thou *art, dost, hast, wilt, shalt, mayst, canst, must*. Past tense is: thou *wast, didst, hadst, wouldst, shouldst, mightst, couldst*. Second person plural uses the pronoun *ye* and verbs the same as above.

MODE
94. DEFINITION

1. **Mode** is the manner in which the action, being, or state is expressed.

2. There are five modes: the *indicative, subjunctive, potential, imperative*, and *infinitive*.

95. INDICATIVE MODE

The **indicative mode** asserts a thing as a fact, or as actually existing; as, "The man *walks*," "The house *was burned*."

Rem.—The indicative mode may be used in interrogative and exclamatory sentences; also, in subordinate propositions, to denote what is actual, or what is assumed as actual; as, "*Is* he a merchant?" "The rascal *has stolen* my horse!" "I hear that you *have moved* from town."

96. SUBJUNCTIVE MODE

The **subjunctive mode** asserts a thing as *doubtful*, as a *wish*, a *supposition*, or a *future contingency*; as, "If this *be* true, all will end well," "*Had* I the wings of a dove," "I shall leave, if you *remain*."

Rem. 1—The subjunctive mode is so called because it is used in *subjoined* or subordinate propositions only. It represents an ideal act, or a real act placed under a condition of more or less doubt, and is joined to the verb of the principal proposition by the subordinate connectives *if, though, except, lest, that, unless*, and some others. These connectives are called the *signs* of the subjunctive.

Rem. 2—The sign is frequently omitted, in which case the auxiliary or copula precedes the subject; as, "*Had* I time," *i.e.*, If I had time; "*Were* I a king," *i.e.*, If I were a king.

Rem. 3—In a subordinate proposition expressing a condition or a supposition, the verb may be in either the indicative or the subjunctive mode. Use the subjunctive mode, *when it is intended to express doubt or denial*; the indicative or potential mode, *when the thing supposed is a fact or is assumed to be a fact*.

Ex.—"If I *go*, I shall return": I may go, or I may not; doubt is implied. "If he *were* honest, he would pay me": the supposition is that he is not honest. "If he *had been* there, I should have seen him": I deny that he was there. In these sentences, the verbs are in the subjunctive mode, doubt or denial being implied. In the sentences, "If he *goes*, you must stay," and "If he *was* there, he fought bravely," "goes" and "was" are in the indicative mode, neither doubt nor denial being implied.

Rem. 4—Comparatively few modern writers observe the distinction between the indicative and the subjunctive modes in stating suppositions. The directions given in Rem. 3 state the usage of the best writers.

97. POTENTIAL MODE

The **potential mode** asserts the *power*, *necessity*, *liberty*, *duty*, or *liability* of acting or being in a certain state; as, "You *can read*," "He *must go*," "You *may retire*," "They *should be* more careful."

Rem. 1—The potential mode, like the indicative, is used in interrogative and exclamatory sentences; also, in subordinate propositions, to represent what is assumed as actual, or what has not been realized; as, "I know that I *may be* disappointed," "He says that I *may study* algebra."

Rem. 2—The *signs* of the potential mode are the auxiliaries *may*, *can*, *must*, *might*, *could*, *would*, and *should*.

1. **Can** or **could** implies power or ability *within* one's self; as, "He *can* do it," *i.e.*, he has ability to do it without assistance from others.

2. **May** or **might** implies an agency *without* or *beyond* one's self; hence, *possibility*, *probability*, *permission*, *wishing*—the act being contingent on something beyond one's own will or power; as, "He *may* go," *i.e.*, all hindrances are removed: "You *may* all go to the picnic," denotes permission: "Oh, that he *might* return," denotes a wish that all hindrance to his return be removed.

3. **Must** denotes *necessity*; as, "We *must* submit to the laws," *i.e.*, there is a necessity for our doing so.

4. **Should** denotes that the act or state is not dependent upon the doer's will, but on that of another; hence, *duty* or *obligation*; as, "He *should* pay his debts," *i.e.*, it is his duty, or he is under a moral obligation to pay his debts.

5. **Would** implies *inclination*, *wish*, or *desire*; as, "He *would* pay his debts, if he could," *i.e.*, he has the inclination or the desire.

98. IMPERATIVE MODE

The **imperative mode** expresses a *command*, an *exhortation*, an *entreaty*, or a *permission*; as, "*Charge*, Chester, *charge!*" "Do *come* to see us," "*Lead* us not into temptation," "God said, *Let* there be light."

Rem. 1—The imperative mode may usually be known by the omission of the subject; as, "*Write*" [*thou, you*, or *ye*]. It denotes a command, when a superior speaks to an inferior; an exhortation, when an equal speaks to an equal; a prayer or supplication, when an inferior addresses a superior. It is used mostly in principal propositions, and is made subordinate in direct quotations only; as, "He said, '*Be* silent.' "

Rem. 2—The expressions "*Let* Ellen come," "*Let* him go," etc., are made up of the imperative of the verb *let*, and the objective case of a noun or pronoun, limited by an infinitive. They are equivalent to "[You] *Permit* Ellen *to* go," etc.

Rem. 3—These expressions are sometimes abridged by dropping the verb *let*, changing the infinitive to the imperative, and the objective case to the nominative; as, "*Come* one, *come* all," *i.e.*, Let one come, *let* all come: "*Sing* we to our God above," *i.e.*, Let us sing to our God above. In such cases, the noun or pronoun should be parsed as the subject of the proposition, the imperative agreeing with it in number and person. This use of the imperative is not uncommon.

Ex.—"Ruin *seize* thee, ruthless king."—*Gray*. "*Laugh* those who may, *weep* those who must."—*Scott*. "Then *turn* we to her latest tribune's name."—*Byron*. "*Proceed* we therefore to our subject."—*Pope*. "*Come* the eleventh plague, rather than this should be."—*Cowley*. "*Be* it enacted."—*Statutes of Ohio*. "Somebody *call* my wife."—*Shakespeare*. "Hallowed *be* thy name."

Rem. 4—The imperative mode is sometimes used to denote a wish, a demand, a grant, a concession, or a precaution.

Ex.—"*Let* all the earth fear the Lord." "*Give* me that knife." "*Let* it be lawful, that law do no wrong."—*Shakespeare*. "*Let* it be admitted." "*Look*, that he hide no weapon."—*Bulwer*.

99. INFINITIVE MODE

The **infinitive mode** expresses the action, being, or state, without affirming it; as, *to write*; *to have written*; "He rose *to speak*."

Rem. 1—The infinitive may usually be known by the sign *to* placed before it. This sign is omitted after the verbs *bid, dare, feel, hear, help, let, make, need, see*, and a few others; as, "*Bid* them *be* quiet," "*Let* them *come* on," "*See* him *run*."

Rem. 2—The infinitive, as an abstract noun, may be the subject or predicate of a sentence; may be in apposition with a noun; and may be the object of a transitive verb or preposition; as, "*To lie* is disgraceful," "To work is *to pray*," "Delightful task, *to rear* the tender thought," "I love *to read*," "Can save the son of Thetis from *to die*."

Although the infinitive has the construction of a noun, it may govern an object, or be modified by an adverb. It is never limited by an adjective attribute, but may have a predicate adjective belonging to it; as, "*To converse* is *pleasant*," "*To suffer* all this wrong is *hard*."

100. EXERCISES

Tell the mode of the verbs in the following sentences.

1. A great storm is raging. 2. You may go or stay. 3. Bring me some flowers. 4. Hope thou in God. 5. If he study, he will excel. 6. If he studies, it is when he is alone. 7. Were I rich, I would purchase that property. 8. Who will go with me? 9. Let me see your book.

10. I must not be tardy. 11. Lift up your heads, O ye gates! 12. Blessed are the poor in spirit; for theirs is the kingdom of heaven. 13. He should have told you. 14. They dare not puzzle us for their own sakes. 15. Let us not, I beseech you, deceive ourselves longer.

16. God help us! What a poor world this would be, if this were the true doctrine. 17. If a line is parallel to a line of a plane, it is parallel to that plane. 18. If a plane intersect two parallel planes, the lines of intersection will be parallel. 19. "Could he have kept his spirit to that flight, he had been happy."—*Byron.*

20. Reign thou in hell, thy kindgom; let me serve
In heaven, God ever blest.—*Milton.*

21. Place me on Sunium's marble steep,
　　Where nothing, save the waves and I,
May hear our mutual murmurs sweep;
　　There, swan-like, let me sing and die.—*Byron.*

TENSE

101. DEFINITION

1. **Tense** denotes the *time* of an action or event.

2. There are three divisions of time: *past, present,* and *future.* Each division has two tenses: an *absolute* and a *relative.*

3. The **absolute tenses** are the *present,* the *past,* and the *future.* They denote indefinite or incomplete action.

4. The **relative tenses** are the *present perfect,* the *past perfect,* and the *future perfect.* They denote completed action.

102. PRESENT TENSE

The **present tense** denotes present time; as, "I *walk,*" "The army *is marching.*"

Rem. 1—The present tense is used in expressing a general truth, or what is habitual; as, "Perseverance *conquers* all things," "The mail *arrives* at six P.M."

Rem. 2—The *historical* present is the present used for the past, to describe more vividly what took place in past time; as, "Tacitus *describes* the manners and customs of the ancient Germans," "Ulysses *wakes*, not knowing where he was."—*Pope.* "Matthew *traces* the descent of Joseph; Luke *traces* that of Mary." Keep in mind that works of literature exist in the present, though their authors may be long dead. Therefore the writers are ordinarily said to speak in the present. Say "Moses *writes* in Exodus, Chapter 20"; but, "Moses, about B.C. 1500, *wrote*."

Rem. 3—The present of the speaker or hearer is what is meant by present time. The present of the reader may not be the same as that of the writer.

Rem. 4—When preceded by a relative pronoun, or by conjunctive adverbs of time, the present tense is sometimes future in its reference; as, "He will please all who *employ* him," "The flowers will bloom when spring *comes*."

103. PRESENT PERFECT TENSE

The **present perfect tense** represents an action or event as past, but connected with present time; as, "I *have learned* my lesson."

Rem. 1—**Have**, the sign of the present perfect tense, originally denoted *possession*. It retains this meaning when used as a principal verb. As an auxiliary, it denotes *completion*; as, "The hunters *have killed* a wolf," "A man *has fallen* from the bridge."

Rem. 2—When preceded by a conjunctive adverb of time, the present perfect tense sometimes denotes future time; as, "He will forward the goods as soon as he *has received* them."

104. PAST TENSE

The **past tense** expresses what took place in time wholly past; as, "I *wrote*," "I *was sailing*."

Rem.—The *past indicative*, like the *present*, denotes what was habitual; as, "We *walked* five miles every morning." In the progressive form, it denotes an act in past time, but not completed; as, "He *was driving* furiously when I saw him."

The *past potential* denotes (1) a duty or obligation, without reference to time; as, "Judges *should* be merciful": (2) a habit or custom; as, "He *would* be absent a week at a time": (3) ability possessed in past time; as, "He *could* walk yesterday'': (4) present possibility or power; as, "I *could* write [now] if I would'': (5) a future possibility; as, "If I *should* write to you [hereafter], you must answer immediately."

105. PAST PERFECT TENSE

The **past perfect tense** represents an act as ended or completed in time fully past; as, "The train *had started* before we reached the depot."

Rem. 1—The past is frequently used instead of the past perfect, to denote the completion of an act at or before a certain past time mentioned; as, "The boat *left* before midnight."

Rem. 2—The *past perfect subjunctive* and *past perfect potential* deny the action or event; as, "If I *had started* sooner, I *should have* overtaken you."

106. FUTURE TENSE

The **future tense** expresses what will take place in future time; as, "I *shall return* soon," "The lion *shall eat* straw like the ox."

Rem. 1—**Shall** and **will** are the *signs* of the future tense. *Shall* expresses the action or event (1) as a duty commanded; as, "He *shall* pay you," "Thou *shalt* not steal": (2) as a prediction; as, "I *shall* make a thousand dollars": (3) as future; as, "I *shall* leave at noon."

Will expresses the action or event (1) as something determined upon; as, "I *will* go: no power on earth can prevent me," "The cause *will* raise up armies": (2) as future; as, "You *will* feel better tomorrow."

Rem. 2—*Shall*, in the first person, and *will*, in the second and third, are usually employed to denote futurity; as, "We *shall arrive* there by noon," "You *will be* glad to see us," "He *will be* with us."

Will is used, in the first person, to denote determination; and *shall*, in the second and third, to denote necessity; as, "I *will write* to you," "I *will* not *do* it, come what may," "Neither he nor you *shall go* without me."

107. FUTURE PERFECT TENSE

The **future perfect tense** represents an action as finished or ended at or before a certain future time; as, "I *shall have finished* my task at three o'clock," "We *shall have dined* before you arrive."

108. TENSES IN ALL THE MODES

1. The indicative mode has the *six* tenses.

2. The subjunctive mode has *three* tenses: the *present*, *past*, and *past perfect*.

3. The potential mode has *four* tenses: the *present*, *present perfect*, *past*, and *past perfect*.

4. The imperative mode has *one* tense: the *present*.

5. The infinitive mode has *two* tenses: the *present* and *present perfect*.

Rem.—Tense does not properly belong to the infinitive mode. Its tenses are mere *forms*, without regard to time. The *present* tense denotes progressive or completed action or state, with reference to past, present, or future time; the *present perfect*, a completed action or state in an unlimited manner.

109. SIGNS OF THE TENSES: ACTIVE VOICE

INDICATIVE MODE

Present ....Simple form of the verb.
Past ....When regular, add *ed* to the simple form.
Future ....Prefix *shall* or *will* to the simple form.
Present Perfect..Prefix *have*, *hast*, or *has* to the perfect participle.
Past Perfect ....Prefix *had* or *hadst* to the perfect participle.
Future Perfect ..Prefix *shall have* or *will have* to the perfect participle.

SUBJUNCTIVE MODE

If, *though*, *except*, *unless*, etc., placed before tense forms given in the conjugation, are called of the subjunctive mode.

POTENTIAL MODE

Present ....Prefix *may*, *can* or *must* to the simple form.
Past ....Prefix *might*, *could*, *would*, or *should* to the simple form.

Present Perfect..Prefix *may, can,* or *must have* to the perfect participle.

Past Perfect ....Prefix *might, could, would,* or *should have* to the perfect participle.

IMPERATIVE MODE

Present ....*Let,* or a *command.*

INFINITIVE MODE

Present ....Prefix *to* to the simple form.

Present Perfect..Prefix *to have* to the perfect participle.

PARTICIPLES

Present ....Add *ing* to the simple form.

Perfect ....When regular, add *ed* or *d* to the simple form.

Compound .....Prefix *having* to the perfect participle.

110. FORMS OF THE VERB

1. **Verbs** have five forms, which may be considered subdivisions of the tenses: the *common,* the *emphatic,* the *progressive,* the *passive,* and the *ancient,* or *solemn style.*

2. The **common form** represents an act as a custom, or as completed without reference to its progress; as, "I *write,*" "I *shall write.*"

3. The **emphatic form** represents an act with emphasis; as, "I *do* write," "He *did* go," "He declared that he *did* not do it."

Rem.—This form is used in the *present* and *past* indicative and subjunctive and in the *present* imperative. It is formed by prefixing the present and past tenses of *to do* to the simple form of the verb.

4. The **progressive form** is used to denote action or state in progress; as, "I *am writing,*" "He *had been singing.*"

Rem.—The progressive form may be used in all the modes and tenses, and is formed by prefixing the various modes and tenses of the verb *to be* to the present participle of the principal verb.

5. The **passive form** denotes the reception of an act by its subject; as, "I *am struck*," "John *was punished*," "I *shall be loved*."

Rem.—The passive form is used in all the modes and tenses, and is formed by prefixing the various modes and tenses of the verb *to be* to the perfect participle of the principal verb.

6. The **ancient form**, or *solemn style*, is used in the Bible, in religious worship, and sometimes in poetry; as, "Thou *art* the man," "So *shalt* thou *rest*."

111. PERSON AND NUMBER

1. The **person** and **number** of verbs are their modifications to mark their agreement with their subjects.

2. A subject in the *second person singular, ancient form*, generally requires the verb, or its auxiliary, to end in *t*, *st*, or *est*; as, "Thou *shalt* not steal," "Thou *canst* read," "Thou *runnest*."

3. *You*, when the subject in the second person singular, requires a plural verb not ending in *s*; as, "You *shall* not *steal*," "You *can read*," "You *run*."

Rem.—In *ancient form*, as in the King James Bible, both *you* and *ye* were generally plural. The singular form was *thou*. In modern usage, therefore, *you* always requires a plural verb, though it may be either singular or plural, depending on its antecedent; as, "John, *you clean* the boards today," "John and Paul, *you clean* the board today" (but, "*Paul cleans* the boards today").

4. A subject in the *third person singular*, generally requires the verb, or its auxiliary, to end in *s*, *es*, or *eth*; as, "Julia *reads*," "The horse *goes*," "God *loveth* us."

5. The personal terminations in the plural are the same as the *first person singular*, except in the verb *to be*.

6. A verb must agree with its subject in person and number.

Rem. 1—When two or more nominatives, differing in person, are taken collectively, the verb prefers the first to the second, and the second to the third. When they are connected by *or* or *nor*, or are taken separately, it prefers the person of the nominative next to it. Courtesy requires the first place to be given to the *second* person, and last place to the *first*.

Ex.—"*You, he*, and *I have* to remain." "*You* and *he have* to learn that long lesson." "*You* or I *am* mistaken." "*Thou* and *thy friends are* to make reparation."

Rem. 2—A verb must be in the singular number when its subject conveys the idea of unity.

Ex.—"Rain *falls*." "The army *is marching*." "*Dombey & Son* [the title of a book] *was* written by Dickens." "The *ten dollars* [a single sum] *was* duly paid." "*Descent* and *fall* [words alike in meaning] to us *is* adverse."

Rem. 3—A verb must be in the plural number when its subject conveys the idea of plurality.

Ex.—"The *rains descend*." "The *multitude pursue* pleasure." "Either the *magistrate* or the *laws are* at fault." "*You, he*, and *I are* here."

112. UNIPERSONAL VERBS

A **unipersonal verb** is one by which an act or state is asserted independently of any particular subject; as, "It *snows*," "It *cleared off*," "It *behooves* us to be careful."

113. CONJUGATION

1. The **conjugation** of a verb is the correct expression, in regular order, of its *modes, tenses, voices, persons*, and *numbers*.

2. There are four forms of conjugation: the *regular*, the *emphatic*, the *progressive*, and the *interrogative*.

3. The **principal parts** of a verb are: the *present indicative*, the *past indicative*, and the *perfect participle*.

4. The **synopsis** of a verb is its variation in form, through the different modes and tenses, in a single number and person.

114. CONJUGATION OF THE VERB "TO BE"

PRINCIPAL PARTS

Present Tense	*Past Tense*	*Perfect Participle*
Be, or am	Was	Been

SYNOPSIS

INDICATIVE MODE

Present . . . . .I am
Present Perfect. .I have been
Past . . . . .I was

Past Perfect ....I had been
Future ....I shall be
Future Perfect ..I shall have been

SUBJUNCTIVE MODE

Present ....If I be
Past ....If I were
Past Perfect ....If I had been

POTENTIAL MODE

Present ....I may, can, or must be
Present Perfect..I may, can, or must have been
Past ....I might, could, would, or should be
Past Perfect ....I might, could, would, or should have been

REGULAR CONJUGATION

Note—*Shall*, in the first person, and *will*, in the second and third, future tenses, are used to denote futurity. When *will* is used in the first person, or *shall*, in the second or third, *determination* or *necessity*, as well as *futurity*, is represented.

INDICATIVE MODE

PRESENT TENSE

Singular	*Plural*
1. I am	1. We are
2. You are	2. You are
3. He is	3. They are

PRESENT PERFECT TENSE

1. I have been	1. We have been
2. You have been	2. You have been
3. He has been	3. They have been

PAST TENSE

1. I was	1. We were
2. You were	2. You were
3. He was	3. They were

PAST PERFECT TENSE

1. I had been	1. We had been
2. You had been	2. You had been
3. He had been	3. They had been

FUTURE TENSE

Singular	*Plural*
1. I shall be	1. We shall be
2. You will be	2. You will be
3. He will be	3. They will be

FUTURE PERFECT TENSE

1. I shall have been	1. We shall have been
2. You will have been	2. You will have been
3. He will have been	3. They will have been

SUBJUNCTIVE MODE

PRESENT TENSE

1. If I be	1. If we be
2. If you be	2. If you be
3. If he be	3. If they be

PAST TENSE

1. If I were	1. If we were
2. If you were	2. If you were
3. If he were	3. If they were

PAST PERFECT TENSE

1. If I had been	1. If we had been
2. If you had been	2. If you had been
3. If he had been	3. If they had been

POTENTIAL MODE

PRESENT TENSE

1. I may be	1. We may be
2. You may be	2. You may be
3. He may be	3. They may be

PRESENT PERFECT TENSE

1. I may have been	1. We may have been
2. You may have been	2. You may have been
3. He may have been	3. They may have been

PAST TENSE

1. I might be	1. We might be
2. You might be	2. You might be
3. He might be	3. They might be

PAST PERFECT TENSE

Singular	Plural
1. I might have been	1. We might have been
2. You might have been	2. You might have been
3. He might have been	3. They might have been

Note—In reviews, use the auxiliary *can* or *must*.

IMPERATIVE MODE

PRESENT TENSE

1. Be   2. Be

INFINITIVE MODE

Present, To be   *Present Perfect*, To have been

PARTICIPLES

Present, Being   *Perfect*, Been   *Compound*, Having been

115. CONJUGATION OF THE VERB "TO LOVE"

ACTIVE VOICE

PRINCIPAL PARTS

Present Tense	Past Tense	Perfect Participle
Love	Loved	Loved

SYNOPSIS

INDICATIVE MODE

Present	I love	*Past Perfect*	I had loved
Present Perfect	I have loved	*Future*	I shall love
Past	I loved	*Future Perfect*	I shall have loved

SUBJUNCTIVE MODE

Present	If I love	*Past*	If I loved
		Past Perfect	If I had loved

POTENTIAL MODE

Present ....I may, can, or must love
Present Perfect..I may, can, or must have loved
Past ....I might, could, would, or should love
Past Perfect ....I might, could, would, or should have loved

REGULAR CONJUGATION

INDICATIVE MODE

PRESENT TENSE

Singular		*Plural*
1. I love		1. We love
2. You love		2. You love
3. He loves		3. They love

PRESENT PERFECT TENSE

1. I have loved		1. We have loved
2. You have loved		2. You have loved
3. He has loved		3. They have loved

PAST TENSE

1. I loved		1. We loved
2. You loved		2. You loved
3. He loved		3. They loved

PAST PERFECT TENSE

1. I had loved		1. We had loved
2. You had loved		2. You had loved
3. He had loved		3. They had loved

FUTURE TENSE

1. I shall love		1. We shall love
2. You will love		2. You will love
3. He will love		3. They will love

FUTURE PERFECT TENSE

1. I shall have loved		1. We shall have loved
2. You will have loved		2. You will have loved
3. He will have loved		3. They will have loved

SUBJUNCTIVE MODE

PRESENT TENSE

1. If I love		1. If we love
2. If you love		2. If you love
3. If he love		3. If they love

PAST TENSE

1. If I loved		1. If we loved
2. If you loved		2. If you loved
3. If he loved		3. If they loved

PAST PERFECT TENSE

Singular	Plural
1. If I had loved	1. If we had loved
2. If you had loved	2. If you had loved
3. If he had loved	3. If they had loved

POTENTIAL MODE

PRESENT TENSE

1. I may love	1. We may love
2. You may love	2. You may love
3. He may love	3. They may love

PRESENT PERFECT TENSE

1. I may have loved	1. We may have loved
2. You may have loved	2. You may have loved
3. He may have loved	3. They may have loved

PAST TENSE

1. I might love	1. We might love
2. You might love	2. You might love
3. He might love	3. They might love

PAST PERFECT TENSE

1. I might have loved	1. We might have loved
2. You might have loved	2. You might have loved
3. He might have loved	3. They might have loved

IMPERATIVE MODE

PRESENT TENSE

1. Love or do (you) love	2. Love or do (you) love

INFINITIVE MODE

Present, To love   *Present Perfect*, To have loved

PARTICIPLES

Present, Loving   *Perfect*, Loved   *Compound*, Having loved

116. CONJUGATION OF THE VERB "TO LOVE"

PASSIVE VOICE

The **passive voice** is formed by prefixing, as an auxiliary, the various forms of the verb *to be*, to the *perfect participle* of a transitive verb. The tense of the verb *to be* determines the tense in the passive voice.

SYNOPSIS

INDICATIVE MODE

Present ....I am loved
Present Perfect...I have been loved
Past ....I was loved
Past Perfect .....I had been loved
Future ....I shall be loved
Future Perfect ...I shall have been loved

SUBJUNCTIVE MODE

Present . . . If I be loved   *Past* . . . If I were loved
Past Perfect . . . If I had been loved

POTENTIAL MODE

Present ....I may be loved
Present Perfect...I may have been loved
Past ....I might be loved
Past Perfect .....I might have been loved

REGULAR CONJUGATION

INDICATIVE MODE

PRESENT TENSE

Singular
1. I am loved
2. You are loved
3. He is loved

Plural
1. We are loved
2. You are loved
3. They are loved

PRESENT PERFECT TENSE

1. I have been loved
2. You have been loved
3. He has been loved

1. We have been loved
2. You have been loved
3. They have been loved

PAST TENSE

1. I was loved
2. You were loved
3. He was loved

1. We were loved
2. You were loved
3. They were loved

PAST PERFECT TENSE

1. I had been loved
2. You have been loved
3. He had been loved

1. We had been loved
2. You had been loved
3. They had been loved

FUTURE TENSE

Singular	*Plural*
1. I shall be loved	1. We shall be loved
2. You will be loved	2. You will be loved
3. He will be loved	3. They will be loved

FUTURE PERFECT TENSE

1. I shall have been loved	1. We shall have been loved
2. You will have been loved	2. You will have been loved
3. He will have been loved	3. They will have been loved

SUBJUNCTIVE MODE

PRESENT TENSE

1. If I be loved	1. If we be loved
2. If you be loved	2. If you be loved
3. If he be loved	3. If they be loved

PAST TENSE

1. If I were loved	1. Were I loved	1. If we were loved
2. If you were loved	2. Were you loved	2. If you were loved
3. If he were loved	3. Were he loved	3. If they were loved

Rem.—For the *past perfect tense*, prefix *if* to the forms of the *past perfect indicative*.

POTENTIAL MODE

PRESENT TENSE

1. I may be loved	1. We may be loved
2. You may be loved	2. You may be loved
3. He may be loved	3. They may be loved

PRESENT PERFECT TENSE

1. I may have been loved	1. We may have been loved
2. You may have been loved	2. You may have been loved
3. He may have been loved	3. They may have been loved

PAST TENSE

1. I might be loved	1. We might be loved
2. You might be loved	2. You might be loved
3. He might be loved	3. They might be loved

PAST PERFECT TENSE

1. I might have been loved	1. We might have been loved
2. You might have been loved	2. You might have been loved
3. He might have been loved	3. They might have been loved

Note—In reviews, use the auxiliary *can* or *must*.

IMPERATIVE MODE

PRESENT TENSE

2. Be loved   2. Be loved

INFINITIVE MODE

Present, To be loved   *Present Perfect,* To have been loved

PARTICIPLES

Present, Being loved   *Perfect,* Loved   *Compound,* Having been loved

117. COORDINATE FORMS OF CONJUGATION

The progressive, the emphatic, and the interrogative are called the *coordinate forms of conjugation.*

SYNOPSIS

PROGRESSIVE FORM

INDICATIVE MODE

Present.................I am loving
Present Perfect..........I have been loving
Past ....I was loving
Past Perfect ....I had been loving
Future ....I shall be loving
Future Perfect ....I shall have been loving

SUBJUNCTIVE MODE

Present . . . If I be loving   *Past*. . . If I were loving
Past Perfect . . . . If I had been loving

POTENTIAL MODE

Present.................I may be loving
Present Perfect...........I may have been loving
Past ....I might be loving
Past Perfect ....I might have been loving

INFINITIVE MODE

Present, To be loving   *Present Perfect,* To have been loving

IMPERATIVE MODE

Present . . . . . . Be thou loving

PARTICIPLES

Present, Loving   *Compound*, Having been loving

THE EMPHATIC FORM
INDICATIVE MODE

Present, I do love   *Past*, I did love

SUBJUNCTIVE MODE

Present, If I do love   *Past*, If I did love

IMPERATIVE MODE

Present . . . . .Do thou love

INTERROGATIVE FORM
INDICATIVE MODE

Present . . . . .Love I? Do I love? Am I loving?
Present Perfect . . . . . .Have I loved? Have I been loving?
Past . . . . .Loved I? Did I love? Was I loving?
Past Perfect . . . . .Had I loved? Had I been loving?
Future . . . . .Shall I love? Shall I be loving?
Future Perfect . . . . . . .Shall I have loved? Shall I have been loving?

POTENTIAL MODE

Present . . . Must I love?   *Past* . . . Might I love?

Present Perfect . . Must I have loved?   *Past Perfect* . . Might I have loved?

118. NEGATIVE FORMS

1. To conjugate a verb *negatively*, place *not* after it or after the first auxiliary, but before the infinitive and the participles.

Ex.—*Indicative*, I learn not, *or*, I do not learn. I have not learned. I learned not, *or*, did not learn, etc.

Infinitive—Not to learn. Not to have learned.

Participle—Not learning. Not learned. Not having learned.

2. To conjugate a verb *interrogatively* and *negatively,* in the indicative and potential modes, place the *subject* and *not* after the verb, or after the first auxiliary.

Ex.—Learn I not? *or,* Do I not learn? Have I not learned? Did I not learn? etc.

119. EXERCISES

Write a synopsis of the transitive verbs *write, think, row, awaken, build, conquer, command, entreat, teach,* and *instruct,* in the indicative, subjunctive, and potential modes, active and passive voices.

As an oral exercise, tell the mode, tense, person, and number of each verb in the following sentences and clauses.

1. He has gone. 2. I might write. 3. We had gone. 4. He had been assured. 5. If I were loved. 6. They may have been left. 7. You were seen. 8. You will have loved. 9. She will have been invited. 10. He might have built. 11. You might have been seen. 12. The ship will have sailed.

13. We might have written. 14. They were loved. 15. If I had been loved. 16. If he is loved. 17. Though he love. 18. Though he is loved. 19. If I may be seen. 20. We can go. 21. Go. 22. Remain. 23. If he return. 24. If he returns.

120. IRREGULAR VERBS

An **irregular verb** is one which does not form its past tense and perfect participle by adding *d* or *ed* to the present tense; as, *do, did, done*; *go, went, gone.*

The following list contains the *principal parts* of common irregular verbs. Those marked R have also the regular forms.

PRESENT	PAST	PERFECT PARTICIPLE	PRESENT	PAST	PERFECT PARTICIPLE
Abide	abode	abode	Beget	begat	begotten
Am	was	been		begot	begot
Arise	arose	arisen	Begin	began	begun
Awake	awoke, R	awoke, R	Behold	beheld	beheld
Bear	bore	born	Bend	bent, R	bent, R
(bring forth)			Bereave	bereft, R	bereft, R
Bear (carry)	bore	borne	Beseech	besought	besought
Beat	beat	beaten	Bet	bet	bet
		beat	Bid	bid	bid
Become	became	become			bidden
Befall	befell	befallen	Bind	bound	bound

PRESENT	PAST	PERFECT PARTICIPLE	PRESENT	PAST	PERFECT PARTICIPLE
Bite	bit	bitten	Go	went	gone
		bit	Grave	graven, R	graven, R
Bleed	bled	bled	Grind	ground	ground
Bless	blest	blest	Grow	grew	grown
Break	broke	broken	Hang	hung	hung
		broke	(R. when it means *to execute*)		
Breed	bred	bred	Have	had	had
Bring	brought	brought	Hear	heard	heard
Build	built, R	built, R	Hew	hewed	hewn, R
Burst	burst	burst	Hide	hid	hidden
Buy	bought	bought			hid
Cast	cast	cast	Hit	hit	hit
Catch	caught	caught	Hold	held	held
Choose	chose	chosen	Hurt	hurt	hurt
Cleave	cleaved	cleaved	Keep	kept	kept
(adhere)			Kneel	knelt, R	knelt
Cleave	cleft	cleft, R	Knit	knit, R	knit, R
(split)	clove, R	cloven	Know	knew	known
Cling	clung	clung	Lay	laid	laid
Clothe	clad, R	clad, R	Lead	led	led
Come	came	come	Lean	leant, R	leant, R
Cost	cost	cost	Leap	leapt, R	leapt, R
Creep	crept	crept	Learn	learnt, R	learnt, R
Crow	crew, R	crowed	Leave	left	left
Cut	cut	cut	Lend	lent	lent
Deal	dealt	dealt	Let	let	let
Dig	dug, R	dug, R	Lie (recline)	lay	lain
Do	did	done	Light	lit, R	lit, R
Draw	drew	drawn	Lose	lost	lost
Dream	dreamt, R	dreamt, R	Load	loaded	laden, R
Drive	drove	driven	Make	made	made
Dwell	dwelt, R	dwelt, R	Mean	meant	meant
Eat	ate	eaten	Meet	met	met
Fall	fell	fallen	Mow	mowed	mown, R
Feed	fed	fed	Pass	past, R	past
Feel	felt	felt	Pay	paid	paid
Fight	fought	fought	Plead	plead, R	plead, R
Find	found	found		pled	pled
Forbear	forbore	forborne	Put	put	put
Forget	forgot	forgotten	Quit	quit, R	quit, R
		forgot	Read	read	read
Forsake	forsook	forsaken	Rend	rent	rent
Flee	fled	fled	Rid	rid, R	rid, R
Fling	flung	flung	Ride	rode	ridden
Fly	flew	flown			rode
Freeze	froze	frozen	Ring	rang	rung
Freight	freighted	fraught, R		rung	
Get	got	got	Rise	rose	risen
		gotten	Rive	riven, R	riven, R
Give	gave	given	Run	ran	run

PRESENT	PAST	PERFECT PARTICIPLE	PRESENT	PAST	PERFECT PARTICIPLE
Saw	sawed	sawn, R	Stand	stood	stood
Say	said	said	Steal	stole	stolen
See	saw	seen	Stick	stuck	stuck
Seek	sought	sought	Sting	stung	stung
Set	set	set	Stride	strode	stridden
Shake	shook	shaken	Strike	struck	struck
Shear	shorn, R	shorn, R			stricken
Shed	shed	shed	String	strung	strung
Shine	shone, R	shone, R	Strive	strove	striven, R
Shoe	shod	shod	Swear	swore	sworn
Shoot	shot	shot		sware	
Show	showed	shown	Sweat	sweat, R	sweat, R
Shred	shred, R	shred, R	Sweep	swept	swept
Shrink	shrunk	shrunk	Swell	swelled	swollen, R
	shrank	shrunken	Swim	swam	swum
Shut	shut	shut		swum	
Sing	sang	sung	Swing	swung	swung
	sung		Take	took	taken
Sink	sank	sunk	Teach	taught	taught
	sunk		Tear	tore	torn
Sit	sat	sat	Tell	told	told
Slay	slew	slain	Think	thought	thought
Sleep	slept	slept	Throw	threw	thrown
Sling	slung	slung	Thrust	thrust	thrust
Slink	slunk	slunk	Tread	trod	trodden
Slit	slit	slit			trod
Smite	smote	smitten	Wake	woke, R	woke, R
		smote	Wear	wore	worn
Sow (scatter)	sowed	sown, R	Weave	wove, R	woven, R
Speak	spoke	spoken	Wed	wed, R	wed, R
Speed	sped	sped, R	Weep	wept	wept
Spend	spent	spent	Wed	wed, R	wed, R
Spin	spun	spun	Wet	wet, R	wet, R
Spit	spit	spit	Whet	whet; R	whet, R
(R. when it means *to impale*)			Win	won	won
	spat		Wind	wound	wound, R
Split	split	split	Work	wrought, R	wrought, R
Spread	spread	spread	Wring	wrung	wrung
Spoil	spoilt, R	spoilt, R	Write	wrote	written
Spring	sprang	sprung			
	sprung				

Rem. 1—The *auxiliaries* are all irregular verbs. Their forms may be found in the paradigm for their conjugation.

Rem. 2—Ancient verb forms include: dare, durst; stay, staid; wit (to know), wist.

121. DEFECTIVE AND REDUNDANT VERBS

1. **Defective verbs** are those which want some of the principal parts.

Ex.—Beware, from *be* and *aware*, used mostly in the imperative mode, but may be used wherever *be* would occur in the conjugation of the verb *to be*; as, *"Beware* the awful avalanche!" "If angels fell, why should not men *beware?"*

Ought, used in both present and past tenses; as, "I know I *ought* to go" (now); "I knew he *ought* to have gone" (then).

Quoth, used for *said*; as, " 'Not I,' *quoth* Sancho." It always stands before its subject. **Quod** is also used in the same sense, by old authors.

2. The **auxiliaries** are also defective, wanting the perfect participle.

3. **Redundant verbs** are those which have more than one form for their past tense or perfect participle.

Ex.—*Cleave*; *cleft, clove,* or *clave*; *cleft, cloven,* or *cleaved.*

122. ORDER OF PARSING

1. A Verb, and why?
2. Regular or irregular, and why?
3. Give its principal parts.
4. Copulative, transitive or intransitive, and why?
5. Voice, and why?
6. Mode, and why?
7. Tense, and why? Inflect the tense.
8. Person and number, and why? Rule.

123. MODELS FOR PARSING

I. "Mary *has recited* her lesson."

Has recited . . . . is a *verb*; it is a word which expresses being, action, or state: *regular*; it forms its past tense and perfect participle by adding *ed*: *principal parts* are pres., *recite,* past, *recited,* perfect participle, *recited*; *transitive*; it requires the addition of an object to complete its meaning: *active voice*; it represents the subject as acting: *common form*; it represents a customary act: *indicative mode*; it asserts a thing as actual: *present perfect tense*; it represents a past act as completed in present time: *third person, singular number*; to agree with its subject "Mary," according to Rule XIII: "A verb must agree with its subject in person and number."

II. "I *shall go* if you *stay*."

Shall go ......is a *verb*; *irregular*; it does not form its past tense and perfect participle by adding *ed*: *principal parts* are *go, went, gone*: *intransitive*; *common form*; *indicative mode*; *future tense*; *first person, singular number*: Rule XIII.

Stay..........is a *verb*; *regular*; *principal parts*; (give them): *intransitive*; *common form*; *subjunctive mode*; it represents an act as conditional: *present tense* in form, but denotes future time: *second person, plural number*; Rule XIII.

III. "He *should have answered* my letter."

Should have answered is a *verb*; *regular*; *principal parts*; (give them): *transitive*; *active voice*; *common form*; *potential mode*; it represents an act as obligatory: *past perfect tense*; it is the form used to represent an act as completed at or before some other act: *third person, singular number*; Rule XIII.

IV. "*Bring* me a glass of water."

Bring.........is a *verb*; *irregular*; *principal parts*; (give them): *transitive*; *active voice*; *common form*; *imperative mode*; *present tense*; *second person, singular number*, to agree with its subject "you" understood: Rule XIII.

V. "He attempted *to ascend* the mountain."

To ascend.....is a *verb*; *regular*; *principal parts*; (give them): *transitive*; *active voice*; *common form*; *infinitive mode*; *present tense*; object of "attempted": Rule VI.

VI. "The letter *was written* yesterday."

Was written ...is a *verb*; *irregular*; *principal parts*; (give them): *transitive*; *passive voice*; it represents the subject as being acted upon: *indicative mode*; *past tense*; *third person, singular number*: Rule XIII.

VII. "Liberty *is* sweet."

Is ....is a *verb*; *irregular*; *principal parts*; (give them): *copulative*; it is used to connect the predicate "sweet" to the subject "liberty": *indicative mode*; *present tense*; *third person, singular number*, to agree with its subject "liberty": Rule XIII.

VIII. "He *was considered* rich."

Was considered is a *verb*; *regular*; *principal parts*; (give them): *passive form*; *copulative*; *indicative mode*; *past tense*; *third person*, *singular number*; Rule XIII.

IX. "The fields *look* green."

Look . . . . .is a *verb*; *regular*; *principal parts*; (give them); *copulative*; it connects the predicate "green" to the subject "fields": *indicative mode*; *present tense*; *third person, plural number*; Rule XIII.

X. "John hastened *to assist* us."

To assist . . . . . .is a *verb*; *regular*; *principal parts*; (give them): *transitive*; *active voice*; *infinitive mode*; it expresses action without affirming it: it depends upon "hastened": Rule XVII.

XI. "*To lie* is disgraceful."

To lie . . . . .is a *verb*; *regular*; *principal parts*; (give them): *infinitive mode*; it is the subject of the sentence "To lie is disgraceful," and is in the *nominative case*: Rule I.

XII. "He *has been reading* Shakespeare."

Has been reading is a *verb*; *irregular*; *principal parts*; (give them): *active voice*; *progressive form*; it denotes continuance of action: *indicative mode*; *present perfect tense*; *third person, singular number*: Rule XIII.

XIII. "That man *did buy* our house."

Did buy . . . . . .is a *verb*; *irregular*; *principal parts*; (give them): *active voice*; *emphatic form*; it denotes assertion with emphasis: *indicative mode*; *past tense*; *third person, singular number*: Rule XIII.

124. EXERCISES

Parse the nouns, pronouns, adjectives, and verbs in the following sentences.

1. They commenced plowing yesterday. 2. I seldom write letters. 3. My father brought me some pineapples when he came from the city. 4.She had gone to walk. 5. When do you intend to return my umbrella? 6. The workmen should have been more careful. 7. Hallowed be thy name. 8. Respect the aged. 9. I could learn to do it.

10. The weather was unpleasant. 11. He should have been more industrious. 12. Shall I assist you? 13. How many regiments were mustered out?

14. Does everyone have the gifts of healing? 15. Remember thy Creator in the days of thy youth. 16. We were speedily convinced that his professions were insincere.

17. Hear, father, hear our prayer!
    Long hath thy goodness our footsteps attended.

18. That very law that molds a tear,
    And bids it trickle from its source,
    That law preserves the earth a sphere,
    And guides the planets in their course.—*Rogers.*

19. Why restless, why cast down, my soul?
    Hope still, and thou shalt sing
    The praise of Him who is thy God,
    Thy Savior, and thy king.

20. If parts allure thee, think how Bacon shined,
    The wisest, brightest, meanest of mankind.—*Pope.*

21. If goodness lead him not, yet weariness
    May toss him to my heart.—*Geo. Herbert.*

Passive Forms.—1. He was beaten with many stripes. 2. The sheep were destroyed by wolves. 3. Every crime should be punished. 4. You, he, and I were invited. 5. America was discovered by Christopher Columbus. 6. He has been elected mayor of our city. 7. The work might have been finished.

Progressive, Emphatic, and Interrogative Forms.—1. He is writing a letter. 2. They should have been studying their lessons. 3. They were digging for gold. 4. I do wish you were here. 5. He did not commit forgery. 6. How do you learn so fast? 7. Why does he persist in denying it? 8. Where were you going when I met you?

125. CAUTIONS

Caution I—General truths should be expressed in the present tense.

Ex.—1. I have always thought that dew fell. 2. He proved that the earth was round. 3. I should think it was time for the bell to ring. 4. He told me that every star was a sun. 5. I did not know that brass was made of zinc and copper. 6. Heat will radiate best from rough substances.

Caution II—Do not use the perfect participle to express past time, nor the past tense form instead of the perfect participle.

Ex.—1. I come here last Saturday. 2. John done it, I seen him. 3. I have saw an old friend today. 4. The bridge had fell; it was broken in two.

5. The cars have ran off the track. 6. The bells ringed when we come into town. 7. The letter was wrote in haste. 8. He has went and brung some snow into the house. 9. The wind has blowed the fence down.

10. His face has wore a sad expression for some time. 11. He laid down a while. 12. Charles winned the prize. 13. The vessel springed a leak. 14. He clumb the tree and shaked the chestnuts down. 15. Have the cattle been drove to pasture? 16. The cloth was weaved beautiful. 17. The boy had swam the river.

Caution III—In the use of words in sentences, a due regard should be paid to expressed or implied relations of time.

Ex.—1. He was tardy every day this week. 2. After I learned my lesson, I took a walk. 3. They have visited us last week. 4. He was under obligations to have assisted me. 5. John was absent all this afternoon. 6. I know the family more than twenty years. 7. I shall live here ten years next October.

Caution IV—Do not use *aint* for *is not*, *haint* for *have not*, *'taint* for *it is not*, *might of* for *might have*, etc.

Ex.—1. I haint learned my lesson. 2. 'Taint right to disturb the meeting. 3. Aint you going east this summer? 4. You might of known that I aint well. 5. He could of helped you, and you should of made him do so.

Caution V—Never use *will* for *shall*, nor *would* for *should*, etc.

Ex.—1. I shall go; no one will prevent me. 2. I should be sorry if you would be sick. 3. If I would earn money, I would save it. 4. I will not be at home tomorrow evening. 5. We will receive our pay next week. 6. Would we have a pleasant time if we should go?

Caution VI—Do not use improper passive forms.

Ex.—1. He was retired from active service. 2. He is possessed of a large amount of bank stock. 3. He was just returned from Boston when I saw him. 4. Evening was come before we reached the shore. 5. The men were all agreed on that.

Caution VII—In expressing a supposition, use the subjunctive mode to denote doubt or denial, and the indicative mode to express a fact or anything assumed as a fact.

Ex.—1. If he were (not *was*) rich, he would be generous. 2. If I were (not *was*) you, I would go.

Rem.—The examples of incorrect grammar in each of these cautions can be used as an oral exercise. Have your students give the correct readings.

THE ADVERB

126. ORAL LESSON

Write this sentence on your papers: "Jane sang a *song*." What element is "song"? *Ans.*—An object. Why? *Ans.*—Because it completes the meaning of the predicate. Write "Jane sang a song *sweetly*." Does "sweetly" complete the meaning of the predicate? *Ans.*—It does not. What word is modified by it, however? *Ans.*—"Sang." How does it modify "sang"? *Ans.*—It tells *how* Jane sang.

Write this sentence: "You are *very* kind." What word is modified by "very"? *Ans.*—"Kind." What part of speech is "kind"? *Ans.*—An adjective. Write, "A letter, *hastily* written, was sent me yesterday." What does "hastily" modify? *Ans.*—"Written." What part of speech is "written"? *Ans.*—A participle. Write, "The letter was written *very* hastily." What does "very" modify? *Ans.*—"Hastily." What does "hastily" modify? *Ans.*—"Was written."

Those words, and all others used in a similar manner, are called *adverbs*.

127. DEFINITION

An **adverb** is a word used to modify the meaning of a verb, adjective, participle, or an adverb; as, "She sings *sweetly*," "The roads are *very* rough," "The ranks were *quickly* broken," "He reads *tolerably* well."

Rem. 1.—An adverb is equivalent to a phrase consisting of a preposition and its object, limited by an adjective.

Ex.—"He walks *rapidly*," *i.e.*, He walks *in a rapid manner*. "He lives *there*," *i.e.*, He lives *at that place*. "The work is *intensely* interesting," *i.e.*, The work is interesting *in an intense degree*.

Rem. 2.—An adverb sometimes modifies a phrase or a clause.

Ex.—"He sailed *nearly* around the globe." "The old man, *likewise*, came to the city." In the first sentence, *nearly* limits the phrase "around the globe"; and in the second, *likewise* modifies the entire proposition.

128. CLASSES

1. With respect to their meaning and use, adverbs are divided into five classes: adverbs of *time*, *place*, *cause*, *manner*, and *degree*.

2. **Adverbs of time** answer the questions, *When? How long? How often?*

Ex.—After, again, ago, always, anon, early, ever, never, forever, frequently, hereafter, hitherto, immediately, lately, now, often, seldom, soon, sometimes, then, when, while, weekly, until, yet, etc.

Rem.—*Today, tomorrow, tonight, yesterday, yesternight* are nouns, not adverbs. When used as modifiers, they should, in most instances, be parsed as nouns in the objective case, without a governing word. (See Rule VIII.)

Ex.—"He will come *today*." "They all left *yesterday*." "We had a severe storm *yesternight*."

3. **Adverbs of place** answer the questions, *Where? Whither? Whence?*

Ex.—Above, below, down, up, hither, thither, here, there, where, herein, therein, wherein, hence, thence, whence, everywhere, nowhere, somewhere, far, yonder, back, forth, aloof, away, aboard, aloft, ashore, backwards, forwards, first, secondly, wherever, etc.

Rem.—*There* is sometimes used as an expletive to introduce a sentence; as, "*There* were giants in those days," "Breathes *there* a man with soul so dead?"

4. **Adverbs of cause** answer the questions, *Why? Wherefore?*

Ex.—Wherefore, therefore, then, why.

5. **Adverbs of manner** answer the question, *How?*

Ex.—Amiss, asunder, anyhow, well, badly, easily, foolishly, sweetly, certainly, indeed, surely, verily, nay, no, not, nowise, haply, perhaps, perchance, peradventure, probably, etc.

Rem.—Most adverbs of *manner* are formed by adding *ly* to adjectives or participles; as, wise, *wisely*; united, *unitedly*.

6. **Adverbs of degree** answer the questions, *How much? How little?*

Ex.—As, almost, altogether, enough, even, equally, much, more, most, little, less, least, wholly, partly, only, quite, scarcely, nearly, excellently, too, chiefly, somewhat, etc.

7. Adverbs which show the manner of the *assertion* are called **modal adverbs**; as, *verily, truly, not, no, yes*, etc.

8. *When, why*, etc., when used in asking questions, are called **interrogative adverbs**.

9. An **adverbial phrase** is a combination of words used as a single adverb.

Ex.—"In general," "hand in hand," "by and by," "through and through," "no more," "for the most part," "as usual," etc. Such combinations may be parsed as single adverbs.

10. **Conjunctive adverbs** are those which connect sentences used as modifiers and the term modified.

Ex.—"I shall see you again *when* I return." "Go *where* glory waits thee." "I have been to Boston *since* I saw you last." "Pay your bills *before* you leave." "The book remained *where* I left it." "I will go *as soon as* I have eaten my dinner."

Rem. 1—The clause introduced by a conjunctive adverb modifies some word in the principal clause; the conjunctive adverb itself modifies some word in the subordinate clause. In the sentence, "He defends himself when he is attacked," the clause "when he is attacked" modifies "defends"; "when" modifies "is attacked" and connects the two clauses.

Rem. 2—The principal conjunctive adverbs are: *as, after, before, how, since, therefore, till, until, when, where, wherefore, while,* and *why.*

129. COMPARISON

Many adverbs admit of comparison.

1. Derivatives ending in *ly* are usually compared by prefixing *more* and *most, less* and *least* to the simple form; as, *wisely, more wisely, most wisely; firmly, less firmly, least firmly.*

2. Three adverbs are compared by adding *er* and *est* to the simple form, viz.: *fast, faster, fastest; often, oftener, oftenest; soon, sooner, soonest.*

3. Some adverbs are compared irregularly; as, *well, better, best; ill, worse, worst; little, less, least; much, more, most,* etc.

GENERAL REMARKS

1. Some adverbs seem to be used *independently*; as, *yes, no, why, well,* etc., in certain constructions. They may be parsed as modifying the entire proposition, the preceding sentence, something understood, or, as independent.

Ex.—"Have you my book?—*No.*" "*Why*, that is strange." "*Well*, I am surprised." "*Yea*, the Lord sitteth King forever."

2. Certain words are used sometimes as adverbs and sometimes as adjectives. They are adverbs when they modify verbs, adjectives, and other adverbs, and adjectives when they modify nouns or pronouns.

Ex.—"I can remain *no* longer." "Let *no* man deceive you." In the first sentence, "no" is an adverb, modifying "longer"; in the second, it is an adjective, modifying "man."

3. In such expressions as "One man *only* was injured," "only" is an adjective, modifying the preceding noun. "He sells medicines and books *also*." Here "also" is an adverb, modifying "sells" understood. "He sells medicines, and he *also* sells books."

130. ORDER OF PARSING

1. An adverb, and why?
2. Compare it.
3. Tell what it modifies.
4. Rule.

131. MODELS FOR PARSING

I. "He acted *wisely*."

Wisely . . . . is an *adverb*; it is used to modify the meaning of a verb: *compared*, wisely, more wisely, most wisely: it is an adverb of *manner*, and modifies "acted": Rule XVIII: "Adverbs modify verbs, adjectives, participles, and adverbs."

II. "*Why* do you laugh?"

Why . . . . is an *adverb*; it is not compared: *interrogative adverb*, and modifies "do laugh": Rule XVIII.

III. "They walk *hand in hand*."

Hand in hand . . is an *adverbial phrase*; it is a combination of words used as a simple adverb: it modifies "walk": Rule XVIII.

IV. "I shall *certainly* recover."

Certainly . . . . . . is an *adverb*; *modal*; it shows the manner in which the assertion is made: it modifies "shall recover": Rule XVIII.

V. "I will go *whenever* you wish."

Whenever . . . . . is an *adverb*; *conjunctive adverb*; it connects two clauses, and modifies "wish": Rule XVIII.

132. EXERCISES

Parse the adverbs in the following sentences.

1. They lived very happily. 2. Why do you look so sad? 3. When spring comes, the flowers will bloom. 4. How rapidly the moments fly! 5. He signed

it then and there. 6. I have read it again and again. 7. He will do so no more. 8. The mystery will be explained by and by. 9. Perhaps you are the man.

10. Where has he gone? 11. They were agreeably disappointed. 12. He lives just over the hill yonder. 13. Henceforth let no man fear that God will forsake us. 14. I saw him before he left. 15. I will not be unjust. 16. I have not seen him since I returned from New York. 17. Doubtless, ye are the people. 18. Perhaps I shall go.

133. CAUTIONS

Caution I—Do not use adjectives as adverbs.

Ex.—1. I feel tolerable well, I thank you. 2. She dresses neat. 3. I was exceeding glad to hear from you. 4. You do not speak distinct enough. 5. He was near famished. 6. We walked careful over the rough ground. 7. You ought to value his friendship higher.

Caution II—Avoid the use of two negatives to express negation (double negatives).

Ex.—1. The train don't wait for no one. 2. We didn't find nobody at home. 3. The boys don't want no holidays. 4. You don't look no older than you did ten years ago. 5. Nothing can't be done about it now. 6. The doctor said she would never be no better. 7. I hadn't no money left when I got home.

THE PREPOSITION

134. ORAL LESSON

Write this sentence on your papers: "Mr. Olds is a wealthy man." What element is "wealthy"? *Ans.*—An adjective. What does it modify? *Ans.*—"Man." Write this sentence: "Mr. Olds is a man of wealth." You see that "of wealth," in this sentence, has the same meaning as "wealthy" in the other. What part of speech is "wealth"? *Ans.*—A noun. The word "of" connects "man" and "wealth," and shows the relation between the ideas expressed by them. In this case, the relation is that of possession: "man" possesses "wealth." Words used in this manner are called *prepositions*, because they are usually *placed before* nouns.

In the sentence "We live in London," what words tell where we live? *Ans.*—"In London." These words constitute what is called a *phrase*, and form an adverbial element. The word limited by the phrase is called the antecedent term of relation, and the noun following the preposition, the *subsequent* term, or *object*. The antecedent term may be anything which can be modified, but the subsequent term must be the objective case of a noun or something used as a noun, such as a pronoun or participle.

In the sentence, "I recite in the afternoon," what is the antecedent term of relation? *Ans.*—"Recite." Why? *Ans.*—Because it is the word which is modified by the phrase "in the afternoon." What is the subsequent term, or object? *Ans.*—"Afternoon." Why? *Ans.*—Because it is the object of the preposition "in."

135. DEFINITION

A **preposition** is a word used to show the relation between its object and some other word; as, "The man *of* Uz," "Ellen is walking *in* the garden."

Rem. 1—A preposition and its object form a separable phrase, which modifies some word or combination of words, called the *antecedent* term of the relation expressed by the preposition; the object of the preposition being the *subsequent* term. In the sentence, "The house stands *on* a hill," "stands" is the antecedent term of relation, and "hill" the subsequent.

Rem. 2—Two prepositions are frequently combined and used as one; as, "He came *from over* the sea," "The church stands *over against* the school-house." In such cases, parse the two prepositions as one, calling the combination a *complex preposition*.

Rem. 3—Sometimes the object of a preposition is omitted; as, "The boys went *out*," "The regiment marched *by*." In such cases, parse the preposition as an adverb.

Rem. 4—The antecedent term is sometimes omitted; as, " '*From* Vermont?' asked the landlord." In such cases, parse the preposition as showing the relation between its object and an antecedent term understood.

For, in the complex phrases, "*For* him to lie," "*For* you to deceive," etc., may be parsed as an *introductory* preposition.

Rem. 5—When the relations between objects of thought are so obvious that they need no expression, the prepositions are usually omitted; as, "I came home *yesterday*." ("I came home *on yesterday*"). In such cases, the subsequent term of relation is said to be in the objective case without a governing word.

136. LIST OF PREPOSITIONS

A = *at*, *on*, or *in*; "Be quiet, and go *a*-angling."
Aboard; "*Aboard* ships, dull shocks are sometimes felt."

About; "It was a day to be at home, crowding *about* the fire."

Above; "*Above* your voices sounds the wail of starving men."

According to; "Proceed *according to* law."

Across; "Their way was *across* a stretch of open meadow."

After; "*After* life's fitful fever, he sleeps well."

Against; "Uplift *against* the sky, your mighty shapes."

Along; "I hear the waves resounding *along* the shore."

Amid, amidst; "A lark reared her brood *amid* the corn."

Among, amongst; "He was always foremost *among* them."

Around; "I hear *around* me cries of fear."

As to; "*As to* the parts of the cargo, they were already made fast."

At; "She is *at* church." "The bell rings *at* noon."

Athwart; "*Athwart* the waste the pleasant home-light shines."

Before; "Who shall go *before* them?" "I left *before* sunrise."

Behind; "We have seen the moon rising *behind* the eastern pines."

Below; "It was on the road to Kennebec, *below* the city of Bath."

Beneath; "The steps creaked *beneath* his noiseless tread."

Beside; "I sat *beside* her." "He is *beside* himself."

Besides; "There is nothing at all *besides* this manna."

Between; "The town is situated *between* two mountains."

Beyond; "His thoughts turned to his home *beyond* the sea."

But = *except*; "He had retained nothing *but* his father's belt."

By; "Strength came *by* working in the mines."

Concerning; "The Lord hath spoken good *concerning* Israel."

Down; "They wandered in throngs *down* the valley."

During; "He stayed at home *during* the war."

Ere; "Nile flowed *ere* the wonted season."

Except; "Are they all gone *except* you?"

For; "I looked up *for* a moment." "I sell *for* cash."

From; "He felt like a leaf torn *from* a romance."

In; "Late *in* life, he began life *in* earnest."

Into; "He gazed *into* the vast surrounding darkness."

Like;. "He ran *like* a deer."

Notwithstanding; "He is proud, *notwithstanding* his poverty."

Of; " 'Tis the middle watch *of* a summer's night."

Off; "The sailing vessel was becalmed *off* Cuba."

On; "I leave *on* Saturday."

Onto; "He sprang *onto* a rock."

Out of; "No one was moving, at least *out of* doors."

Over; "The billows had rolled *over* him." "He rules *over* us."

Past; "He drove *past* our house this morning."

Round; "A shoreless ocean tumbled *round* the globe."

Save; "All is silent *save* the dropping rain."

Since; "The Lord hath blessed thee *since* my coming."
Through; "Then stept she down *through* town and field."
Throughout; "There was much anxiety felt *throughout* the land."
To; "Let the old tree go down *to* the earth."
Toward, towards; "He turned me *toward* the moonlight."
Under; "He stands erect *under* the curved roof."
Until; "Not *until* the next morning did the boys appear."
Unto; "Verily, I say *unto* you."
Up; "He sailed *up* the river."
Upon; "They were walking *upon* the hurricane deck."
With; "The sky was red *with* flame."
Without; "The morning broke *without* a sun."

Rem. 1—The following prepositions, less commonly used, may be added to the foregoing list:

Aloft, alongside, afore, adown, aloof, aslant, despite, inside, outside, minus, plus, per, sans, underneath, versus, via, as for, along with, from among, from before, from betwixt, from off, from under, over against, round about, but for; and the participial forms *excepting, regarding, touching, respecting*, etc., when followed by objects.

Rem. 2—*But, for, since* and some others, are frequently used as conjunctions; as, "I must go, *for* it is late."

Rem. 3—*A* as a preposition is now rare except in colloquial conversation or as a part of such compound words as *abed, asleep*, and *aloud*. The King James Bible uses it occasionally (e.g. "I go a fishing," Jn. 20:3).

137. ORDER OF PARSING

1. A preposition, and why?
2. What relation does it show?
3. Rule.

138. MODELS FOR PARSING

I. "The horse ran *over* the hill."

Over . . . . is a *preposition*; it is a word used to show the relation between its object and some other word: it shows the relation between "hill" and "ran": Rule XIX: "A preposition shows the relation of its object to the word upon which the latter depends."

II. "He came out *from under* the bridge."

From under..is a *complex preposition*; it shows the relation between "bridge" and "came." Rule XIX.

139. EXERCISES

Parse the prepositions in the following sentences:

1. Will you go with me into the garden? 2. In my Father's house are many mansions. 3. We went over the river, through the cornfields, into the woods. 4. I am not satisfied as to that affair. 5. All came but Mary. 6. The Rhone flows out from among the Alps. 7. He went from St. Louis, across the plains, and over the Rockies to California. 8. Light moves in straight lines, and in all directions from the point of emission. 9. They went aboard the ship.

10. Night, sable goddess! from her ebon throne,
In rayless majesty, now stretches forth
Her leaden scepter o'er a slumbering world.—*Young.*

140. CAUTION

Caution—Care should be taken to select such prepositions as express the relations intended.

Ex.—*Among, amongst,* are applicable to more than two objects; as, "He divided the estate *among* the four brothers." *Between, betwixt,* are applicable to two objects only; as, "He divided the estate *between* the two brothers."

During should be used when the event continues through all the period mentioned; as, "I have examined law papers *during* the day": *in, at,* or *within,* when the event does not continue during the whole period; as, "I alluded to that *in* my remarks this morning," "The debt must be paid *within* the year."

Of denotes possession of a quality or thing; as, "He is a friend *of* mine": *to* denotes that the quality or thing is directed towards something else; as, "He has been a friend *to* me."

In or *at* is used before the names of countries, cities, and towns; as, "She lives *in* New York," "They reside *at* Glendale," "We stayed *in* London."

Into should be used after verbs denoting entrance; as, "He came *into* the office," "He put the knife *into* his pocket."

At is generally used after *to be,* not followed by a predicate; as, "They are *at* home," "She is *at* church." When a predicate is understood, or clearly implied, *to* should be used; as, "I have been *to* Cincinnati," *i.e.,* I have been (traveling) to Cincinnati.

Upon should follow *bestow* and *dependent*; as, "Many favors were bestowed *upon* me," "He is dependent *upon* his friends."

From should follow *differ* and *dissent*; as, "I differ *from* you," "I dissent *from* that decision."

Of should follow *diminution*; as, "Any diminution *of* expenses is impossible."

In should follow *confide*; as, "I confide *in* you."

Of should be used when we are disappointed in obtaining a thing; as, "I was disappointed *of* money": *in*, when we are disappointed in the quality of a thing, or the character of a person; as, "I am disappointed *in* that mower," "I am disappointed *in* Mr. Johnson."

With denotes an *instrument*; *by*, a *cause*: *with*, the immediate, *by*, the remoter means; as, "A man is killed *with* a sword, and dies *by* violence," "He walks *with* a cane *by* moonlight."

Correct the following exercises.

1. Divide the money among the two boys. 2. I will pay you sometime during next week. 3. Washington was a friend of his country. 4. He put the money in his pocket. 5. Where is the key to that trunk? 6. Never depart out of the straight path. 7. He went out of a fine morning with a bundle in his hand.

8. I wish I had stayed to home. 9. He depends on his daily labor for his support. 10. He boasted about his standing in society. 11. My father and mother are to church. 12. The still, sultry morning was followed with a hailstorm. 13. He was eager of making money. 14. I can make no diminution in my tuition rates. 15. He has gone west, accompanied with his wife. 16. We ought to profit from the errors of others. 17. You look different to what I supposed.

THE CONJUNCTION

141. ORAL LESSON

In the sentence, "Emma *and* Eva study algebra," what is the subject? *Ans.*—"Emma and Eva." Why? *Ans.*—Because something is affirmed of them. That is right. They are both subjects of the same predicate; and to show that they both have the same relation to the rest of the sentence, they are joined by the word "and." This is called a *conjunction*, because its use is to join words. It is a *coordinate conjunction*, because it joins elements of the same rank or name.

In the sentence, "Emma will study algebra, *if* Eva does not," "if" is a conjunction, but it joins elements of different rank or name. It connects "will study" and "Eva does not." Those conjunctions which join elements of different rank or name are called *subordinate* conjunctions.

In the sentence, "*Both* Emma *and* Eva study algebra," "both" and "and" are called *correlative* conjunctions, because each answers or refers to the other.

142. DEFINITION

A **conjunction** is a word used to connect words, sentences, and parts of sentences.

Ex.—"The horse *and* stagecoach were captured, *but* the driver escaped." "He lives out of town, *and* on a farm." In the first sentence, "and" connects "horse" and "stagecoach" and "but" connects the two propositions, "the horse and stagecoach were captured" and "the driver escaped." In the second sentence, "and" connects the phrases "out of town" and "on a farm."

Rem.—Conjunctions sometimes merely introduce sentences; as, "*And* it came to pass in those days," "*That* the times are hard is undeniable."

143. CLASSES OF CONJUNCTIONS

1. Conjunctions are divided into two general classes: *coordinate* and *subordinate*.

2. **Coordinate conjunctions** are those which join elements of the same rank or name.

Rem.—Coordinate conjunctions form no part of the material of which a sentence is composed—their use being to unite the material into a single sentence. They may be classified as follows:

1. **Copulative**, denoting addition merely; as, *and*, *also*, *further*, *moreover*, etc.

2. **Adversative**, denoting opposition of meaning; as, *but*, *still*, *yet*, *only*, *however*, *notwithstanding*, etc.

3. **Alternative**, denoting that which may be chosen or omitted; as, *else*, *otherwise*, *or*, *nor*, *either*, etc.

4. **Illative**, implying a consequence or inference following from what has been said; as, *hence*, *thence*, *then*, *therefore*, *wherefore*, *for*, *because*, *so*, *consequently*, *accordingly*, etc.

3. **Subordinate conjunctions** are those which join elements of different ranks or names.

Rem.—Subordinate conjunctions may be classified as follows:

1. **Causal**, denoting effect, condition, reason, result, or purpose; as, *that, so that, if, unless, except, as, because, since, although, though, for, whereas, inasmuch as, lest,* etc.

2. **Temporal**, denoting time; as, *ere, after, before, until, whilst, while, when,* etc.

3. **Local**, denoting rest in, or motion to or from place; as, *where, there, whence, thence, whither, thither,* etc.

4. Of **manner** or **degree**, denoting likeness, equality, and excess or deficiency; as, *as, as if, how, although, than, so as,* etc.

Rem. 1—**Correlative conjunctions** are coordinate or subordinate conjunctions used in pairs, one referring or answering to the other; as, *both . . . and, as . . . as, if . . . then, so . . . as, notwithstanding . . . yet, though . . . yet, either . . . or, nor . . . nor, neither . . . nor,* etc.

Ex.—1. He is *both* learned *and* wise. 2. I am *as* tall *as* you. 3. *As* it was then, *so* it is now. 4. *Though* deep, *yet* clear. 5. *If* he confessed it, *then* forgive him.

Rem. 2—Many of the subordinate conjunctions are frequently used as adverbs or conjunctive adverbs. (See Sec. 128.)

Rem. 3—Certain combinations of words have the force of connectives, and should be parsed as conjunctions or conjunctive adverbs. They are: *as if, as well as, except that, forasmuch as, but also, but likewise, notwithstanding that, not only,* etc.

Ex.—1. Facts may be transmitted by tradition *as well as* by history. 2. You talk *as if* you know your lesson.

144. ORDER OF PARSING

1. A conjunction, and why?
2. Coordinate or subordinate, and why?
3. What does it connect?
4. Rule.

145. MODELS FOR PARSING

I. "He came *and* went like a pleasant thought."

And . . . . is a *conjunction*; it connects words; *coordinate*; it denotes addition: it connects "came" and "went." Rule XX: "Coordinate conjunctions join similar elements."

II. "He learns, *because* he is studious."

Because . . . . . . is a *conjunction*; *subordinate*; it joins dissimilar elements; it connects "learns" and "he is studious." Rule XXI.

III. "*Neither* James *nor* John had his lesson."

Neither . . nor are *conjunctions*; *correlative*; one refers or answers to the other: "neither" introduces the sentence, and "nor" connects "James" and "John." Rule XX.

IV. "Unto us was the gospel preached, *as well as* unto them."—*Hebrews* 4:2.

As well as . . . . is a *conjunction*; *copulative*; it connects and emphatically distinguishes the two phrases, "unto us" and "unto them": Rule XX.

146. EXERCISES

Parse all the words in the following sentences.

1. He'd sooner die than ask you or any man for a shilling. 2. Talent is something, but tact is everything. 3. Neither military nor civil pomp was wanting. 4. The truth is, that I am tired of ticking. 5. I remember a mass of things, but nothing distinctly.

6. I alone was solitary and idle. 7. Both the ties of nature and the dictates of policy demand this. 8. There was no reply, for fear was upon every man. 9. No man more highly esteems or honors the British troops than I do. 10. The soldier marches on and on, inflicting pain and suffering, as before. 11. There may be wisdom with knowledge, and there may be knowledge without wisdom.

12. Not a having and resting, but a growing and becoming, is the true character of perfection as culture conceives it.—*Shairp*. 13. Men must be taught as if you taught them not.—*Pope*. 14. Essex had neither the virtues nor the vices which enable men to retain greatness long.—*Macaulay*. 15. How long didst thou think that his silence was slumber?—*Scott*.

16.   Vice is a monster of so frightful mien,
       As to be hated needs but to be seen;
       But seen too oft, familiar with her face,
       We first endure, then pity, then embrace.—*Pope*.

147. CAUTIONS

Caution I—Do not use *like* or *with* for *as*, *but* for *than*, or *without* for *unless*, as in these incorrect examples.

Ex.—1. They live in houses like we do. 2. We ought to be industrious and economical, like our forefathers were. 3. The answer is the same with that in the book. 4. He reads for no other purpose but to pass away the time. 5. I shall not go without you go with me.

Caution II—Do not use *as well as* or *together with* for *and*, nor *how* for *that*, or in its stead.

Ex.—1. I, as well as my sister, were at the concert last evening. 2. Mr. Brown, together with Mr. Shriver, are opening a new coal mine. 3. He told me how that he was going to Oregon. 4. Father said how he believed he would sell his farm.

Note—Strunk and White speak to the problem of the first two examples: "Omit needless words."

THE INTERJECTION

148. DEFINITION

An **interjection** is a word used to denote some sudden or strong emotion; as, "Shh! Someone comes." "Nonsense! That is ridiculous."

The principal interjections are the following.

Ah, aha, hurrah; oh; ha, indeed, ha, ha, ha (laughter); begone; hail, all hail; adieu, farewell, goodby; hello, ahoy, lo, hark; hush, tush; avast, hold; eh? hey? ouch, nonsense, shh, scat, scram, amen, and ho.

Rem. 1—Interjections have no definite meaning or grammatical construction. They occur frequently in colloquial or impassioned discourse, but are expressions of emotion only, and cannot be used as signs of thought. As their name imports, they may be *thrown in between* connected parts of discourse, but are generally found at the commencement of sentences.

Rem. 2—Other parts of speech, when used as exclamations, may be treated as interjections; as, "*What*! Art thou mad?" "*My stars*! What can all this be?" "*Revenge*! *About,—seek,—burn,—fire,—kill,—slay*!—let not a traitor live!" In most cases, however, words thus used may be parsed otherwise; as, " '*Magnificent*!' cried all at once." "Magnificent" may be parsed as an adjective, the predicate of the sentence, "*It is magnificent.*" "*Behold*! Your house is left unto you desolate!" "Behold" may be parsed as a verb in the imperative mode.

149. ORDER OF PARSING

1. An interjection, and why?
2. Rule.

150. MODEL FOR PARSING

I. "Oh, let me live."

Oh . . . . is an *interjection*; it denotes some strong emotion: Rule XXII: "An interjection has no dependence upon other words."

151. EXERCISES

Parse all the words in the following sentences.

1. Ha! Laughest thou? 2. Hey! Sirs, what a noise you make here. 3. Hurrah! Hurrah! Long live Lord Robin! 4. Hah! It is a sight to freeze one. 5. Let them be desolate for a reward of their shame which say unto me. Aha! Aha!

6. Oh, that the salvation of Israel were come out of Zion! 7. Alas! All earthly good still blends itself with home! 8. Tush, tush, man! I made no reference to you. 9. Hark! What nearer war drum shakes the gale? 10. Soft! I did but dream!

11. What! Old acquaintance! Could not all this flesh
Keep in a little life? Poor Jack, farewell!
I could have better spared a better man.—*Shakespeare.*

152. MISCELLANEOUS EXERCISES

1. A mercenary informer knows no distinction. 2. I send you here a sort of allegory. 3. Our island home is far beyond the sea. 4. Love took up the harp of life, and smote on all the chords with might. 5. Your *If* is the only peacemaker: much virtue in *If*. 6. He is very prodigal of his *ohs* and *ahs*.

7. He looked upward at the rugged heights that towered above him in the gloom. 8. He possessed that rare union of reason, simplicity, and vehemence, which formed the prince of orators. 9. Mark well my fall, and that that ruined me.—*Shakespeare.* 10. The jingling of the guinea helps the hurt that honor feels.—*Tennyson.*

11. His qualities were so happily blended, that the result was a great and perfect whole. 12. There is no joy but calm. 13. Why are we weighed upon with heaviness? 14. Now blessings light on him that first invented sleep: it covers a man all over, thoughts and all, like a cloak.—*Cervantes.*

15. Many a morning on the moorlands did we hear the copses ring.—*Tennyson.* 16. He stretched out his right hand at these words, and laid it gently on the boy's head.—*Dickens.* 17. He acted ever as if his country's welfare, and that alone, was the moving spirit. 18. The great contention of criticism is to find the faults of the moderns and the beauties of the ancients. Whilst an author is yet living, we estimate his powers by his worst performance; and when he is dead, we estimate them by his best.—*Johnson.*

19. I will work in my own sphere, nor wish it other than it is. 20. As his authority was undisputed, so it required no jealous precautions, no rigorous severity. 21. Like all men of genius, he delighted to take refuge in poetry. 22. To know how to say what other people only think, is what makes men poets and sages; and to dare to say what others only dare to think, makes men martyrs or reformers, or both. 23. That done, she turned to the old man with a lovely smile upon her face—such, they said, as they had never seen, and never could forget—and clung with both her arms about his neck.—*Dickens.*

24. To live in hearts we leave behind,
    Is not to die.—*Campbell.*

25. But war's a game which, were their subjects wise,
    Kings would not play at.—*Cowper.*

26. Whoever thinks a faultless piece to see,
    Thinks what ne'er was, nor is, nor e'er shall be.—*Pope.*

27. The Niobe of nations, there she stands,
    Childless and crownless, in her voiceless woe;
    An empty urn within her withered hands,
    Whose holy dust was scattered long ago.—*Byron.*

28. Can storied urn or animated bust
    Back to its mansion call the fleeting breath?
    Can Honor's voice provoke the sleeping dust,
    Or Flattery soothe the dull, cold ear of death?—*Gray.*

29. Forth from his dark and lonely hiding place,
    (Portentous sight!) the owlet Atheism,
    Sailing on obscure wings athwart the noon,
    Drops his blue-fringed lids, and holds them close,
    And hooting at the glorious sun in heaven,
    Cries out, "Where is it?"—*Coleridge.*

30. A thing of beauty is a joy forever:
Its loveliness increases; it will never
Pass into nothingness.—*Keats.*

31. Dry clank'd his harness in the icy caves
And barren chasms, and all to left and right
The bare black cliff clang'd round him, as he based
His feet on jets of slippery crag that rang
Sharp smitten with the dint of armed heels.—*Tennyson.*

32.   Then came wandering by
A shadow like an angel with bright hair
Dabbled in blood; and he shriek'd out aloud:
"Clarence is come! false, fleeting, perjur'd Clarence!
That stabbed me in the field by Tewksbury:
Seize on him, furies, take him to your torments!"—*Shakespeare.*

33. There are things of which I may not speak:
     There are dreams that cannot die:
There are thoughts that make the strong heart weak,
     And bring a pallor upon the cheek,
          And a mist before the eye
          And the words of that fatal song
     Come over me like a chill:
          "A boy's will is the wind's will,
And the thoughts of youth are long, long thoughts."—*Longfellow.*

34. These ages have no memory, but they left
     A record in the desert—columns strown
On the waste sands, and statues fallen and cleft.
     Heap'd like a host in battle overthrown;
Vast ruins, where the mountain's ribs of stone
     Were hewn into a city: streets that spread
In the dark earth, where never breath has blown
     Of heaven's sweet air, nor foot of man dares tread,
The long and perilous ways—the Cities of the Dead.—*Bryant.*

PART III

SYNTAX

153. PRELIMINARY ORAL LESSONS

Note to teachers—The object of these lessons is: (1) To exercise pupils in the construction of simple sentences; (2) To teach the uses and definitions of the elements of a sentence; (3) To teach the analysis of sentences containing elements of the first class.

Use Oral Lesson on page 19 as introductory to these.

LESSON I

I hold in my hand a piece of chalk. What is its color? *Ans.*—It is *white*. It breaks easily. What else can be said of it? *Ans.*—It is *brittle*. It crumbles readily; hence, we say it is *friable*. Each of the words, *white*, *brittle*, *friable*, expresses some quality belonging to chalk: what shall we call them? *Ans.*— *Quality words*. We will now unite these *quality words* with "chalk" by the word "is," thus:

> Chalk is white.
> Chalk is brittle.
> Chalk is friable.

Each of these groups of words is called a *sentence*; for

"A **sentence** is an assemblage of words making complete sense."

Write the definition in your notebooks. Now repeat it in concert. Each group is also called a *proposition*; for

"A **proposition** is a thought expressed in words."

Write this definition in your notebooks. Repeat it in concert.

In the proposition "Chalk is white," the noun "chalk" is called the *subject*; for

"The **subject** of a proposition is that of which something is affirmed."

"White" is called the *predicate*; for

"The **predicate** of a proposition is that which is affirmed of the subject."

The word "is" is called the *copula*; for

"The **copula** is a word or group of words used to join a predicate to a subject, and to make an assertion."

In this sentence it affirms that the quality "white" belongs to "chalk."

Write these definitions in your notebooks. Repeat them in concert.

In the proposition, "Chalk is brittle," what is the subject? *Ans.*—"Chalk." Why? *Ans.*—It is that of which something is affirmed. What is the predicate? *Ans.*—"Brittle." Why? *Ans.*—It is that which is affirmed of the subject.

Affirm **qualities** *of the following subjects.*

Iron, gold, silver, lead, ink, cork, sugar, vinegar, grass, books, lessons.

Model—Iron is *heavy.*

Affirm the following qualities of appropriate **subjects.**

Transparent, opaque, hard, round, square, good, bad, bitter, heavy, rough, smooth, red, yellow, green.

Model—*Glass* is transparent.

Rem.—The *copula* is also called a *copulative* or *linking verb.* The most commonly used copula/copulative verb is *to be.* Its parts include *am, is, are, was, were, be, being,* and *been.*

LESSON II

In the sentence "Iron is a metal," is any quality affirmed of "iron"? *Ans.*—There is not. That is right. The predicate "metal" denotes *kind* or *class,* not *quality.* It is a predicate, however, because it is affirmed of the subject "iron."

In the sentence "Horses are animals," what is the subject? *Ans.*—"Horses." Why? *Ans.*—Because it is that of which something is affirmed. What is the predicate? *Ans.*—"Animals." Why? *Ans.*—Because it is that which is affirmed of the subject. What is the copula? *Ans.*—The word "are."

Affirm **class** *of the following subjects.*

Horses, oxen, coal, wood, hay, oats, wheat, ax, hoe, locomotive, dogs, sheep, copper, gold, apples, trees, wagons, houses.

Model—Wheat is a *grain.*

Affirm **qualities** *of the same subjects.*

LESSON III

Write this sentence on your papers: "Horses run." You see that the predicate "run" is affirmed *directly* of the subject without the use of the copula. The copula and predicate are united in one word; for "Horses run" means the same as "Horses are running."

What is the subject in this sentence: "Boys learn"? *Ans.*—"Boys." What is the predicate? *Ans.*—"Learn." Why? *Ans.*—It is that which is affirmed of the subject. Words which affirm anything of subjects are called verbs. What are the words "run" and "learn"? *Ans.*—Verbs. Why? *Ans.*—Because they affirm something of their subjects.

Write sentences, using the following verbs as predicates.

Walk, sing, whistle, swim, wrestle, play, write, study, plow, reap, drive, neigh, cackle, whine, snarl, gobble, quarrel, fight.

Model—Cattle *walk*.

LESSON IV

Write on your papers and then repeat in concert:

"An **element** is one of the distinct parts of a sentence."

The *subject* and *predicate* are called *principal elements*, because no sentence can be formed without them.

The *copula* is not an element; it is used merely to join a predicate to a subject and to make an assertion.

Separating a sentence into its elements is called **analysis.** We will now analyze some sentences according to the following models.

MODELS

I. "Apples are ripe."

Apples....is the subject; it is that of which something is affirmed. **Ripe** is the predicate; it is that which is affirmed of the subject: **Are** is the copula.

II. "Birds fly."

Birds .....is the subject; (why?). **Fly** is the predicate (why?).

EXERCISES

1. Ink is black. 2. Gold is yellow. 3. Lead is a metal. 4. Birds sing. 5. Vessels sail. 6. Trees are plants. 7. Fishes swim. 8. Elihu was tardy. 9. Mary was studious. 10. Enoch may be angry. 11. Snow falls. 12. Houses stand.

LESSON V

Write this sentence: "Horses eat." While you were writing did you not think some word should be added, representing *what* horses eat? *Ans.*—We did. What word shall we add? *Ans.*—Oats. Write "oats" after the verb.

This word *completes* the meaning of the verb, and is called an *objective element*, or *object*. In the sentence "Pupils study arithmetic," what word completes the meaning of the predicate or verb? *Ans.*—An objective element. Why? *Ans.*—Because it completes the meaning of the verb.

Write ten sentences, each containing an objective element.

Model—Indians hunt *buffaloes.*

Analyze the sentences you have written, using this model:

"Children love play."

Children . . is the subject; (why?). **Love**, the predicate; (why?). The predicate is modified by **play**, an objective element.

Analyze also the following sentences:

1. Heat melts lead. 2. Men love money. 3. I study botany. 4. Haste makes waste. 5. Cats catch mice. 6. Mr. Jones sells encyclopedias. 7. Clouds bring rain.

LESSON VI

Write this sentence on your papers: "Apples are ripe." What is the subject of the sentence? *Ans.*—"Apples." Why? *Ans.*—It is that of which something is affirmed. What is the word "apples"? *Ans.*—It is a noun. Why? *Ans.*—It is a name. What is the predicate? *Ans.*—"Ripe." Why? *Ans.*—It is that which is affirmed of the subject. Now write these words: "Ripe apples." Is this a sentence? *Ans.*—It is not. Why? *Ans.*—There is nothing affirmed. That is correct. The word "ripe" is here used to modify the meaning of "apples," as an *attribute*, not as a *predicate*: that is, it is *assumed*, or *taken for granted*, that it belongs to "apples." All words which modify the meaning of nouns in this manner, are called *adjective elements*.

Write this sentence: "Ripe apples are cheap." What is "ripe?" *Ans.*—An adjective element. Why? *Ans.*—It modifies the meaning of a noun. "Samuel's hat is torn." What element is "Samuel's"? *Ans.*—An adjective element. Why? *Ans.*—It modifies the meaning of the noun "hat." "Mr. Smith, the mason, is sick." What is "mason"? *Ans.*—An adjective element. Why? *Ans.*—It modifies the meaning of "Mr. Smith," a noun. What are the words "Samuel's" and "mason"? *Ans.*—They are nouns. Nouns, then, are adjective elements when they modify nouns.

Write five sentences, limiting the subjects by adjective elements denoting quality.

Models—*Cross* dogs bite. *Cold* winter comes.

Write five sentences, limiting their subjects by adjective elements denoting number.

Models—*Two* boys fought. *Three* men left.

Write five sentences, limiting their subjects by words which merely point them out.

Models—*That* boy is studious. *This* boy is lazy.

Write five sentences, limiting both subjects and objects by adjective elements.

Model—*Emma's* mother bought a *new* bonnet.

Analyze the following sentences, using these models:

I. "Milton, the poet, was blind."

Milton . . . . .is the subject; **blind** is the predicate; "Milton" is modified by **poet**, an adjective element, and "poet" by **the**, an adjective element: **was** is the copula.

II. "Evil companions corrupt good morals."

Companions . . . . .is the subject; **corrupt**, the predicate. "Companions" is modified by **evil**, an adjective; "corrupt," by **morals**, an objective element; and "morals," by **good**, an adjective.

EXERCISES

1. Sarah's book is lost. 2. Mrs. Elkins, the seamstress, found Sarah's book. 3. Old people love quiet. 4. Young children love play. 5. I like ripe cherries. 6. You have found my pencil.

LESSON VII

Write this sentence: "Birds sing sweetly." Does "sweetly" denote *what* the birds sing? *Ans.*—It does not; it tells *how* they sing. That is right. "Sweetly" does not complete the meaning of "sing," like an objective element; but it modifies its meaning in another way. All words used in such a manner are called *adverbial elements*, or *adverbs*. Words which modify adjectives are called adverbs also. In this sentence, "The storm rages violently," what is the subject? *Ans.*—"Storm." What is the predicate? *Ans.*—"Rages." What is "violently"? *Ans.*—An adverb. Why? *Ans.*—It modifies a verb, but does not complete its meaning.

In the sentence, "Very large vessels were seen," what is modified by "very"? *Ans.*—"Large." What is "large"? *Ans.*—An adjective. What element, then, is "very"? *Ans.*—An adverb. Why? *Ans.*—It modifies an adjective. Adverbs also modify other adverbs.

Write ten sentences, modifying the verbs by adverbs.

Model—The wind blows *furiously.*

Write ten sentences, containing adjectives modified by adverbs.

Model—James recited a *very* long lesson.

Analyze the following sentences, using these models:

I. "The wind blows violently."

Wind . . is the subject; **blows**, the predicate. "Wind" is modified by **the**, an adjective; "blows" is modified by **violently**, an adverb.

II. "Emma has a very severe headache."

Emma. . is the subject; **has**, the predicate. "Has" is modified by **headache**, an object; "headache" by **a** and **severe**, adjectives; and "severe" by **very**, an adverb.

EXERCISES

1. A sluggard sleeps soundly. 2. The horses were much fatigued. 3. Very loud reports were heard. 4. That boy spends his money foolishly. 5. You may go now. 6. He then left the country.

7. The river rose rapidly. 8. The troops marched forward. 9. Their parents live there. 10. How far did the horses run? 11. He acted wisely. 12. Mr. Mason is a truly good man. 13. He will be heard from presently. 14. The men were very much fatigued. 15. The doctor will be here immediately.

154. DEFINITIONS

1. **Syntax** treats of the construction of sentences.

2. A **sentence** is an assemblage of words making complete sense.

Ex.—Birds fly. Man is mortal. "The great throat of the chimney laughed." "When the farmer came down in the morning, he declared that his watch had gained half an hour in the night."

3. A **proposition** or **clause** is a thought expressed in words.

Ex.—The weather is pleasant. The boy seems frightened.

Rem.—The term *sentence* is applied to any group of words so arranged as to make complete sense; *proposition*, to the thought which those words express.

4. **Propositions** or **clauses** are either *principal* or *subordinate*.

5. A **principal proposition/clause** is one which makes complete sense when standing alone.

6. A **subordinate proposition/clause** is one which does not make complete sense when standing alone, but which must be connected with another proposition/clause.

Ex.—"The man who does no good, does harm." Here "the man does harm" is the principal clause, for it makes complete sense when standing alone: "who does no good" is a subordinate clause, for it does not make complete sense when standing alone.

7. A **phrase** is an assemblage of words forming a single expression but not making complete sense.

Ex.—Till lately; in haste; since then; year by year; little by little; to see; to have seen; to be seen.

8. A **discourse** is a series of sentences on the same subject, arranged in logical order.

9. A **paragraph** is a series of sentences on the same branch of a subject.

10. An **element** is one of the component parts of a sentence.

11. **Analysis** is the separation of a sentence into its elements.

12. **Synthesis** is the construction of sentences from words.

SENTENCES

155. CLASSIFICATION WITH RESPECT TO USE

1. With respect to *use*, sentences are divided into four classes: *declarative*, *interrogative*, *imperative*, and *exclamatory*.

2. A **declarative sentence** is one used to affirm or deny something.

Ex.—Fish swim. Fish do not walk.

Rem.—**Direct discourse** is telling what somebody thinks or says, by using his own words; as, "Our teacher said, '*Be frank, honest, and truthful.*' "

Indirect discourse is giving the substance of what somebody thinks or says, but not using his own words; as, "Our teacher said *that we should be frank, honest, and truthful.*"

3. An **interrogative sentence** is one used to ask a question.

Ex.—Are you angry? Where does that man live?

Rem.— A **direct question** is one which can be answered by *yes* or *no*; as, "Has the money been paid?"

An **indirect question** is one which cannot be answered by *yes* or *no*; as, "Who paid the money?"

4. An **imperative sentence** is one used to express a command or an entreaty.

Ex.—Bring me that book. Do not strike me.

5. An **exclamatory sentence** is one used in exclamations, or in the expression of strong emotion.

Ex.—Oh, how glad I am to see you!

156. EXERCISES

Tell to which class each of the following sentences belongs:

Model—"The dews bring their jewels."

This is a *declarative sentence*; it is used to affirm something.

1. The days are calm. 2. How many quarts are there in a gallon? 3. The winds bring perfumes. 4. Study diligently. 5. He waved his arm. 6. And the fellow calls himself a painter! 7. He deserved punishment rather than pity.

8. Oh, how careless you are! 9. What was the Rubicon? 10. How brightly the sun shines! 11. Alas for the man who has not learned to work! 12. Bring forth the prisoner now. 13. I had a dream which was not all a dream.—*Byron.* 14. A plague of cowards, still say I.—*Shakespeare.*

15. Attend to the duties I have assigned you. 16. Many fell by thy arm: they were consumed in the flame of thy wrath. 17. When shall it be morn in the grave, to bid the slumberer awake? 18. The Commons, faithful to their system, remained in a wise and masterly inactivity.—*Mackintosh.*

157. CLASSIFICATION WITH RESPECT TO FORM

1. With respect to *form*, sentences are divided into three classes: *simple*, *complex*, and *compound*.

2. A **simple sentence** consists of a single proposition/clause.

Ex.—Flowers bloom. Who is he? Tread lightly. How glad I am!

3. A **complex sentence** is one some element of which contains a subject and a predicate.

Ex.—Flowers bloom *when spring returns.* He *who is diligent* shall be rewarded. I hear *that you have sold your farm, and that you are going to California.*

Rem.—The propositions in complex sentences, called **clauses**, are named and numbered according to the order of their subordination.

Ex.—"I believe that he is honest." In this sentence, "I believe" is the *principal* clause, and "that he is honest" is the *subordinate*.

4. A **compound sentence** consists of two or more simple or complex sentences, joined by coordinate conjunctions.

Ex.—Spring comes, *and* the flowers bloom. "I go, *but* I return." "Though Truth is fearless and absolute, *yet* she is meek and modest."

Rem. 1—The simple or complex sentences, of which compound sentences are composed, are called **members**. They are numbered according to their place in the sentence.

Ex.—"Every man desires to live long; but no man would be old." In this sentence, "every man desires to live long" is the *first* member, and "no man would be old" is the *second*.

Rem. 2—The clauses of complex sentences are connected by *relative pronouns*, *conjunctions*, and *conjunctive adverbs*. The members of compound sentences are connected by conjunctions.

Rem. 3—The connectives are sometimes omitted; as, "I thought [that] he was absent"; "Talent is power; [but] tact is skill."

Rem. 4—A sentence whose members are complex, is a *compound-complex* sentence.

158. MODELS FOR CLASSIFICATION

I. "The nights are tranquil."

This is a *sentence*; it is a group of words making complete sense: *declarative*; it is used to affirm something: *simple*; it consists of a single proposition.

II. "Shall I return the book which you lent me?"

This is a *sentence*; *interrogative*; it is used to ask a question: *complex*; it is composed of a principal and a subordinate clause. "*Shall I return the book*" is the principal clause, and "*which you lent me*," the subordinate, limiting "book." "Which" is the connective.

III. "She counseled him that when he arose in the morning
he should beat them without mercy."—*Bunyan*.

This is a *sentence*; *declarative*; *complex*; "*She counseled him*" is the principal proposition; "*that he should beat them without mercy*" the first subordinate, modifying "counseled." "*When he arose in the morning*" is the second subordinate, modifying "beat." "That" and "when" are connectives.

IV. "Pope had perhaps the judgment of Dryden; but Dryden
certainly wanted the diligence of Pope."—*Johnson*.

This is a *sentence*; *declarative*; *compound*; it is composed of two propositions, joined by a coordinate connective. *"Pope had perhaps the judgment of Dryden"* is the first member, and *"Dryden certainly wanted the diligence of Pope"* is the second. "But" is the connective.

159. EXERCISES

1. Thy feet are fetterless. 2. Level spread the lake before him. 3. He waved his broad felt hat for silence. 4. A soldier of the Legion lay dying in Algiers. 5. It sank from sight before it set.—*Whittier.* 6. Ye softening dews, ye tender showers, descend! 7. None will flatter the poor. 8. These are the things that count. 9. The house was wrapped in flames.

10. Hope and fear are the bane of human life. 11. The village all declared how much he knew.—*Goldsmith.* 12. He that refuseth instruction despiseth his own soul. 13. Is it for thee the lark ascends and sings? 14. How dreadful is this place, for God is here! 15. He dares not touch a hair of Catiline. 16. What can compensate for the loss of character? 17. Lead us not into temptation, but deliver us from evil.

18. Time slept on flowers and lent his glass to Hope. 19. All were sealed with the seal which is never to be broken till the great day! 20. O God, we are but leaves on thy stream, clouds in thy sky. 21. Talk to the point, and stop when you have reached it.

22. "It was now the Sabbath day, and a small congregation of about a hundred souls had met for divine service in a place more magnificent than any temple that human hands had ever built to Deity."—*Wilson.*

23. I know thou art gone where the weary are blest,
    And the mourner looks up and is glad.

24. What matter how the night behaved?
    What matter how the north wind raved?—*Whittier.*

25. Bird of the broad and sweeping wing,
    Thy home is high in heaven,
    Where the wide storms their banners fling,
    And the tempest clouds are driven.—*Percival.*

ELEMENTS

160. PRINCIPAL ELEMENTS

1. The **principal elements** of a proposition or clause are those which are necessary to its construction. They are the *subject* and the *predicate*.

2. The **subject** of a proposition/clause is that of which something is affirmed.

Ex.—*"Time* is precious." "Time" is the *subject*; it is that of which "precious" is affirmed.

3. The **predicate** of a proposition is that which is affirmed of the subject.

Ex.—"Time is *precious."* "Precious" is the *predicate*; it is that which is affirmed of the subject.

Rem.—In these definitions, the term "affirm" is meant to include *say, ask for, command, entreat,* or *exclaim.*

4. The subject may be a *word*, a *phrase*, or a *clause.*

Ex.—*Winter* is coming. *H* is a letter. *To steal* is base. *"Pay as you go"* is a good rule. *"Why will he persist?"* is often asked.

Rem.—The subject of a proposition may be known by its answering the question formed by using *Who?* or *What?* with the predicate.

Ex.—"John is careless." *Who* is careless? *Ans.*—"John." "John," therefore, is the subject. *"To be sick* is disagreeable." *What* is disagreeable? *Ans.*—"To be sick." "To be sick," therefore, is the subject.

5. The **copula** is some form of the verb *to be* (*is, was, might be,* etc.) or of some other *copulative* verb. Its office is to affirm the predicate of the subject.

Ex.—"Silence *is* impressive." "Is" is the *copula* and "impressive" the *predicate.* "He *may have been* injudicious." "May have been" is the *copula* and "injudicious" the *predicate.* "The fields *look* green." "Look" is the *copula* and "green" the *predicate.*

6. In affirming *action, being,* or *state,* the copula and predicate are generally united in one word, or one form, called a *verb.*

Ex.—Pupils *study.* I *am.* The house *stands.* Rain *is falling.* Letters *are written.*

7. The copula is sometimes followed by the infinitive of the verb *to be* or of some other copulative verb; as, "The boy seems *to be* sick"; "The detective was *to appear* inattentive." The infinitive depends upon the copula, and is an adverbial element; the entire expression is called a **strengthened copula.**

8. The predicate may be a *word*, a *phrase*, or a *clause.*

Ex.—Horses *gallop.* Wheat is a *grain.* The sun *was shining.* "To obey is *to enjoy."* He seems *honest.* My desire is *that you attend school.*

Rem.—The predicate is sometimes erroneously called the *attribute* of a proposition, and the copula and predicate, taken together, the *predicate*.

161. MODELS FOR ANALYSIS

I. "Birds sing."

This is a *sentence*; *declarative*; *simple*.

Birds is the subject; it is that of which something is affirmed. **Sing** is the predicate; it is that which is affirmed of the subject.

II. "Scholars should be studious."

This is a *sentence*; *declarative*; *simple*.

Scholars is the subject; **studious** is the predicate; **should be** is the copula.

III. "Franklin was a philosopher."

This is a *sentence*; *declarative*; *simple*.

Franklin is the subject; **philosopher** is the predicate; **was** is the copula.

IV. "He was considered responsible."

This is a *sentence*; *declarative*; *simple*.

He is the subject; **responsible** is the predicate; **was considered** is the copula.

V. "Be truthful."

This is a *sentence*; *imperative*; *simple*.

You, understood, is the subject; **truthful** is the predicate; **be** is the copula.

162. EXERCISES IN ANALYSIS

1. Children play. 2. Virtue ennobles. 3. Spring has come. 4. Winter has departed. 5. You may go. 6. Mary might have sung. 7. Horses can run. 8. Flowers are blooming. 9. Money may be loaned. 10. Books will be bought. 11. Stars were shining. 12. John should have been studying.

13. Glass is brittle. 14. Water is transparent. 15. Savages may be merciful. 16. Men should be just. 17. Samuel should have been obedient. 18. Geography is interesting. 19. Job was patient. 20. I will be industrious. 21. They have been successful.

22. Iron is a metal. 23. Flies are insects. 24. Napoleon was a general. 25. Ostriches are birds. 26. "Men would be angels; angels would be gods." 27. They may have been truants. 28. Howard was a philanthropist. 29. He might have been a lawyer. 30. George had been a captain.

31. John looks cold. 32. I feel anguish. 33. Ants appear industrious. 34. Washington was elected president. 35. Avarice has become his master. 36. He seems dejected. 37. He became wealthy. 38. It was deemed inexpedient.

163. ARRANGEMENT OF ELEMENTS

1. **Arrangement** is the correct *placing* of elements.

2. Elements are arranged in *natural* or *inverted* order.

3. The **natural** order of arrangement is that which is most customary.

4. The **inverted** order of arrangement is any departure from the natural order.

Rem.—In inverted order, the elements are said to be transposed.

5. The *natural* order of arrangement is:

In **declarative sentences**:

1. *Subject . . . predicate*; as, "Winds blow."
2. *Subject . . . copula . . . predicate*; as, "Chalk is white."
3. *Subject . . . auxiliary . . . predicate*; as, "You may go."

In **interrogative sentences**:

1. *Copula . . . subject . . . predicate*; as, "Is he wise?"
2. *Auxiliary . . . subject . . . predicate*; as, "May I go?"
3. *Predicate . . . subject*; as, "Say you so?"
4. *Subject . . . predicate*; as, "Who remained?"

In **imperative sentences**;

1. *Predicate . . . subject*; as, "Go thou."
2. *Copula . . . subject . . . predicate*; as, "Be ye merciful."

In **exclamatory sentences**, the arrangement is the same as in *declarative, interrogative*, and *imperative* sentences.

6. The *inverted* order is used when the predicate is made emphatic.

Rem.—**Inversion** occurs in declarative and exclamatory sentences. The usual order of arrangement is: *predicate . . . copula . . . subject*; as, "Great was our wonder," "Known unto God are all his works."

164. EXERCISES IN SYNTHESIS

Affirm **actions** *of the following subjects:*

Winds, waters, stars, fire, light, acorns, sheep, rabbits, fish, men, women, boys, girls, children, thunder, lightning, storms, pastors, kings, merchants.

Models—Winds *blow*. Storms *rage*.

Affirm **quality** *of the following subjects:*

Apples, cherries, peaches, fruit, books, desks, winter, spring, summer, autumn, sugar, quinine, vinegar, grammar, writing, evenings, darkness, chemistry, geography.

Models—Apples *are ripe*. Vinegar *is sour*.

Ascertain all the distinguishing properties of five substances. Affirm them of the substances to which they belong.

Models—Chalk *is white*; chalk *is opaque*; chalk *is brittle*; chalk *is incombustible*, etc.

Affirm **class** *or* **kind** *of the following subjects:*

Oranges, horses, hens, flies, Henry, Washington, ships, gold, silver, sharks, water, air, table.

Models—Oranges *are fruit*. Henry *is a clerk*.

165. SUBORDINATE ELEMENTS

1. A **modifier** is a word, phrase, or clause joined to a term to limit or restrict its meaning or application.

Ex.—A *wealthy* man. Chairs *to mend*. A man *who is wealthy*.

2. **Subordinate elements** are those which modify other elements. They are distinguished as *objective*, *adjective*, and *adverbial*.

166. OBJECTIVE ELEMENT

An **objective element** is a word or group of words which completes the meaning of a transitive verb in the active voice, or of its participles. It is usually called the **object**.

Ex.—Heat melts *metals*. Men love *money*. I wish *to be quiet*. Alice knew *that we were not at home*. *Him* they sought.

Rem. 1—The object answers the question formed by using *Whom*? or *What*? with the predicate or with the subject and predicate.

Ex.—"John writes letters." Writes *what*? *Ans.*—"Letters" = the *object*. "Brutus killed Caesar." Brutus killed *whom*? *Ans.*—"Caesar" = the *object*.

Rem. 2—By "completing the meaning of a verb" is meant restricting its application by stating that on which its action terminates. In the sentence

"John writes," the predicate "writes" is taken in its most general sense: *what* John writes is not mentioned. In the sentence "John writes letters," the application of the predicate is restricted to the single act of writing letters. "Letters" being the object on which the act of writing terminates, it is called the *objective element*.

Rem. 3—Some verbs are followed by two objects: one denoting a person or thing; the other, the rank, office, occupation, or character, of the person, or the species of the thing.

Ex.—They elected *Charles captain*. He called *him a scoundrel*. He makes the *sea* his *home*. They declared *self government a delusion*.

Rem. 4—Another class of verbs is followed by two objects: one denoting a person or thing; the other, that *to* or *from* which the act tends. The former is called the *direct*, the latter the *indirect* object. (See, also, Sec. 32, Rem.)

Ex.—He taught *me arithmetic*. He sold *me a horse*. I gave *him money*. They sent *John a telegram*.

167. MODELS FOR ANALYSIS

VI. "Columbus discovered America."

This is a *sentence*; *declarative*; *simple*.

Columbus is the subject; **discovered** is the predicate. The predicate is modified by **America**, an object.

VII. "Whom did you see?"

This is a *sentence*; *interrogative*; *simple*.

You is the subject; **did see** is the predicate. The predicate is modified by **whom**, an object.

VIII. "Bring me flowers."

This is a *sentence*; *imperative*; *simple*.

You, understood, is the subject; **bring** is the predicate. The predicate is modified by **me**, an indirect, and by **flowers**, a direct object.

IX. "They have chosen Mr. Ames speaker."

This is a *sentence; declarative; simple*.

They is the subject; **have chosen** is the predicate. The predicate is modified by **Mr. Ames**, a direct object, and by **speaker**, an indirect object, denoting office.

168. EXERCISES IN ANALYSIS

1. He examined the books. 2. Silas studied geology. 3. They watched the storm. 4. You must obey the laws. 5. We earn money. 6. Merchants sell goods. 7. Engineers run locomotives. 8. Blacksmiths shoe horses.

9. Farmers sow grain. 10. Give me music. 11. They chose him. 12. We have chosen him director. 13. Bring him a book. 14. Whom did you call? 15. I sold him a horse. 16. He taught me algebra. 17. Henry gave Eli his velocipede. 18. The teacher has appointed John monitor. 19. God called the light day. 20. They made him their leader.

169. EXERCISES IN SYNTHESIS

Sentences containing objective elements are arranged as follows:

Declarative; *Subject . . . predicate . . . object*; as, "I found it."

Interrogative; 1. *Object . . . predicate . . . subject*; as, "What see you?" 2. *Object . . . auxiliary . . . subject. . . verb*; as, "What did you see?"

Imperative; *Predicate . . . object*; as, "Practice economy."

Rem. 1—In inverted order, the arrangement of declarative sentences is: *object . . . subject . . . predicate*; as, "Him they found."

Write sentences containing an objective element, using the following words as subjects.

Men, boys, heat, lightning, horses, locomotives, scythe, knife, shears, clerks, merchants, blacksmith, tailor, mason, doctors, lion, oxen, eagles.

Models—Men drive *horses*. Boys fly *kites*. Merchants sell *goods*.

Write sentences containing two objects, using the above or any other nouns.

Models—Charles calls *doctors physicians*. Frank calls a *sleigh* a *cutter*. I consider *William* a *genius*.

Write sentences containing a direct and an indirect object, using the following verbs:

Ask, buy, bring, do, draw, deny, find, get, leave, make, pass, pour, promise, provide, present, sell, send, show, refuse, teach, tell, throw, write.

Models—I *was asked* a question. A *pony was bought* for Charles.

Analyze the sentences you have written.

170. ADJECTIVE ELEMENT

An **adjective element** is a word or group of words which modifies a noun or any expression used as a noun.

Ex.—A *good* man. Mr. Myers, the *banker*. *Friend* Hiram. "If you can: a *sensible* if." "Done gone," a *vulgarism*, is frequently heard. *My* book is on *Ellen's* desk. A letter, *written* in haste. She came, *laughing*.

Rem. 1—An adjective element is a definitive or descriptive term used to modify the meaning of a noun or its substitute. The relation which a *predicate attribute* sustains to the subject is *affirmed*: the relation which an *adjective* sustains to the term it modifies is *assumed* or taken for granted.

Ex.—"That man is *wealthy*." The predicate "wealthy" is *affirmed* to belong to "man." "A *wealthy* man." The attribute "wealthy" is here *assumed* to belong to "man," and is an *adjective*.

Rem. 2—An adjective, containing a single word, may be:

1. An **adjective**; as, "*Ripe* apples."

2. A **participle**; as, "Hats *made* to order."

3. A **noun in apposition**; as, "Powers, the *sculptor*."

4. A **possessive**; as, "*Eli's* pen." "*His* hat."

171. MODELS FOR ANALYSIS

X. "Small lakes are abundant."

This is a *sentence*; *declarative*; *simple*.

Lakes is the subject; **abundant** is the predicate; **are** is the copula. The subject is modified by **small**, an adjective element.

XI. "The steamship Hibernia has arrived."

This is a *sentence*: *declarative*; *simple*.

Steamship is the subject; **has arrived** is the predicate. The subject is modified by **the** and **Hibernia**, both adjectives.

XII. "My brother broke Stephen's model."

This is a *sentence*; *declarative*; *simple*.

Brother is the subject; **broke** is the predicate. The subject is modified by **my**, an adjective. The predicate is modified by **model**, an object, and "model" is modified by **Stephen's**, an adjective.

XIII. "The old man, laughing, said 'Yes.' "

This is a *sentence*; *declarative; simple*.

Man is the subject; **said** is the predicate. The subject is modified by **the**, **old**, and **laughing**, adjectives. The predicate is modified by **yes**, an object.

172. EXERCISES IN ANALYSIS

1. A large house was burned. 2. I wrote a long letter. 3. This land is government property. 4. Many hands make quick work. 5. A wise son maketh a glad father. 6. Man's necessity is God's opportunity. 7. Mr. Hodge, the farmer, hired Mr. Olds, the mason.

8. Mary has chosen the better part. 9. Carlo's barking wakened the family. 10. I saw six swans. 11. This is my fourteenth birthday. 12. Every man received a penny.

173. EXERCISES IN SYNTHESIS

Adjectives and possessives are usually placed before, and participles and nouns in apposition after, the nouns they modify.

Write seven sentences, limiting the subject by one of the following adjectives:

Round, square, oval, rough, smooth, transparent, translucent, white, green, sour, sweet, old, young, new, wise, foolish, careful, careless.

Models—A *round* table was purchased. A *square* box was found.

Write seven sentences, limiting both subject and object by an adjective.

Model—A *stout* horse draws *heavy* loads.

Write seven sentences, limiting the subject or object by the possessive case of one of the following nouns:

Elephant, swan, hawk, sparrow, summer, winter, father, mother, uncle, aunt, John, Samuel, Celia, Harriet, Jackson, teacher, doctor, pupil, merchant.

Models—An *elephant's* tusks are white. A *swan's* movements are graceful.

Write seven sentences, limiting the subject or object, or both, by a noun in apposition.

Models—Mr. Sledge, the *blacksmith*, is sick. Wilson, the *burgler*, robbed Wilson, the *banker*.

Analyze the sentences you have written.

174. ADVERBIAL ELEMENT

An **adverbial element** is a word or group of words used to modify a verb, participle, adjective, or adverb.

Ex.—The stranger was *very* kind. The wind blows *fiercely*. Come *here*. Who goes *there*?

Rem. 1—Adverbial elements/adverbs, when they modify the meaning of verbs, usually denote some circumstance of *time*, *place*, *cause*, *degree*, or *manner*.

Ex.—He calls *frequently*. There is no night *there*. *Why* are you angry? The teacher labored *faithfully*.

Rem. 2—Adverbs which modify the manner of the assertion, and not the predicate itself, are called *modal adverbs*.

Ex.—He has *not* come. *Perhaps* I shall go. He was absent, *probably*. He will *certainly* resign.

175. MODELS FOR ANALYSIS

XIV. "He is strictly honest."

This is a *sentence*; *declarative*; *simple*.

He is the subject; **honest** is the predicate. The predicate is modified by **strictly**, an adverb.

XV. "The sun shines brightly."

This is a *sentence*; *declarative*; *simple*.

Sun is the subject; **shines** is the predicate. The subject is modified by **the**, an adjective; the predicate by **brightly**, an adverb.

XVI. "He is not handsome."

This is a *sentence*; *declarative*; *simple*.

He is the subject; **handsome** is the predicate. The copula **is** is modified by **not**, an adverb.

176. EXERCISES IN ANALYSIS

1. The birds sing sweetly. 2. We struck the vessel just amidships. 3. I now require your votes. 4. He formerly lived here. 5. The fire went out. 6. He seems very sad. 7. The boy wrote the letter carelessly. 8. They have been long absent. 9. I shall certainly defend you.

177. EXERCISES IN SYNTHESIS

In the natural order of arrangement, the adverbial element is placed after the word or group of words it limits.

Ex.—He denied the charge *vehemently*.

Rem.—In inverted order, the adverb is placed between the subject and predicate, or at the head of the sentence.

Ex.—He *vehemently* denied the charge. *Vehemently* did he deny the charge.

Write seven sentences, limiting the predicates by an adverb of **manner**.

Models—She writes *rapidly*. He does his work *thoroughly*.

Write seven sentences, limiting the predicates by an adverb of **place**.

Models—He lives *there*. *Where* do you live?

Write seven sentences, limiting the predicates by an adverb of **time**.

Models—I was very happy *then*. *When* will you come?

Write seven sentences, limiting the predicates by an adverb of **cause** *or* **degree**.

Models—*Why* are you sad? The work is *scarcely* commenced.

Write seven sentences, limiting the copulas by a **modal** *adverb*.

Models—He is *certainly* insane. James is *not* a truant.

Write seven sentences, containing adjectives modified by adverbs.

Models—That tree is *very* tall. It is a *remarkably* fine gem.

Analyze the sentences you have written.

178. ATTENDANT ELEMENTS

Attendant or **independent elements** are words or expressions not used as principal or subordinate elements of the sentences in which they are found. They are:

1. Nouns and pronouns in the nominative absolute case; as, "*Children*, obey your parents," "*Rome*, her glory has departed," "*He* having arrived, we returned."

2. Interjections and nouns used in broken exclamations; as, "*Phooey*, what *nonsense*!" "Wretched *man* that I am!"

3. Expletives, and words used to introduce sentences in a peculiar way; as, "*Now*, Barabbas was a robber," "*There* is no report of any disaster," "*It* is a shameful thing to tell a lie."

4. All phrases and clauses which have no perceptible connection with the rest of the sentence.

Rem.—Attendant elements should be omitted in the analysis of the sentences containing them. They have no grammatical connection with other words, except in certain constructions in which they are used as antecedents of pronouns. Sometimes the entire group of words of which they form a part has the force of an adverbial element.

Ex.—"*Gad*, a troop shall overcome him." The attendant element "Gad," is the antecedent of the pronoun "him." "*They* having left, order was restored." The attendant element "they," is connected with "having left," and the combination has the force of the adverbial clause "after they left."

179. WORDS, PHRASES, AND CLAUSES

1. Elements are divided into three classes: *words*, *phrases*, and *clauses*.

2. An element may consist of a single word.

Ex.—"A careless boy seldom learns his lesson." In this sentence all the elements are single words.

3. An element may consist of a *phrase*, which may be an infinitive or a preposition and its objects.

Rem.—There are two kinds of phrases: *separable* and *inseparable*.

A **separable phrase** is one whose words should always be parsed separately; as, "He rode *in a wagon*." The three words composing the phrase "in a wagon," should be parsed separately—"in" as a preposition; "a" as an adjective; "wagon" as a noun.

An **inseparable phrase** is one whose words need not be separated in parsing; as, "I will come *by and by*," "He labors *in vain*." The phrases "by and by" and "in vain" may be parsed as single words. All the forms of the infinitive mode are *inseparable* phrases.

4. An element may consist of a *clause*, or subordinate proposition.

Ex.—"A man *who is indolent* will not prosper"; "I learn *that you are out of employment*." The subordinate propositions "who is indolent" and "you are out of employment" are subordinate *clauses*.

180. MODELS FOR ANALYSIS
SINGLE WORDS

XVII. "Tumultuous murder shook the midnight air."

This is a *sentence; declarative; simple.*

Murder is the subject, **shook** is the predicate. The subject, "murder," is modified by **tumultuous**, an adjective; the predicate "shook" is modified by **air**, an object; "air" is modified by **the** and **midnight**, adjectives.

181. EXERCISES

1. Thou hast uttered cruel words. 2. Every heart knows its sorrows. 3. Gratitude is a delightful emotion. 4. This generous bounty was well bestowed. 5. The best men often experience disappointments. 6. A disposition so amiable will secure universal regard. 7. His brother's offense will not condemn him.

182. PHRASES — ADJECTIVE ELEMENTS

XVIII. "A life of prayer is a life of heaven."

Life is the subject; **life** is the predicate; **is** is the copula. The subject, "life," is modified by **a**, an adjective and by the phrase **of prayer**, an adjective. The predicate, "life," is modified by **a**, an adjective and by the phrase **of heaven**, an adjective.

183. EXERCISES

1. Black crags behind thee pierce the clear blue sky. 2. Vicissitudes of good and evil fill up the life of man. 3. He had a remarkably good view of their features. 4. He shakes the woods on the mountain side. 5. The fate of gods may well be thine.—*Byron.* 6. He had endured three months of nights.—*Ware.* 7. His architecture has become a mere framework for the setting of delicate sculpture.—*Ruskin.*

184. PHRASES — ADVERBIAL ELEMENTS

XIX. "Many actions apt to procure fame, are not conducive to our ultimate happiness."

This is a *sentence*; *declarative*; *simple.*

Actions is the subject; **conducive** is the predicate; **are** is the copula. The subject, "actions," is modified by **many** and **apt**, adjectives; "apt" is modified by the phrase **to procure**, an adverb, and "to procure," by **fame**, an object. The copula, "are," is modified by **not**, a modal adverb; and the predicate, "conducive," by the phrase **to happiness**, an adverb, and "happiness," by **our** and **ultimate**, adjectives.

XX. "I will go tomorrow."

This is a *sentence*; *declarative*; *simple.*

I is the subject: **will go** is the predicate. The predicate, "will go," is modified by **tomorrow**, an adverb—**tomorrow** being a noun in the objective case without a governing word. (See Sec. 219, Rule VIII.)

185. EXERCISES

1. I bow reverently to thy decrees. 2. Heaven burns with the descending sun. 3. The panther's track is fresh in the snow. 4. His home lay low in the valley. 5. We one day descried some shapeless object floating at a distance. 6. The horses ran two miles without stopping. 7. We sailed south four days. 8. See what a grace is seated on his brow.—*Shakespeare*. 9. There is a very life in our despair.—*Byron*. 10. Eternal sunshine settles on his head.—*Goldsmith*. 11. Heaven first taught letters for some wretch's aid.—

Pope.

186. PHRASES — INFINITIVES

XXI. "To love is to obey."

This is a *sentence*; *declarative*; *simple*.

To love is the subject; it is a phrase: **to obey** is the predicate; it is a phrase: **is** is the copula.

XXII. "He wishes to go to the house."

This is a *sentence*; *declarative*; *simple*.

He is the subject; **wishes** is the predicate. The predicate, "wishes," is modified by the phrase **to go**, an objective element; "to go" is modified by the phrase **to the house**, an adverbial element, and "house" by **the**, an adjective.

XXIII. "Clarence seemed to be their leader."

This is a *sentence*; *declarative*; *simple*.

Clarence is the subject; **leader** is the predicate; **seemed to be** is the strengthened copula. The predicate, "leader," is modified by "their," an adjective. "Seemed" is modified by the phrase "to be," an adverbial element.

187. EXERCISES

1. To doubt the promise of a friend is a sin. 2. He has gone to his office to write a letter. 3. How pleasant it is to see the sun. 4. Not to know me argues yourselves unknown.—*Milton*. 5. 'Tis not in mortals to command success.—*Addison*. 6. Music hath charms to soothe the savage breast.—*Congreve*. 7. I was not hardened enough to venture a quarrel with him then.—*Cowley*. 8. A thousand years scarce serve to found a state.—*Byron*.

188. CLAUSES

XXIV. "The credulity which has faith in goodness is a sign of goodness."

This is a *sentence*; *declarative*; *complex*. "Credulity is a sign of goodness" is the principal clause, and "which has faith in goodness," the subordinate clause.

Credulity is the subject of the principal clause; **sign** is the predicate; **is** is the copula. The subject "credulity," is modified by **the**, an adjective, and by the clause **which has faith in goodness**, an adjective element, "sign," the predicate, is modified by **a**, an adjective, and by the prepositional phrase **of goodness**, an adjective element. **Which** is the subject of the subordinate clause; **has** is the predicate. The predicate, "has," is modified by **faith**, an object, and by the prepositional phrase **in goodness**, an adverbial element.

XXV. "I thought, when I saw you last, that I should never see you again."

This is a *sentence*; *declarative*; *complex*. "I thought" is the principal proposition; "when I saw you last" and "that I should never see you again" are subordinate propositions.

I is the subject of the principal proposition; **thought** is the predicate. The predicate, "thought," is modified by the clause **when I saw you last**, an adverbial element, and by the clause **that I should never see you again**, an objective element. **I** is the subject of the objective clause; **should see** is the predicate; "should see" is modified by **you**, an object, and by **never** and **again**, adverbs. **I** is the subject of the adverbial clause; **saw** is the predicate; "saw" is modified by **you**, an object, and by **when** and **last**, adverbs. **When** and **that** are connectives, joining the clauses they introduce to "thought."

189. EXERCISES

1. Soon rested those who fought. 2. All said that Love had suffered wrong. 3. He builds a palace of ice where the torrents fall. 4. It was now a matter of curiosity who the old gentleman was. 5. The fires of the bivouac complete what the fires kindled by the battle have not consumed. 6. Towards night, the schoolmaster walked over to the cottage where his little friend lay sick.

7. The sound of the wind among the leaves was no longer the sound of the wind, but of the sea.—*Longfellow*. 8. These are follies on which it would be greater folly to remark.—*Landor*. 9. I am now at liberty to confess that much which I have heard objected to my late friend's writings was well founded. 10. One of his favorite maxims was that the only way to keep a secret is never to let anyone suspect that you have one. 11. How his essays will read, now they are brought together, is a question for the publishers, who have thus ventured to draw out into one piece his "weaved-up follies."—*Lamb*.

12. Merciful wind, sing me a hoarse, rough song,
For there is other music made tonight
That I would fain not hear.

13. Woe worth the chase! woe worth the day!
That cost thy life, my gallant gray.—*Scott*

14. The mountain arose, with its lofty brow,
While its shadow was sleeping in vales below.—*Clark*.

190. EXERCISES IN SYNTHESIS

Write seven sentences, limiting their subjects by an adjective phrase.

Models—Love *of display* is a sin. Greed *of gain* is wrong.

Write seven sentences, limiting their subjects by an adjective clause.

Model—The house *which you see yonder* belongs to my father.

Write seven sentences, limiting their predicates by an objective phrase or clause.

Models—I wish *to remain*. He says *that he cannot walk*.

Write seven sentences, limiting their predicates by an adverbial phrase or clause.

Models—I study *to learn*. I will come *when you call me*.

Write seven sentences, introducing attendant elements.

Model—I think, *my dear friend*, that you are mistaken.

Analyze the sentences you have written.

KINDS OF ELEMENTS

191. SIMPLE ELEMENTS

1. A **simple element** is one which is not restricted by a modifier.

Ex.—"A *rich* man"; "A man *of wealth*"; "A man *who is wealthy*." The word "rich," the phrase "of wealth," and the clause "who is wealthy," are simple *adjective elements*.

2. The **grammatical subject** is the *simple* subject.

3. The **grammatical predicate** is the *simple* predicate.

Rem.—The same distinction may be made in the other elements.

192. MODELS FOR COMPLETE ANALYSIS

XXVI. "To err is human."

This is a *sentence*; *declarative*; *simple*.

To err is the grammatical subject; **human** is the grammatical predicate; **is** is the copula.

XXVII. "I am in danger."

This is a *sentence*; *declarative*; *simple*.

I is the grammatical subject; **am** is the grammatical predicate. The predicate, "am," is modified by the phrase **in danger**, an adverbial element.

193. EXERCISES

1. Banners were waving. 2. To forgive is divine. 3. It is pleasant to read. 4. Stars have been shining. 5. Weapons were procured. 6. To covet is sinful. 7. To quarrel is disgraceful. 8. To rob is to plunder. 9. Vessels are in sight.

194. COMPLEX ELEMENTS

1. A **complex element** is one which contains a leading element, restricted in meaning by one or more modifiers.

2. The leading element is called the **basis**.

Ex.—"A *very rich* man." "Rich" is the basis of the adjective element, and it is modified by "very," an adverb. "A man *faithful when others were faithless*." "Faithful" is the basis of the adjective element, and it is modified by the clause "when others were faithless."

Rem.—The basis of an element need not be pointed out or mentioned in analysis.

3. The **complex, logical,** or **complete subject** is the simple subject taken with all its modifiers.

Rem. 1—The simple subject, when a noun, may be modified:

1. By an *adjective*; as, "*Loud* reports followed."

2. By a *participle*; as, "The hour *appointed* has come."

3. By a *possessive*; as, "*George's* plan succeeded."

4. By a *noun in the same case*; as, "Byron, the *poet*, is dead."

5. By a *phrase*; as, "A storm *of applause* followed."

6. By a *clause*; as, "Money *which I earn* is my own."

Rem. 2—A subject may have all the preceding modifications in the same sentence.

Rem. 3—When the simple subject is a pronoun, it may have all the modifications of a noun, except that made by a noun or pronoun in the possessive case.

Rem. 4—An infinitive or participial noun, used as a subject, may be modified (1) *as a noun*, by a word, phrase, or clause in the nominative case, in apposition with it; (2) *as a verb*, by the modifiers of a verb.

4. The **complex** or **logical predicate** is the simple predicate taken with all its modifiers.

Rem. 1—The simple predicate, when a verb, may be modified:

1. If transitive, by an *object*; as, "He saves *money*."

2. By an *adverb*; as, "The horse runs *swiftly*."

3. By a *phrase*; as, "He lives *in Troy*," "He studies *to learn*."

4. By a *clause*; as, "He knows *where the mushrooms grow*."

Rem. 2—When the predicate is an adjective, a participle, a noun, or anything used as a noun, it may have all the modifications of the part of speech with which it is classed.

Rem. 3—The copula is usually, but not always, modified by modal adverbs and adverbs of time.

Rem. 4—A predicate may have all the modifications given above in the same sentence.

5. A **complex objective element** is the simple object taken with all its modifiers.

Rem.—A complex objective element may be:

1. A **word**, modified by words, phrases, or clauses: as, "We found *much gold*"; "He owns the *house on the hill*"; "I love *those who are frank*."

2. A **phrase**, modified by single words, phrases, or clauses; as, "He desires *to learn rapidly*"; "He desires *to learn to write*"; "He desires *to repeat what he has heard*."

3. A **clause**, some part of which is modified by another clause; as, "I said *that he was present when the assault was made*."

6. A **complex adjective element** is the simple adjective taken with all its modifiers.

Rem.—A complex adjective element may be:

1. An **adjective**, modified by an adverb; as, "A *very large* lot."

2. A **participle**, with all the modifiers of a verb; as, "The young man was seen *clandestinely entering a tavern.*"

3. A **noun** or **pronoun**, with the modifications of a noun or pronoun; as, "*Mr. Elder's* house"; "Thompson, *the faithful guardian of our cousins*"; "*Our own* dear native land."

4. A **phrase**, modified by a word, phrase, or clause; as, "A time *to make friends*"; "A time *to learn to write*"; "A time *to repeat what you have learned.*"

5. A **clause**, some part of which is modified by another clause; as, "A man *who is angry whenever his views are contradicted.*"

7. A **complex adverbial element** is the simple adverb taken with all its modifiers.

Rem.—A complex adverbial element may be:

1. An **adverb**, modified by a single word, phrase, or clause; as, "I am ready *to begin* the work"; "I shall be ready *to commence* work *by daylight*"; "I am ready *to go wherever the Lord calls me.*"

2. A **phrase**, modified by a single word, phrase, or clause; as "We rode *very rapidly*"; "It is too *badly* done *to last*"; "He spoke so *distinctively that we could not understand him.*"

3. A **clause**, some part of which is modified by another clause; as, "He is afraid *that you will not return before he leaves.*"

195. MODELS FOR COMPLETE ANALYSIS

XXVIII. "A lad, made orphan by a winter shipwreck,
played among the debris."

This is a *sentence*; *declarative*; *simple*.

"A lad, made orphan by a winter shipwreck," is the logical or complete subject, and "played among the debris" is the logical or complete predicate.

Lad is the grammatical or simple subject; **played** is the grammatical predicate. The subject, "lad," is modified by **a**, a simple adjective element, and by **made orphan by a winter shipwreck**, a complex adjective element. "Made orphan" is modified by the phrase **by a winter shipwreck**, an adverbial element: "shipwreck" is modified by **a** and **winter**, adjectives.

The predicate, "played," is modified by the phrase **among the debris**, an adverbial element, and "debris" by **the**, an adjective element. "Made orphan" is an abridged proposition, equivalent to "that was made an orphan." (See Sec. 206.)

XXIX. "He who does as he desires, without regard to the wishes of others, will soon cease to do well."

This is a *sentence*; *declarative*; *complex*.

"He will soon cease to do well" is the principal proposition or clause: "who does as he desires, without regard to the wishes of others," the complex subordinate proposition or clause.

"He who does as he desires, without regard to the wishes of others," is the logical or complete subject, and "will soon cease to do well," the logical predicate.

He is the grammatical subject of the principal, main clause; **will cease** is the predicate. The subject, "he," is modified by the clause **who does as he desires**, etc., a complex adjective element.

Who is the subject of this dependent clause; **does** is the predicate; "does" is modified by the clause **as he desires**, an adverbial element; of which **as** is the connective, **he** is the subject, and **desires** is the predicate; also by the phrase **without regard to the wishes of others**, a complex adverbial element, of which **regard** is modified by the phrase **to the wishes of others**, a complex adjective element. **Wishes** is modified by **the**, an adjective, and by the phrase **of others**, an adjective element.

"Will cease," the predicate, is modified by **soon**, an adverb, and by the phrase **to do well**, a complex objective element; of which **to do** is modified by **well**, an adverb.

196. EXERCISES

1. There is a limit at which forbearance ceases to be a virtue. 2. If ye love me, keep my commandments. 3. Were I not Alexander, I would be Diogenes. 4. Unless he reforms soon, he is a ruined man. 5. Except ye repent, ye shall all likewise perish.

6. Withdraw thy foot from thy neighbor's house, lest he weary of thee, and so hate thee. 7. I am quite sure that Mr. Hutchins rode through the village this morning. 8. He never knows his lesson because he is too lazy to study. 9. Do not forget to write when you reach home. 10. Even by means of our sorrows, we belong to the eternal plan.

11. The gentleman who was dressed in brown-once-black had a sort of medico-theological exterior, which we afterward found to be representative of the inward man.

12. Every art was practiced to make them pleased with their own condition.—*Johnson*.

13. The man that blushes is not quite a brute.—*Young.*

14. My soul is an enchanted boat,
      Which, like a sleeping swan, doth float
Upon the silver waves of thy sweet singing.—*Shelly.*

197. COMPOUND ELEMENTS

A compound element consists of two or more independent simple or complex elements, joined by coordinate conjunctions.

Ex.—The *moon* and *stars* are shining. You may **go** or **stay**.

Rem.—All the elements of a sentence may be compound.

198. MODELS FOR COMPLETE ANALYSIS

XXX. "Industry, honesty, and economy generally insure success."

This is a *sentence*; *declarative*; *simple*.

"Industry, honesty, and economy" is the logical subject; "generally insure success" is the logical predicate.

Industry, honesty, and economy is the compound grammatical subject; **insure** is the grammatical predicate. The subject is not modified. The predicate, "insure," is modified by **generally**, an adverb, and by **success**, an object.

XXXI. "The charities that soothe, and heal, and bless,
      Are scattered at the feet of man like flowers."—*Wordsworth.*

This is a *sentence*; *declarative*; *complex*. Name the principal and the subordinate clause.

"The charities that soothe, and heal, and bless" is the complete subject: "Are scattered at the feet of man like flowers" is the complete predicate.

Charities is the simple subject of the principal proposition; **are scattered** is the simple predicate. The subject, "charities," is modified by **the**, an adjective, and by the clause **that soothe, and heal, and bless**, an adjective element; of which **that** is the subject, and **soothe, and heal, and bless** is the compound predicate; **and** being the connective.

The predicate, "are scattered," is modified (1) by the phrase **at the feet of man**, a complex adverbial element; of which "feet" is modified by **the**, an adjective, and by the phrase **of man**, an adjective element; (2) by the phrase **like flowers**, an adverbial element.

199. EXERCISES

1. Exercise and temperance strengthen the constitution. 2. Youth is bright and lovely. 3. He is neither old nor infirm. 4. He is not angry, but excited. 5. They wash, iron, cook, eat, and sleep in the same room. 6. I want to be quiet and to be let alone. 7. The book which I loaned you, and which you lost, was a present from my father. 8. To live in a fine house and drive fast cars is the height of his ambition.

9. There was another tap at the door—a smart, potential tap, which seemed to say, "Here I am, and in I'm coming."

10. Not a truth has to art or to science been given,
But brows have ached for it, and souls toiled and striven.—*Lytton*.

200. CLASSIFICATION OF PHRASES

1. Complex elements and abridged clauses are sometimes called **phrases**.

Rem.—The basis of the element, the manner in which it modifies, the connective, or the leading word, determines the name of the phrase.

2. Phrases may be:

1. **Appositive**; as, "Washington, *the father of his country.*"
2. **Adjective**; as, "A man, *tenacious of principle.*"
3. **Adverbial**; as, "He lives *just around the corner.*"
4. **Prepositional**; as, "We walked *on the bank of the river.*"
5. **Infinitive**; as, "He hoped *to receive a telegram.*"
6. **Participial**; as, "*Being unwell*, he remained at home."
7. **Absolute**; as, "*He being sick,* I remained."
8. **Independent**; as, "Oh *my ducats!*"

Rem. 1—The infinitive, or participial phrase, when used as subject, is called the *subject phrase*: when used as predicate, the *predicate phrase*.

Rem. 2—The absolute phrase is an abridged clause. It usually modifies the predicate of the sentence of which it forms a part, but it may modify the subject and predicate combined.

201. CLASSIFICATION OF CLAUSES

Clauses are classified with reference to their use or position in sentences. They are:

1. The **subject clause**: a proposition used as the subject of a sentence; as, "*How the accident occurred* is not known."

2. The **predicate clause**: a proposition used as the predicate of a sentence; as, "The question is, *How did he obtain the money?*"

3. The **relative clause**: a dependent proposition introduced by a relative pronoun; as, "The vessel *which you see yonder* is a sloop."

4. The **appositive clause**: a proposition put in apposition with a noun; as, "The question, *Are we a nation?* is now answered."

5. The **interrogative clause**: a proposition introduced by an interrogative word; as, "*Who* said so?" "*What* vessel is that?" "*Where* do you live?"

6. The **objective clause**: a proposition used as an objective element; as, "The chairman declared *that the motion was lost.*"

7. The **adverbial clause**: a proposition used as an adverbial element; as, "I will pay you *when I receive my week's wages.*"

Rem. 1—*Subject, predicate*, and *objective* clauses are used as nouns.

Rem. 2—*Relative* clauses are either *restrictive* or *explanatory*. If restrictive, the antecedent is usually modified by *a, the*, or *that*; as, "*The* vessel *which capsized* was a bark." If explanatory, the antecedent is not so modified; as, "Steamships, *which are a modern invention*, make quick voyages."

A clause introduced by a compound relative is frequently equivalent to an adverb; as, "He will succeed, *whoever may oppose him.*"

Rem. 3—*Interrogative* clauses may be introduced by interrogative pronouns, interrogative adjectives, or interrogative adverbs.

Rem. 4—*Adverbial* clauses may be classified as follows:

1. **Temporal**: dependent clauses denoting *time*; as, "I was absent *when the accident occurred.*"

2. **Local**: dependent clauses denoting *place*; as, "Go *where duty calls you.*"

3. **Causal**: dependent clauses denoting *cause*; as, "He is beloved, *for he is good.*"

4. **Final**: dependent clauses denoting a *purpose* or a *result*; as, "We came *that we might assist you*"; "Love not sleep, *lest thou come to poverty.*"

5. **Comparative**: dependent clauses expressing *comparison*; as, "He is older *than* I [am]"; "Men generally die *as they live.*"

6. **Conditional**: dependent clauses modifying propositions containing *deductions* or *conclusions*; as, "He will be ruined *unless he reform*"; "I would pay you *if I could.*"

7. **Concessive**: dependent clauses denoting a *concession* or *admission*; as, "*Though he slay me*, yet will I trust in him."

Rem. 5—Two clauses which mutually qualify are called **correlative**; as, "The deeper the well, the cooler the water."

202. EXERCISES

Classify the phrases and clauses in the following sentences.

1. No one came to his assistance. 2. He were no lion, were not Romans hinds. 3. I would that ye all spake with tongues. 4. Thou shalt love thy neighbor as thyself. 5. Launch thy bark, mariner! 6. He made them give up their spoils. 7. Go quickly, that you may meet them.

8. Voltaire, who might have seen him, speaks repeatedly of his majestic stature. 9. The French, a mighty people, combined for the regeneration of Europe. 10. Not many generations ago, where you now sit circled with all that exalts and embellishes civilized life, the rank thistle nodded in the wind, and the wild fox dug his hole unscared.—*Sprague.*

11. Very few men, properly speaking, live at present: most are preparing to live another time. 12. I lisped in numbers, for the numbers came. 13. While the bridegroom tarried, they all slumbered and slept. 14. Study nature, whose laws and phenomena are all deeply interesting. 15. Its qualities exist, since they are known, and are known because they exist. 16. At ten o'clock, my task being finished, I went down to the river.

17. Some say, that ever 'gainst that season comes
Wherein our Savior's birth is celebrated,
This bird of warning singeth all night long:
And then no spirit dares stir abroad;
The nights are wholesome: then no planets strike,
No fairy tales, nor witch hath power to charm,
So hallowed and so gracious is the time.—*Shakespeare.*

CONTRACTED SENTENCES

Sentences are contracted by ellipsis, abridgment, or by substituting a different expression.

Rem.—The object of contraction is to secure conciseness of expression by means of brevity in the construction of sentences.

203. ELLIPSIS

1. **Ellipsis** is the omission of one or more words of a sentence. The words omitted are said to be *understood*.

Rem.—If required in analysis or parsing, the words omitted must be supplied.

2. A **simple sentence** is contracted by omitting all, or nearly all, but the most important part.

1. The *subject* may be omitted; as, "Come" = "You come."

2. The *predicate* may be omitted; as, "Who will go? He [*will go*]." "I'll [*go*] hence to London," "Ye are Christ's [*disciples*]."

3. Both *subject* and *predicate* may be omitted; as, "Water!" = *Give me some* water; "Forward!" = *You march* forward.

4. The *object* may be omitted; as, "Whose book have you? *John's*" = *I have* John's *book*.

5. The verb *to be*, in all its forms, may be omitted; as, "Where now [*are*] her glittering towers?" "A professed Catholic, he imprisoned the Pope" = *Being* a professed Catholic, etc.

6. *Prepositions* and *conjunctions* may be omitted; as, "Build [*for*] me here seven altars"; "Woe is [*to*] me"; "I know [*that*] you are honest"; "Each officer, [*and*] each private did his duty."

Rem.—A complex sentence, whose subject or predicate is a clause, may be contracted by changing the clause to an infinitive or participial phrase; as, "*That I may remain here*, is my desire" = *To remain here* is my desire; "My desire is, *that I may remain here*" = My desire is, *to remain here*.

3. A **compound sentence** may be contracted by uniting the parts not common to all its members, and using the common parts but once.

Ex.—"Exercise strengthens the constitution, and temperance strengthens the constitution" = Exercise and temperance strengthen the constitution. "Behold my mother and behold my brethren" = Behold my mother and my brethren.

204. MODELS FOR ANALYSIS

XXXII. "Rest."

This is a *sentence*; *imperative*; *simple*.

You, understood, is the subject; **rest** is the predicate.

XXXIII. "Build me here seven altars."

This is a *sentence*; *imperative*; *simple*.

You, understood, is the subject; **build** is the predicate. The predicate, "build," is modified by **altars**, an object, which is modified by **seven**, an adjective. "Build" is also modified by **here** and the phrase **for me**, adverbial elements.

XXXIV. "He spake as one having authority."

This is a *sentence*; *declarative*; *complex*.

"He spake" is the principal clause; "as one having authority speaks," the subordinate clause.

He is the subject of the principal clause; **spake** is the predicate. The predicate, "spake," is modified by the clause **as one having authority speaks**, an adverbial element. **One** is the subject of the subordinate clause; **speaks** is the predicate. The subject, "one," is modified by **having**, an adjective, which is modified by **authority**, an object. **As** is the connective.

XXXV. "He is worth more than you."

This is a *sentence*; *declarative*; *complex*.

"He is worth more" is the principal clause; "than you are worth," the subordinate clause.

He is the subject of the principal clause; **worth** is the predicate; **is** is the copula. The predicate, "worth," is modified by **more**, an adverb, "more" being an adjective used as a noun in the objective case without a governing word. "More," as an adjective in the comparative degree, is modified by the clause **than you are worth**, an adverbial element. **You** is the subject of the subordinate clause; **worth** is the predicate; **are** is the copula. **Than** is the connective.

205. EXERCISES

1. Advance. 2. Up, comrades, up. 3. Quick, quick, or we are lost. 4. Honest, my lord? 5. Impossible! 6. This done, we instantly departed. 7. Thou denied a grave! 8. What would content you? Talent? 9. How, now, Jenkinson? 10. A rope to the side! 11. Rather he than I. 12. The orphan of St. Louis, he became the adopted child of the Republic.

13. Do you see a man wise in his own conceit? There is more hope for a fool than for him. 14. Are you fond of skating? Somewhat. 15. Horace is older than I? 16. That building is as large as the capitol.

17.   Multitudes of little floating clouds,
    Ere we, who saw, of change were conscious, pierced
    Through their ethereal texture, had become
    Vivid as fire.—*Wordsworth.*

18. Then here's to our boyhood, its gold and its gray!
    The stars of its winter, the dews of its May!
    And when we have done with our life-lasting toys,
    Dear Father, take care of thy children, the Boys!—*O. W. Holmes*

19. Wisdom, judgment, prudence, and firmness were his predominant traits. 20. Rural employments are certainly natural, amusing, and healthy. 21. He had a good mind, a sound judgment, and a vivid imagination. 22. He is a good, faithful, and generous boy. 23. Man is fearfully and wonderfully made.

24. To love God and to do good to men are the leading purposes of every Christian. 25. Education expands and elevates the mind. 26. Learn to labor and to wait. 27. I am not the advocate of indolence and improvidence. 28. During our voyage, we whiled away our time in reading, in writing a journal, and in studying navigation.

29. The writings of the sages show that the best empire is self government, and that subduing our passions is the noblest of conquests.

30. The chastity of honor, which felt a stain like a wound, which inspired courage while it mitigated ferocity, which enobled whatever it touched, and under which vice itself lost half its evil by losing its grossness, is gone.
—*Burke.*

31. When public bodies are to be addressed on momentous occasions, when great interests are at stake and strong passions excited, nothing is valuable in speech further than it is connected with high intellectual and moral endowments.—*Webster.*

206. ABRIDGMENT

1. **Complex sentences** are often changed into simple sentences by abridging their subordinate clauses.

2. Contracted clauses are called *abridged propositions*.

Ex.—"We came *that we might assist you*" = We came *to assist you.* "I believe *that he is honest*" = I believe *him to be honest.*

Rem.—There is an essential difference between a sentence shortened by ellipsis and an abridged proposition. In the former, the omitted words are clearly implied, and must be restored before the sentence can be analyzed or parsed; in the latter, an equivalent expression is substituted for an entire proposition. The predicate is always retained, but is used as an *assumed* attribute, the *assertion* being wholly omitted.

3. To abridge a subordinate clause:

1st. Drop the subject, if it be already expressed in the principal clause; if not, retain it—changing its case to the possessive, objective, or absolute.

2d. Drop the connective, and change the copula or principal verb to a participle, a participial noun, or an infinitive.

Rem. 1—In abridging a proposition, when the copula or principal verb is changed to the infinitive mode, a noun or pronoun used as subject or predicate must be changed to the objective case.

Ex.—1. "I knew that it was he" = I knew *it* to be *him*. 2. "The merchant ordered that the goods should be shipped" = The merchant ordered the *goods* to be shipped.

When the copula or principal verb is changed to a participial noun, the subject is changed to the possessive case; but a noun or pronoun used as the predicate remains unchanged in the nominative.

Ex.—1. "I was not aware that it was he" = I was not aware of *its* being *he*. 2. "That he was a farmer aided his election" = *His* being a *farmer* aided his election.

When the copula or principal verb is changed to a participle, the subject is put in the nominative case absolute with it.

Ex.—1. "The fair was not held, because the weather was unfavorable" = The *weather* being unfavorable, the fair was not held. 2. "When the sun rose, we continued our journey" = The *sun* being risen, we continued our journey.

Rem. 2—Sometimes an infinitive is an abridged proposition, the subject being omitted because it is contained in the principal clause.

Ex.—"I told him *to go*"; equivalent to, I told him that he should go. In this sentence, *to go* is the direct object of *told*, and *him* the indirect object. The expression "him to go" resembles an abridged proposition in form only.

Rem. 3—The abridged form of an *adjective clause* is a participial, infinitive, or prepositional phrase.

Ex.—"Our friends *who live in the city*" = Our friends *living in the city* = Our friends *in the city*. "A book *that may amuse you*" = A book *to amuse you*.

Rem. 4—The abridged form of an *adverbial clause* is a participial, infinitive, prepositional, or absolute phrase.

Ex.—"*When we heard the explosion*, we hastened to the spot" = *hearing the explosion,* we hastened, etc; "I attend school *that I may learn*" = I attend school *to learn*; "*If he be economical*, he will become rich" = He will become rich *by being economical*; "*When the soldiers arrived*, the mob dispersed" = *The soldiers having arrived*, etc.

Rem. 5—The abridged form of an *adjective clause* is a noun or pronoun modified by an infinitive phrase.

Ex.—"We wish *that you would stay*" = We wish you *to stay*. "I thought *that he was a merchant*" = I thought *him to be a merchant*.

207. MODELS FOR ANALYSIS

XXXVI. "I know him to be a sailor."

This is a *sentence, declarative, simple*.

I is the subject; **know** is the predicate. The predicate is modified by the abridged clause **him to be a sailor**, equivalent to "that he is a sailor," an objective element. **Him** is modified by the phrase **to be a sailor**, an adjective element; **sailor** by **a**, an adjective.

XXXVII. "I was aware of his being my enemy."

This is a *sentence, declarative, simple*.

I is the subject; **aware** is the predicate; **was** is the copula. The predicate, "aware," is modified by the abridged clause **of his being my enemy**, an adverbial element, equivalent to, "that he was my enemy." **Being** is modified by **his**, an adjective; **enemy**, by **my**, an adjective.

XXXVIII. "The shower having passed, we resumed our journey."

This is a *sentence, declarative, simple*.

We is the subject; **resumed** is the predicate. "Resumed" is modified by **journey**, an object, which is modified by our, an adjective. "Resumed" is also modified by the abridged proposition **the shower having passed**, equivalent to "when the shower had passed." "Shower" is modified by **the** and **having passed**, adjective elements.

208. EXERCISES

Analyze the following sentences, giving equivalent clauses for the abridged propositions.

1. Caesar having crossed the Rubicon, Pompey prepared for battle.
2. Having accumulated a large fortune, he retired from business. 3. Being but dust, be humble and wise. 4. Judging from his dress, I should pronounce him an artisan.

5. I believe him to be an honest man. 6. There is no hope of his recovering his health. 7. There is no prospect of the storm's abating. 8. Having been detained by this accident, he lost the opportunity of seeing them.

9. Having annoyed us thus for a time, they began to form themselves into close columns, six or eight abreast.—*Jane Taylor.*

10.   My story being done,
She gave me for my pains a world of sighs.—*Shakespeare.*

209. DIRECTIONS FOR ANALYSIS

SENTENCES

I. In analyzing:

1. Read the sentence.
2. Determine, from its form and use, whether it is *declarative, interrogative, imperative,* or *exclamatory.*
3. Determine whether it is *simple, complex,* or *compound.*
4. Arrange all the parts in natural order.
5. If necessary for analysis or parsing, supply all ellipses.

II. If it is a *simple* sentence:

1. Point out the logical/complete subject and logical/complete predicate.
2. Point out the grammatical/simple subject and grammatical/simple predicate.
3. Determine whether the subject is *simple, complex,* or *compound*; and when complex, point out and classify its modifiers with their qualifications.
4. Determine whether the predicate is *simple, complex,* or *compound*; and when complex, point out and classify (1) its objective modifiers, (2) its adverbial modifiers, with their qualifications.
5. Point out the attendant elements, and all the connectives.

III. If it is a *complex* sentence:

1. Analyze the principal clause as in II.
2. Analyze the subordinate clause or clauses as in II.

IV. If it is a *compound* sentence, each member should be analyzed as a simple or complex sentence, as II or III.

ELEMENTS

V. In an element of a sentence:

1. If it is a *single word*, it is completely reduced.

2. If it is a phrase or a clause, determine:
   a. The *connective*, and the parts it joins.
   b. In a *phrase*, determine the antecedent and subsequent terms of relation of the preposition.
   c. In a *clause*, point out the subject and predicate.
3. If an element is *complex*, reduce it to simple elements.
4. If an element is *compound:*
   a. Separate it into its component simple elements.
   b. Point out and classify the connective which joins them.
   c. Dispose of each element separately, as in 1 and 2 above.

Rem.—Once the sentence is reduced by analysis to the parts of speech of which it is composed, let the teacher select words to be parsed, and instruct his pupils how to deal with them according to the "models for parsing."

210. MODEL FOR COMPLETE ANALYSIS

"The patriot, whom the corrupt tremble to see arise, may well feel a grateful satisfaction in the mighty power which heaven has delegated to him, when he thinks that he has used it for those purposes only which heaven approves."

This is a *sentence, declarative, complex.* It is composed of six clauses. The *principal clause* is:

The patriot may well feel a grateful satisfaction in the mighty power.

The *subordinate clauses* are:

1. *Whom the corrupt tremble to see arise;*
2. *Which heaven has delegated to him;*
3. *When he thinks;*
4. *That he has used it for those purposes only;*
5. *Which heaven approves.*

"*Patriot*" is the subject of the principal clause; "*may feel*" is the predicate.

The subject, "*patriot*," is modified (1) by "*the*," an adjective, and (2) by the clause "*whom the corrupt tremble to see arise*," an adjective element; of which "*whom*" is the connective, "*corrupt*" is the subject, and "*tremble*" is the predicate. "*Corrupt*" is modified by "*the*," an adjective; "*tremble*" is modified by the phrase "*to see*," an adverbial element; which is modified by "*whom*," an object, and "*whom*" is modified by the phrase "*[to] arise*," an adjective element.

The predicate, "*may feel*," is modified (1) by "*well*," an adverb; (2) by "*satisfaction*," an object which is modified by "*a*" and "*grateful*," adjectives; and (3) by the phrase "*in the mighty power which heaven has delegated* to him," an adverbial element. "*Power*" is modified (1) by "*the*" and "*mighty*," adjectives; (2) by the clause "*which heaven has delegated to him*," an adjective element; of which "*which*" is the connective, "*heaven*" is the subject, and "*has delegated*" is the predicate; "*has delegated*" is modified (1) by "*which*," an object; (2) by the phrase "*to him*," an adverbial element; of which "*to*" is the connective, and "*him*" is the object.

"*May feel*" is modified (4) by the clause "*when he thinks*," etc., an adverbial element; of which "*when*" is the connective, "*he*" is the subject, and "*thinks*" is the predicate. "*Thinks*" is modified by the clause "*that he has used it*," etc., an objective element; of which "*that*" is the connective, "*he*" is the subject, and "*has used*" is the predicate. "*Has used*" is modified (1) by "*it*," an object; (2) by the phrase "*for those purposes only*," etc., an adverbial element. "*Purposes*" is modified (1) by "*those*" and "*only*," adjectives and (2) by the clause "*which heaven approves*," an adjective element; of which "*which*" is the connective, "*heaven*" is the subject, and "*approves*" is the predicate. "*Approves*" is modified by "*which*" an object.

211. BRIEF METHOD OF ANALYSIS

"*Patriot*" is the subject; "*may feel*" is the predicate.

The subject, "*patriot*," is modified (1) by "*the*," an adjective, and (2) by the clause "*whom the corrupt tremble to see arise*," an adjective element.

The predicate, "*may feel*" is modified (1) by "*well*," an adverb, denoting *manner*; (2) by "*a grateful satisfaction*," a complex objective element; (3) by the phrase "*in the mighty power which . . . him*," a complex adverbial element; and (4) by the clause "*when he thinks . . . approves*," a complex adverbial element, denoting *time*.

212. MISCELLANEOUS EXAMPLES

1. Hypocrisy is a sort of homage that vice pays to virtue. 2. He was a very young boy; quite a little child.

3. "Well, what is it?" said my lady Brook. 4. Suddenly the watch gave the alarm of "A sail ahead!" 5. He saw a star shoot from heaven, and glittering in its fall, vanish upon the earth. 6. Sweet are thy murmurs, O stream!—*Ossian*.

7. Their slumbers are sound, and their wakings cheerful. 8. This were a wicked pretension, even though the whole family were destroyed.—*Cowley*. 9. And behold there came a voice unto him, and said, What doest thou here, Elijah?—*Bible*.

10. I passed the house many successive days. 11. He wore an ample cloak of black sheep's wool, which, having faded into a dull brown, had been refreshed by an enormous patch of the original color. His countenance was that of the faded part of his cloak.—*Bryant.*

12. The line which bisects the vertical angle of a triangle, divides the base into segments proportional to the adjacent sides. 13. He is so good, he is good for nothing. 14. The clouds are divided in heaven: over the green hills flies the inconstant sun: red, through the stony vale, comes down the stream of the hills.—*Ossian.*

15. In the marvelous mystery of human life, it is a consolation sometimes to believe that our mistakes, perhaps even our sins, are permitted to be instruments of our education for immortality.

16. No ax had leveled the giant progeny of the crowded groves, in which the fantastic forms of withered limbs, that had been blasted and riven by lightning, contrasted strangely with the verdant freshness of a younger growth of branches.—*Bancroft.*

17. The sun was now resting his huge disk upon the edge of the level ocean, and gilding the accumulation of clouds through which he had traveled the livelong day; and which now assembled on all sides, like misfortunes and disasters around a sinking empire and falling monarch.—*Scott.*

18. It is, therefore, a certain and a very curious fact, that the representative, at this time, of any great whig family, who probably imagines that he is treading in the footsteps of his forefathers, in reality, while adhering to their party names, is acting against almost every one of their party principles.—*Lord Mahon.*

19. Rivers will always have one shingly shore to play over, where they may be shallow, and foolish, and childlike; and another steep shore, under which they can pause, and purify themselves, and get their strength of waves fully together for due occasion.—*Ruskin.*

20. I seem to have been only like a boy playing on the seashore, and diverting myself in now and then finding a smoother pebble or a prettier shell than ordinary, whilst the great ocean of truth lay all undiscovered before me.—*Newton.*

21.   We're nettles, some of us,
And give offense by the act of springing up.—*Browning.*

22. The twilight deepened round us. Still and black
The great woods climbed the mountain at our back.

23. Honor and shame from no condition rise;
Act well your part, there all the honor lies.—*Pope.*

24.   Better far
Pursue a frivolous trade by serious means,
Than a sublime art frivolously.

25.   With grave
Aspect he rose, and in his rising seemed
A pillar of state; deep on his front engraven,
Deliberation sat, and public care;
And princely counsel in his face yet shone,
Majestic, though in ruin.—*Milton.*

26. Near yonder copse, where once the garden smiled,
And still where many a garden flower grows wild,
There, where a few torn shrubs the place disclose,
The village preacher's modest mansion rose.
A man he was to all the country dear,
And passing rich with forty pounds a year.—*Goldsmith.*

27. As when upon a tranced summer night
Those green-robed senators of mighty woods.
Tall oaks, branch-charmed by the earnest stars,
Dream, and so dream all night without a stir,
Save from one gradual, solitary gust,
Which comes upon the silence, and dies off,
As if the ebbing air had but one wave
So came these words, and went.—*Keats.*

28. When Freedom, from her mountain height,
    Unfurled her standard to the air,
She tore the azure robe of night
    And set the stars of glory there.
She mingled with its gorgeous dyes
The milky baldric of the skies,
And striped its pure, celestial white,
With streakings of the morning light.—*Drake.*

RULES OF SYNTAX

Rule I. The subject of a proposition/clause is in the nominative case.

Rule II. A noun or pronoun, used as the predicate of a proposition/clause is in the nominative case.

Rule III. A noun or pronoun, used to limit the meaning of a noun denoting a different person or thing, is in the possessive case.

Rule IV. A noun or pronoun, used to limit the meaning of a noun or pronoun denoting the same person or thing, is in the same case.

Rule V. A noun or pronoun, used independently, is in the nominative absolute case.

Rule VI. The object of a transitive verb, in the active voice, or of its participles, is in the objective case.

Rule VII. The object of a preposition is in the objective case.

Rule VIII. Nouns denoting time, distance, measure, direction, or value, after verbs and adjectives, are in the objective case without a governing word.

Rule IX. Pronouns must agree with their antecedents in person, gender, and number.

Rule X. A pronoun, with two or more antecedents in the singular, connected by *and*, must be plural.

Rule XI. A pronoun, with two or more antecedents in the singular, connected by *or* or *nor*, must be singular.

Rule XII. An adjective or a participle belongs to some noun or pronoun.

Rule XIII. A verb must agree with its subject in person and number.

Rule XIV. A verb, with two or more subjects in the singular, connected by *and*, must be plural.

Rule XV. A verb, with two or more subjects in the singular, connected by *or* or *nor*, must be singular.

Rule XVI. An infinitive may be used as a noun in any case except the possessive.

Rule XVII. An infinitive not used as a noun, depends upon the word it limits.

Rule XVIII. Adverbs modify verbs, adjectives, participles, and adverbs.

Rule XIX. A preposition shows the relation of its object to the word upon which the latter depends.

Rule XX. Coordinate conjunctions join similar elements.

Rule XXI. Subordinate conjunctions join dissimilar elements.

Rule XXII. An interjection has no dependence upon other words.

213. SUBJECT-NOMINATIVE

Rule I—The subject of a proposition is in the nominative case.

Rem. 1—Anything that may be used as a noun, may be the subject; as, "*A* is a vowel," "*To lie* is base," "*What time he took orders* doth not appear."

Rem. 2—The subject generally precedes the predicate, but is placed after it, or the first auxiliary, (1) When a wish is expressed by the potential; as, "May *you* prosper," (2) When *if* or *though*, denoting a supposition, is suppressed; as, "Had *they* been wise, they would have listened to me," (3) When the verb is in the imperative mode, or is used interrogatively; as, "Rest *ye*," "Why do *you* persist?"

Rem. 3—The subject of the imperative mode is usually omitted; as, "*Depart!*" "*Shut* the door." It is also omitted after *while, when, if, though*, or *than*, when the verb is made one of the terms of a comparison; as, "He talks *while* [he is] writing," "He is kind *when* [he is] sober," "I will come, *if* [it be] possible," "They are honest, *though* [they are] poor," "He has more knowledge *than* [he has] wisdom."

To be corrected, analyzed, and parsed:

1. Him and me study grammar. 2. I never saw larger horses than them are. 3. Me and John sit together. 4. Whom besides I do you suppose got a prize? 5. I am as tall as he, but she is taller than him. 6. Whom do you suppose has come to visit us?

7. Thrice is he armed who hath his quarrel just: and him but naked, though locked up in steel, whose conscience with injustice is corrupted. 8. Who wants an orange? Me. 9. No other pupil is so studious as her. 10. He is older than me. 11. I know not whom else are expected. 12. None of his companions is more beloved than him.

214. PREDICATE-NOMINATIVE

Rule II—A noun or pronoun, used as the predicate of a proposition, is in the nominative case.

Rem. 1—The predicate nominative denotes the same person or thing as the subject; and must agree with it in case, and usually in gender and number. It may be anything that may be used as a noun; as, "That letter is *B*," "To work is *to pray*," "The command was, '*Storm the fort at daybreak.*' "

Rem. 2—In questions, and when the predicate is emphatically distinguished, the subject and predicate change places; as, "*Who* is that *man*?" "Are *you* the ticket *agent*?" "His *pavilion* round about him were dark *waters* and thick *clouds* of the sky."

Rem. 3—The neuter pronoun *it*, as subject, may represent a noun or pronoun of any person, number, or gender, as predicate; as, *"It* was *you,"* *"It* is *Sarah."*

EXERCISES

To be corrected, analyzed, and parsed:

1. It is me. 2. It was her and him who you saw. 3. If I were him, I would go to Europe. 4. Whom do you say they were? 5. I do not know whom they are?

6. It was not me nor him who played truant. 7. It is not them who are to blame. 8. I have no doubt of its being them.

215. POSSESSIVE CASE

Rule III—A noun or pronoun, used to limit the meaning of a noun denoting a different person or thing, is in the possessive case.

Rem. 1—The possessive term is always an adjective element. It may limit a noun of any class or form; as, *"Our* houses," "Oh *my* ducats!" *"Our* country's welfare," "All *their* dearest hopes were blasted," *"His* being a foreigner should not induce us to underrate him."

Rem. 2—The relation of possession may be expressed by the preposition *of* with the objective; as, "My friend's house" = The house *of my friend*. This form should be used when two or more nouns in the possessive would otherwise come together; as, "My *friend's father's* house" = The house *of my friend's father*.

Rem. 3—The limited noun is sometimes omitted; as, "This house is the doctor's [house]," "We visited St. Paul's [church]," "This is a farm of my father's [farms]."

Rem. 4—The limited noun need not be plural because the possessive is plural; as, "Their *judgment* is good," "Our *decision* is made," "The women's *hope* failed."

Rem. 5—In some compound words, formed from the possessive and the word limited by it, both the hyphen and sign of possession are omitted; as, *hogshead* cheese, etc.

To be corrected and parsed:

1. The boys story was believed. 2. He wore the knight's templar's costume. 3. The goods were sent by the Merchants Union Express. 4. That book is his'n. 5. The Bishop's of Dublin's palace. 6. My fathers health is not good. 7. My book is larger than your's. 8. The mistake was the teacher, not the pupil's.

9. The general's aide's horse was killed. 10. No one could prevent him escaping. 11. I purchased this at Penfields', the bookseller's. 12. Some people regret the King of France's Louis XVI, being beheaded. 13. She bought a pound of hog's head cheese. 14. William's and Mary's reign was prosperous. 15. It was John, not Emma's fault.

216. APPOSITION

Rule IV—A noun or pronoun, used to limit the meaning of a noun or pronoun denoting the same person or thing, is in the same case.

Rem. 1—A noun may be in apposition with a sentence, and a sentence with a noun; as, "*I resolved to practice temperance—a resolution* I have always kept." "Remember Franklin's *maxim: 'God helps them that help themselves.'* "

Rem. 2—A noun in apposition sometimes precedes the noun it identifies; as, "*Child* of the Sun, refulgent *Summer*, comes."

Rem. 3—Though a noun or pronoun usually agrees with the noun it identifies, in *number* and *gender*, it is not necessary that it agree with it in anything else than *case*; as, "My *lunch—fried oysters* and *crackers*—was soon eaten."

Rem. 4—When possessives are in apposition, the sign of possession is used only with the one next to the noun limited by the entire possessive term; as, "Peter the *Hermit's* eloquence."

Rem. 5—Sometimes the noun in apposition is separated from the limited noun by *as*, denoting *rank*, *office*, or *capacity*; as, "Mr. Jones, as my *attorney*, sold the land," "My son sails as *supercargo*." Equivalent terms are sometimes introduced by *or*; as, "The *puma*, or American *lion*, is found in South America."

Rem. 6—A noun or pronoun repeated for emphasis, or for the purpose of arresting and fixing the attention, is frequently an appositive; as, "There was another tap at the door—a smart, potential *tap*," "He, *he* alone, can do this." A compound personal pronoun is also sometimes in apposition with a simple personal pronoun which precedes it; as, "I, *myself*, told you so."

EXERCISES

To be corrected, analyzed, and parsed:

1. Will you desert me—I who have always been your friend? 2. Who was the General; him you wished to see? 3. I bought it of Mrs. Wilson; she who

keeps the milliner's shop. 4. Ira Jacobs, him who you punished, was not to be blamed. 5. Whom shall we praise—they who do their duty? 6. My watch was lost near Wilkins's the blacksmith's shop.

7. They are the lovely, them in whom unite
Youth's fleeting charms, with virtue's lovely light.

217. NOMINATIVE ABSOLUTE CASE

Rule V—A noun or pronoun, used independently, is in the nominative absolute case.

Rem. 1—For the five forms of the absolute case, see Sec. 33.

Rem. 2—The nominative absolute with a participle is generally equivalent to an adverbial clause, commencing with *if*, *because*, *since*, *when*, or *while*; as, "*He being rich*, they feared his influence" = They feared his influence *because he was rich*. "*The sun being risen*, we pursued our journey" = *When the sun had risen*, we pursued our journey.

Rem. 3—In mottoes and abbreviated sayings, and frequently in exclamations, nouns in the nominative absolute case seem to have relation to something understood; as, "Laird's Bloom of Youth" = *Use* Laird's Bloom of Youth; "Confidence" (a motto) = *This is a token of* confidence; "A rat! A rat!" = *There is* a rat. It is better, however, to recognize the nominative absolute case as a distinct use of a noun, than to destroy the force of an expression by supplying an awkward ellipsis.

EXERCISES

Examples to be parsed:

1. Soldier, rest! Thy warfare o'er. 2. "Stop! My hat!" he exclaims. 3. Our fathers, where are they? 4. My being a child was a plea for my admission. 5. The north and the south, thou hast created them. 6. John, James, and Henry, they are my scholars. 7. Oh Nelly Gray! Oh Nelly Gray! 8. "The Moon and the Stars—A Fable." 9. PROBLEM III—To construct a mean proportional between two given lines.

218. OBJECTIVE CASE

Rule VI—The object of a transitive verb, in the active voice, or of its participles, is in the objective case.

Rem. 1—The natural order of arrangement is, *subject—verb—object*; but in poetry, or when it is made emphatic, the object precedes the subject;

as, "*Myself* I cannot save," "*Silver* and *gold* have I none." To avoid ambiguity, the natural order should be observed when the subject and object are both nouns. Say, "Alexander conquered Darius," not "Alexander Darius conquered." A relative or interrogative pronoun is placed at the head of its clause; as, "I am he *whom* you seek," "*Whom* shall I invite?"

Rem. 2—The object may be a participial noun, a phrase, or a clause; as, "I like *skating* and *skiing* better than *studying*," "He hopes *to succeed*."

Rem. 3— A phrase beginning with a noun or pronoun, may be the object of a transitive verb; as, "I want *books to read*," "The merchant ordered *the goods to be shipped*," "I heard the *water lapping on the crag*," "I want *him to go*." In such cases, the entire phrase is the object of the verb; but it is best to apply the first paragraph of Remark 1, Section 206, in parsing the noun or pronoun beginning the phrase, Rule XVII in parsing the infinitive, and Rule XII in parsing the participle.

Rem. 4—Some verbs used as copulatives in the passive voice, have two objects, one representing a person or thing, the other a thing; as, "They made *him* their *leader*," "They chose *him chairman*." In such cases, the object closest to the verb is the *direct object*; the object next in line is the *indirect object*.

Rem. 5—A transitive verb may have several objects connected by conjunctions; as, "He owns *houses*, *lands*, and *stock*."

Rem. 6—Participial nouns may be limited by objective elements; as, "*Writing notes* is forbidden," "I like *hunting buffaloes*."

EXERCISES

Examples to be corrected:

1. Who did you write to? 2. Please let him and I sit together. 3. I do not know who to trust. 4. He who did the mischief you should punish, not I. 5. I saw she and him at the concert last evening. 6. And me, what shall I do?

7. We will go at once, him and me. 8. Every one can master a grief but he that hath it. 9. He was presented a gold watch by his employers. 10. Who are you looking for?

Examples to be analyzed and parsed:

1. We will build new homes. 2. The parting words shall pass my lips no more. 3. I said that at sea all is vacancy. 4. They have left unstained what there they found. 5. Bring forth this counterfeit model. 6. Mad frenzy fires him now.

7. Reading makes a full man, conference a ready man, and writing an exact man.—*Bacon*. 8. Thou hast left no son—but thy song shall preserve thy name. 9. His disciples said, Who, then, can be saved?

10. "But what good came of it at last?"
    Quoth little Peterkin.
    "Why, that I cannot tell," said he;
    "But 'twas a famous victory."—*Southey.*

219. OBJECTIVE AFTER PREPOSITIONS

Rule VII—The object of a preposition is in the objective case.

Rem. 1—A preposition usually precedes its object; but in poetry this order is often reversed; as, "From crag to crag, *the rattling peaks among*" = among the rattling peaks; "Come walk with me the jungle *through*."

Rem. 2—Interrogative pronouns frequently precede the prepositions which govern them; as, "*What* are you laughing *at*?"

Such expressions as, "Whom are you talking to?" "Which house do you live in?" are inelegant. The better construction is, "To whom are you talking?" "In which house do you live?"

Rem. 3—Some phrases consist of a preposition, followed by an adjective or an adverb; as, *in vain, at once, in secret, from below, on high, from above, till now, till lately,* etc. In such phrases, an object may be understood; the word following the preposition, parsed as an adjective or adverb *used as a noun*; or the entire expression may be regarded as an *inseparable phrase.*

Rem. 4—A preposition should never be placed between a verb and its object; as, "He does not want *for* anything." Say "He does not *want* anything."

Rem. 5—A noun or pronoun which is the object of two or more prepositions, or of a preposition and a transitive verb, should be placed after the first verb or preposition, and be represented by a pronoun following each of the others. "He came *into* and passed *through* the cars" should be, "He came *into* the cars, and passed *through them.*" "He first *called,* and then *sent for,* the *sergeant*" should be, "He first *called* the *sergeant,* and then *sent for* him."

Rem. 6—A preposition may follow its object in difficult cases where the usual preposition-object construction would result in an awkward sentence; as, "This is the sort of pedantic nonsense up with which I will not put."
—*Churchill.*

EXERCISES

To be corrected:

1. The army shall not want for supplies. 2. Which school do you go to? 3. What firm are you agent for? 4. What country are you a native of? 5. I will not permit of such conduct.

6. It is our duty to assist and sympathize with those in distress. 7. The convicts are hired by and employed for the benefit of a few speculators. 8. He lives in and came from Pittsburgh.

To be analyzed and parsed:

1. We cruised about for several hours in the dense fog. 2. Here rests his head upon the lap of earth. 3. He will steal, sir, an egg out of a cloister. 4. The pile sank down into the opening earth.

5. The ground lifts like a sea. 6. The clouds are driven about in the sky like squadrons of combatants rushing to the conflict. 7. In vain does the old dragon rage. 8. I had supposed till lately that you were my friend. 9. A shoreless ocean tumbled round the globe. 10. The morning broke without a sun.

Rule VIII—Nouns denoting *time, distance, measure, direction*, or *value*, after verbs and adjectives, are in the objective case without a governing word.

Rem. 1—The relations between nouns and verbs, as well as those between nouns and adjectives, are usually expressed by prepositions. Sometimes, however, these relations are so obvious that they are not expressed, but implied. An implied relation and its subsequent term form an adverbial phrase, the *term* being the object of the *relation*. As there is no preposition in the English language that exactly expresses this relation, the noun is said to be in the objective case *without a governing word*.

Rem. 2—A preposition is frequently omitted. The subsequent term is not then in the objective case without a governing word, but is governed by a preposition understood.

Ex.—"Van Antwerp, Bragg & Co., No. 137 Walnut Street, Cincinnati, OH." = *To* Van Antwerp, Bragg & Co., *at* No. 137 Walnut Street, *in* Cincinnati, *in* Ohio. "July 4, 1776" = *On the* 4th *day of* July, *in the year* 1776.

Rem. 3—*Home* and nouns denoting *manner* are frequently in the objective case without a governing word; as, "We drove *home* in a storm," "They marched *Indian file.*"

Rem. 4—The names of *things*, following the passive forms of the verbs *ask, lend, teach, refuse, provide*, and some others, are in the objective case without a governing word, or in the objective case governed by a preposition understood; as, "He was asked a *question*," "John was refused *admittance*," "I was taught *grammar.*"

EXERCISES

To be analyzed and parsed:

1. The horse ran a mile. 2. I do not care a straw. 3. He is worth a million dollars. 4. The child is nine years old. 5. He wore his coat cloak fashion.

6. Spring has already covered her grave twelve times with flowers. 7. The ship sailed four knots an hour.

8. This is worth remembering. 9. The tower is two hundred fifty feet high. 10. How many square yards of plastering in a room twenty-one feet long, fifteen feet wide, and ten feet high? 11. The poor, dissipated student was refused his diploma.

220. PRONOUNS

Rule IX—Pronouns must agree with their antecedents in person, gender, and number.

Rem. 1—The person, gender, and number of an interrogative pronoun are indeterminate when no answer is given to the question in which it is found; as, "*Who* owns that vessel?" The answer may be, "*Mr. Gordon* owns it," "*Jones & Smith* own it," "*I* own it," "*He* and *I* own it," or "*You yourself* own it." The interrogative, however, should be parsed as being in the third person and singular number, because it requires the verb to be in the third person and singular number. Its gender is indeterminate. When an answer is given, or when one can be inferred from well-known facts, these properties are determinate; as, "*Who* owns that vessel? *I* own it." "Who" is the first person, common gender, singular number, agreeing with "I." "*Who* commanded the Allied forces at the Battle of the Bulge?" "Who" is in the third person, masculine gender, singular number—the answer, Eisenhower, though not given, being well known.

Rem. 2—There being no pronoun of the third person singular used in common for either sex, the masculine forms, *he*, *his*, *him*, are used in its place. Do not say, "Each pupil should learn *his* or *her* lesson." Use *his* alone. Say, "Should anyone desire to consult me, let *him* call at my office," even though the invitation be intended for both sexes. Should the gender of the person referred to be known, use a masculine or feminine pronoun, as the case requires.

Rem. 3—Things personified should be represented as masculine or feminine by the pronouns referring to them; as, "Night, sable goddess, from *her* ebon throne"; "Grim-visaged War hath smoothed *his* wrinkled front."

Rem. 4—A pronoun sometimes precedes its antecedent; as, "*Thy* chosen temple, Lord, how fair!" "Hark! *They* whisper, angels say."

Rem. 5—The relative pronoun is frequently omitted; as, "That is the house [*which*] we live in," "This is the book [*which*] you inquired for."

Rem. 6—*That*, as a relative, should generally be used after *a*, *all*, *every*, *same*, and *very*; after *who*, used interrogatively; after an adjective in the superlative degree; and when both persons and things are referred to.

Ex.—"He is a man *that* all respect." "I gave him *all that* I had." "Is this the *same* book *that* I lent you?" "It is the *very* book *that* you lent me." "He is the *wisest that* says the least." "*Who that* has once heard him does not wish to hear him once again?" "Here are the *persons* and *things that* were sent for."

Rem. 7—Unless great emphasis is required, a noun or pronoun should not be used redundantly in the nominative absolute case. Say, "The horse ran away," not "The horse, *it* ran away." Say, "Many words darken speech," not "Many words, *they* darken speech."

Rem. 8—To avoid ambiguity, a relative pronoun should be placed as near as possible to its antecedent.

Ex.—"A purse was lost in the street, *which* contained a large sum of money." The clause introduced by "which," should be placed immediately after "purse."

Rem. 9—A pronoun whose antecedent is a collective noun conveying the idea of unity, should be in the neuter singular; one whose antecedent is a collective noun conveying the idea of plurality, should be plural, taking the gender of the individuals composing the collection.

Rem. 10—*It* is used to represent (1) a noun or pronoun in any person, in either number, or of any gender; (2) a sentence, or a part of a sentence; or (3) it may be used to represent an indefinite antecedent.

Ex.—"*It* is *I*." "*It* was *land warrants* that I purchased." "*You have wronged me* and will repent of *it*." "*It* snows." "We roughed *it* in the woods."

EXERCISES

To be corrected:

1. James, he has been whispering. 2. Whom, when they had washed, they laid her in an upper chamber. 3. The names I called you, I am now sorry for them. 4. If anyone has not paid their fare, let them call at the captain's office. 5. Everyone should have his or her life insured.

6. Everyone should have their lives insured. 7. That book is in the bookcase, which contains pictures. 8. This is the dog whom my father bought. 9. These are the men and the guns which we captured. 10. That is the same pen which I sold you. 11. He is the wisest which lives the most nobly.

12. The moon took its station still higher. 13. The jury could not agree in its verdict. 14. The news came of defeat, but no one believed them. 15. If you see an error or a fault in my conduct, remind me of them.

To be parsed:

1. The hand that governs in April, governed in January. 2. I perish by this people which I made. 3. Many a man shall envy him who henceforth limps. 4. I venerate the man whose heart is warm. 5. Your sorrows are our gladness. 6. The blooming morning opened her dewy eyes.

7. Men are like birds that build their nests in trees that hang over rivers. 8. He was followed by another worthless rogue, who flung away his modesty instead of his ignorance.

9.   Remorseless Time!
   Fierce spirit of the glass and scythe! What power
   Can stay him in his silent course, or melt
   His iron heart to pity?—*Prentice.*

221. ANTECEDENTS CONNECTED BY "AND"

Rule X—A pronoun, with two or more antecedents in the singular, connected by *and*, must be plural.

Rem. 1—When the antecedents are but different names for the same person or thing, the pronoun must be singular; as, "The eminent lawyer and statesman has resigned *his* office."

Rem. 2—When the antecedents are emphatically distinguished, the pronoun should be singular; as, "The mind *as well as* the body has *its* diseases," "The country *and not* the government has *its* admirers."

Rem. 3—When the antecedents are limited by *each*, *every*, or *no*, the pronoun must be singular; as, "Each man and each boy did *his* duty," "Every hill and every mountain has *its* echo," "There is no day and no hour without *its* cares."

Rem. 4—When the antecedents taken together are regarded as a single thing, the pronoun must be singular; as, "The horse and wagon is in *its* place;" "The punch and ice cream is in *its* bowl."

EXERCISES

To be analyzed and parsed:

1. Charles and Henry are flying their kites. 2. You and I should study our lessons. 3. The child wants some bread and milk. Will you get it? 4. The good man, and the sinner, too, shall have his reward. 5. The great philosopher and statesman is laid in his grave. 6. He bought a horse and a wagon, and sold them at a profit. 7. Every house and lot has its price set opposite its number.

222. ANTECEDENTS CONNECTED BY "OR" OR "NOR"

Rule XI—A pronoun, with two or more antecedents in the singular, connected by *or* or *nor*, must be singular.

Rem. 1—When the two antecedents are of different genders, the use of a singular masculine pronoun to represent them is improper. In such cases:

1. Use a plural pronoun that may represent both genders; as, "Not on outward charms could *he* or *she* build *their* pretensions to please."

2. Use different pronouns; as, "No boy or girl should whisper to *his* or *her* neighbor."

3. Substitute a general term, including both, for the two antecedents, and represent this general term by a singular masculine pronoun; as, "No *pupil* (boy or girl) should whisper to *his* neighbor."

Rem. 2—When one of the antecedents is plural, it should be placed last, and the pronoun should be plural; as, "Neither the farmer nor his sons were aware of *their* danger."

EXERCISES

To be corrected:

1. No father or mother lives that does not love his or her children. 2. George or Charles are diligent in their business. 3. If an Aristotle, a Pythagoras, or a Galileo suffer for their opinions, they are martyrs. 4. If you see my son or my daughter, send them home. 5. Poverty or wealth have their own temptations.

To be analyzed and parsed:

1. Henry or Samuel will lend you his book. 2. If thy hand or thy foot offend thee, cut it off and cast it from thee. 3. Neither James nor John has gained much credit for himself.

4. Either Mary or Sarah will recite her lesson. 5. Even a rugged rock, or a barren heath, though in itself disagreeable, contributes by contrast to the beauty of the whole.

6. Either James or his father was mistaken in his opinion. 7. Neither the teacher nor the students used their books in the class.

223. ADJECTIVES AND PARTICIPLES

Rule XII—An adjective or a participle belongs to some noun or pronoun.

Rem. 1—An adjective used as the predicate of a sentence, may modify an infinitive or a substantive clause, used as the subject; as, "To lie is *sinful*," "That all men are created equal, is *self evident*."

Rem. 2—After infinitives and participles, adjectives are frequently used which do not belong to any particular noun or pronoun; as, "To be *good* is to be *happy*," "The main secret of being *sublime* is to say great things in few and plain words." In parsing, say that they modify some noun or pronoun not expressed.

Rem. 3—An adjective should agree in number with the noun to which it belongs; as, *that* kind, *those* kinds; *one* man, *two* men. To denote a collective number, a singular adjective may precede a plural noun; as, "*One* thousand dollars," "The census is taken *every* ten years." To denote plurality, *many a* is used instead of *many*; as, "*Many a* time," "*Many a* morning."

Rem. 4—In poetry, an adjective relating to a noun or pronoun is sometimes used instead of an adverb modifying a verb or a participle; as, "*Incessant* still you flow," "*Swift* on his downy pinions [he] flies from woe."

Rem. 5—Adjectives are sometimes used as nouns; as, "The *rich* and the *poor* here meet together," "*One* said, 'Let us go'; *another*, 'No, let us remain.' "

Rem. 6—Two adjectives are frequently connected by a hyphen, forming a compound adjective; as, "A *sweet-faced* girl." Such adjectives are used before the nouns they modify only, but never elsewhere in a sentence; as, "*Sweet-faced* girl," but, "That girl is *sweet faced*" (no hyphen).

Rem. 7—Numeral and pronominal adjectives precede another adjective which modifies the same noun; as, "The *seven* wise men," "*That* old house."

EXERCISES

To be analyzed and parsed:

1. His spirit was so birdlike and so pure. 2. Dim, cheerless is the scene my path around. 3. This life of ours is a wild Eolian harp of many a joyous strain. 4. Every treetop has its shadow.

5. With fleecy clouds the sky is blanched. 6. Still stands the forest primeval. 7. 'Tis impious in a good man to be sad. 8. To hope the best is pious, brave, and wise. 9. Time wasted is existence; used, is life.

10.   Thoughts shut up, want air,
    And spoil, like bales unopened to the sun.—*Young*.

11. Tell me not in mournful numbers,
    Life is but an empty dream.—*Longfellow*.

12. Pray for the living, in whose breast
    The struggle between right and wrong
    Is raging terrible and strong.

13. Petulant she spoke, and at herself she laughed;
    A rosebud set with little willful thorns,
    And sweet as English air could make her.

14. The hills are dearest which our childish feet
    Have climbed the earliest, and the streams most sweet
    Are ever those at which our young lips drank—
    Stoop'd to their waters o'er the grassy bank.

15. Sometimes her narrow kitchen walls
    Stretched away into stately halls.—*Whittier.*

224. VERBS

Rule XIII—A verb must agree with its subject in person and number.

Rem. 1—When the subject is a collective noun, conveying plurality of idea, the verb should be plural; as, "In France the peasantry *go* barefooted, while the middle class *wear* wooden shoes."

Rem. 2—When a subject, plural in form, represents a single thing, the verb must be singular; as, "The *'Pleasures of Memory'* was published in 1792," "*Politics* is his career," "The *news* is confirmed."

Rem. 3—When the subject is a mere word or sign, an infinitive, or a substantive clause, the verb should be in the third person singular; as, "*They* is a personal pronoun," " *+* is the sign of addition," "*To deceive* is wrong," " *'Who comes there*?' was heard from within."

Rem. 4—A verb in the imperative mode usually agrees with *thou, you,* or *ye,* expressed or understood; as, "*Look* [*ye*] to your hearths, my lord!" "*Smooth* [*thou*] thy brow," "[*Do thou*] let brighter thoughts be with the virtuous dead."—*Hemans.* "[You] watch out!"

EXERCISES

To be corrected:

1. You and I was walking together. 2. The horses has been fed. 3. I called, but you was not at home. 4. He help me when he can. 5. There was mountains where I came from. 6. A committee were appointed to report resolutions. 7. The fleet were seen off Hatteras.

8. The legislature have adjourned. 9. The corporation is individually responsible. 10. The "Pleasures of Hope" are a fine poem. 11. The scissors

is dull. 12. *We* are a personal pronoun. 13. The derivation of these words are uncertain. 14. The board of trustees have a meeting tonight.

To be analyzed and parsed:

1. Thus many a sad tomorrow came and went. 2. Return, O beautiful days of youth! 3. I alone was solitary and idle. 4. This well deserves meditating. 5. At an early hour, arrive the diligences. 6. He waved his arm.

7. Every rational creature has all nature for his dowry and estate. 8. The present needs us. 9. The jury were not unanimous. 10. Generation after generation passes away. 11. The public are respectfully invited to attend.

12.   Every age
Bequeaths the next for heritage,
No lazy luxury or delight.

13. There's not a beggar in the street
Makes such a sorry sight.

14. He that attends to his interior self,
That has a heart, and keeps it—has a mind
That hungers and supplies it, and who seeks
A social, not a dissipated life,
Has business.

15. Between Nose and Eyes a strange contest arose.
The spectacles set them unhappily wrong;
The point in dispute was, as all the world knows,
To which the said spectacles ought to belong.—*Cowper.*

225. SUBJECTS CONNECTED BY "AND"

Rule XIV—A verb, with two or more subjects in the singular, connected by *and*, must be plural.

Rem. 1—When two or more subjects in the singular, connected by *and*, are but different names for the same person or thing, or, when taken together, they represent a single idea, the verb should be singular; as, "*Descent* and *fall* to us is adverse," "A *hue* and *cry* was raised."

Rem. 2—When two or more singular subjects are emphatically distinguished, or are preceded by *each*, *every*, or *no*, the verb should be singular; as, "The father, *as well as* the son, *was* in fault," "All work and no play *makes* Jack a dull boy," "*Every* bird and beast *cowers* before the icy blast."

Rem. 3—When two or more subjects, of different numbers, are emphatically distinguished, the verb agrees with the first; as, "Diligent industry, *and not* mean savings, *constitutes* honorable competence."

EXERCISES

To be corrected:

1. Mr. Johnson and his brother was at the meeting. 2. Time and tide waits for no man. 3. Bread and milk are good food. 4. Each man, each child, and each woman know the hour. 5. The boy's mother, but not his father, deserve great praise.

6. Patience and diligence removes mountains. 7. Neither of them are remarkable for precision. 8. Salmon and trout has become scarce in these waters. 9. A number of horses, together with a large amount of other property, were stolen last night.

To be analyzed and parsed:

1. Her beauty, and not her talents, attracts attention. 2. No wife and no mother was there to comfort him. 3. Out of the same mouth proceed blessing and cursing. 4. You and I look alike.

5. My uncle, with his wife, is in town. 6. Charles and Emma are good scholars. 7. Charles, together with his sister Emma, is studying botany. 8. The crime, not the scaffold, makes the shame. 9. The ambition and avarice of man are the sources of his unhappiness.

10. Fire of imagination, strength of mind, and firmness of soul are gifts of nature. 11. A coach and six is, in our time, never seen, except as a part of some pageant.—*Macaulay.*

12. A day, an hour of virtuous liberty,
Is worth a whole eternity of bondage.—*Addison.*

226. SUBJECTS CONNECTED BY "OR" OR "NOR"

Rule XV—A verb, with two or more subjects in the singular, connected by *or* or *nor*, must be singular.

Rem. 1—When the subjects are of different persons or numbers, the verb must agree with the nearest, unless another be the principal term; as, "Neither you nor I *am* to blame," "Neither you nor he *is* in his place."

Rem. 2—When two or more infinitives, or substantive clauses, are connected by *or* or *nor*, the verb must be singular, and a predicate nominative, following the verb, must be singular also; as, "Why we are detained or why we receive no message from home, *is* mysterious"; "To be, or not to be, that *is* the question."

Rem. 3—When the subjects are singular, but of different genders, the verb is singular, relating to them taken separately; but a pronoun may be plural, relating to them taken conjointly; as, "Mary or her sister *has* lost *their* umbrella"—the umbrella being theirs by joint ownership.

EXERCISES

To be corrected:

1. Has the horses or the cattle been found? 2. Were the boy or the girl badly bruised? 3. The ax or the hammer were lost. 4. Poverty or misfortune have been his lot. 5. Neither the horse nor the wagon are worth much. 6. Either you or I are to blame. 7. Neither the mule nor the horses is found. 8. He comes—nor want nor cold his course delay. 9. Neither avarice nor pleasure move me. 10. A lucky anecdote, or an enlivening tale, relieve the book's page.

11. Not the Mogul, or Czar of Muscovy,
    Not Prester John, or Cham of Tartary,
    Are in their houses monarchs more than I.

To be analyzed and parsed:

1. Neither he nor she has spoken to him. 2. To reveal secrets, or to betray one's friends, is contemptible perfidy. 3. Either ability or ambition was wanting.

4. Hatred or revenge deserves censure. 5. Neither poverty nor riches is desirable. 6. The vanity, the ambition, or the pride of some men keeps them always in trouble. 7. Emma or Jane has lost her dictionary.

8. The breezy call of incense-breathing morn,
    The swallow twittering from the straw-built shed,
    The cock's shrill clarion, or the echoing horn,
    No more shall rouse them from their lowly bed.—*Gray.*

9.   From the high host
    Of stars to the lulled lake, and mountain coast,
        All is concentered in a life intense,
    Where not a beam, nor air, nor leaf is lost.—*Byron.*

10. Time, nor Eternity, hath seen
    A repetition of delight
    In all its phases; ne'er hath been
    For men or angels that which *is*.

227. INFINITIVES

Rule XVI—An infinitive may be used as a noun in any case except the possessive.

Rem. 1—An infinitive represents being, action, or state abstractly. It is the mere verb, without limitation. As such, it may be used:

1. As the *subject* of a proposition; as, "*To err* is human."

2. As the *predicate* of a proposition; as, "To obey is *to enjoy.*"

3. As the object of a transitive verb or of its participles; as, "He loves *to play*," "He is trying *to learn.*"

4. In *apposition with a noun*; as, "Delightful task, *to rear* the tender thought."

5. *Abstractly*, or *independently*; as, "*To tell* the truth, I was inattentive."

Rem. 2—The infinitive always retains its verbal signification. Hence, *as a noun*, it may be limited by a predicate adjective or predicate nominative, and, *as a verb*, be followed by an object, or modified by an adverb; as, "*To spend* money recklessly is criminal."

Rem. 3—The sign *to* should ordinarily not be separated from the rest of the infinitive. "*To correctly report* a speech is difficult," should be "*To report* a speech *correctly* is difficult." The skilled writer, however, will learn that occasionally a split infinitive strengthens the sense of a sentence by stressing an important adverb; as, "to diligently inquire."—Strunk and White.

Rem. 4—The preposition *for* should not be used immediately before the infinitive. "I study *for to learn*," should be "I study *to learn.*"

Rem. 5—After the verbs *bid*, *dare* (venture), *hear, feel, let, make, need, see*, in the active voice, and *let* in the passive, the sign *to* is generally omitted; as, "He bade him *depart*," "I saw him *fall.*" The sign *to* is sometimes omitted after several other verbs.

Rem. 6—Verbs expressing *hope, expectation, command, intention*, etc., require the present infinitive after them; as, "I *hoped to see* you," "I *intended to call* for you," "He *expected to see* you yesterday."

EXERCISES

To be corrected:

1. He came for to see us. 2. To greedily eat one's dinner is ill-mannered. 3. I dared him come to me. 4. He dared not to leave his room. 5. I saw him to write in his book.

6. I have known him to frequently be tardy. 7. He made his horses to go very fast. 8. He needs study more carefully. 9. He need not to remain long. 10. He intended to have written to you. 11. They had hoped to have seen you before they left.

To be analyzed and parsed:

1. To do right, is to do that which is ordered to be done. 2. To die is to be banished from myself. 3. To do justice and judgment is more acceptable to the Lord than sacrifice. 4. It is our duty to try, and our determination to succeed. 5. He had dared to think for himself.

6. It is the curse of kings to be attended
By slaves that take their humors for a warrant
To break within the bloody house of life,
And on the winking of authority,
To understand a law.—*Shakespeare.*

7. Have ye brave sons? Look in the next fierce brawl
To see them die. Have ye fair daughters? Look
To see them live, torn from your arms, distained,
Dishonored, and if ye dare call for justice,
Be answered by the lash.—*Mitford.*

228. INFINITIVES NOT USED AS NOUNS

Rule XVII—An infinitive not used as a noun, depends upon the word it limits.

Rem. 1—An infinitive may depend upon:

1. A *noun*; as, "Flee from the *wrath to come.*"
2. A *pronoun*; as, "I heard *him preach.*"
3. A *verb*; as, "He *went to see* the show."
4. An *adjective*; as, "Grammar is *easy to learn.*"
5. A *participle*; as, "The rain *threatening to fall*, we left."
6. An *adverb*; as, "He told me *when to come.*"

Rem. 2—The infinitive is often understood; as, "I considered him [*to be*] honest."

Rem. 3—The sign *to* may be omitted before all but the first of two or more infinitives in the same construction; as, "They tried *to cheat, rob,* and *murder* me."

EXERCISES

To be parsed:

1. I come not here to talk. 2. I cannot see to spin my flax. 3. In truth, deceit makes no mortal glad.

4. He lived to die, and died to live. 5. It is a brave thing to understand something of what we see. 6. It is better to fight for the good than to rail at the ill.

7.　　　Let us be content in work,
To do the thing we can, and not presume
To fret because it's little.

8. One day with life and heart,
Is more than time enough to find a world.

9. Needful auxiliars are our friends, to give
   To social man true relish of himself.

10. Learn well to know how much need not be known,
    And what that knowledge which impairs your sense.

11. Let him not violate kind nature's laws,
    But own man born to live as well as die.

12.   The blood more stirs
    To rouse a lion than to start a hare.

13. He that lacks time to mourn, lacks time to mend.
    Eternity mourns that.—*Henry Taylor*

229. ADVERBS

Rule XVIII—Adverbs modify verbs, adjectives, participles, and adverbs.

Rem. 1—Adverbs sometimes modify phrases and entire propositions; as, "He lives *just* over the hill," "*Certainly* you are the people."

Rem. 2—Adverbs are frequently used as expletives; as, "*Well*, that is a strange story," "*There, now*, you have said enough."

Rem. 3—The adverbs *yes, no, aye, yea*, and *nay* are generally answers to questions, and are equivalent to a whole sentence. They are then used independently, or modify the sentences preceding or following them.

Ex.—"Are you angry? No." "*Yea*, they shall sing in the ways of the Lord," "*Nay*; but it is really true."

Rem. 4—Two contradictory negatives in the same clause are equivalent to an affirmative; as, "I can*not* write *no* more" = I can write more. Hence, two negatives should never be employed to express a negation. Say, "I want *no* assistance," not, "I *don't* want *no* assistance." Two or more negatives, not contradictory, do not destroy the negative character of a sentence; as, "He will *never* consent, *no*, *never*, *not* he, *nor* I *neither*."

Rem. 5—When the quality of an object, and not the manner of an action, is to be expressed, an adjective should be used as the predicate; as, "He arrived *safe*," not "*safely*"; "She looks *beautiful*," not "beautifully." To test your usage, if a form of *to be* can be substituted for the verb, an adjective should be used.

Rem. 6—Though sanctioned by good authority, the use of *from* before *whence, hence*, and *thence* should be avoided. Say, "*Whence* came you?" not "*From whence* came you."

Rem. 7—The word modified by an adverb is sometimes omitted; as, "*Down*, royal state!" Supply "fall." "*Up* in the morning early." Supply "get" or "rise." "I'll *hence* to London." Supply "go." In some cases, adverbs thus used seem to have the force of verbs in the imperative mode, but not always. *Up* and *out*, followed by the preposition *with*, take the place of verbs in declarative sentences; as, "*Out with* him!"

Rem. 8—*There* is frequently used as an expletive to introduce a sentence; as, "*There* was no grass there," "*There* were three of us."

Rem. 9—An adverbial phrase should not be parsed as a single word when its parts can be parsed separately; as, "They walked *hand in hand*." Place "with" before the phrase.

Rem. 10—The comparative and superlative forms of adjectives, preceded by the definite article, are often used as adverbs; as, "*The longer* I study, *the better* I like it," "He lives *best* who acts *the noblest*." The articles in these expressions are used adverbially.

Rem. 11—Adverbs should be so placed as to render the sentence clear, correct, and elegant. The sense intended to be conveyed depends upon their position. Compare "He is thought to be *generally* honest," with "He is *generally* thought to be honest."

EXERCISES

To be corrected:

1. He won't give me no satisfaction. 2. We didn't find nobody at home. 3. Nobody never saw such a crowd of people. 4. The nation never was more prosperous, nor never was more ungrateful. 5. The velvet feels smoothly. 6. He speaks slow and distinct. 7. The children all looked beautifully. 8. You did splendid last examination. 9. I am tolerable well, thank you. 10. I scarce know what I am saying.

11. He did handsomer than he promised. 12. I only want to borrow your umbrella. 13. The dog wanted in, but he now wants out. 14. It rains most every day. 15. I would not have believed no one but Hubert. 16. They said that he was generally cheerful. 17. Our dog is very good natured usually. 18. Sometimes are you despondent?

To be analyzed and parsed:

1. All the world was ours once more. 2. Therein the patient must minister to himself.—*Shakespeare*. 3. I saw the blue Rhine sweep along. 4. Death erects his batteries right over against our homes. 5. Slowly the throng moves o'er the tomb-paved ground.

6. People desire not only to be loved, but to be lovely. 7. Westward the course of empire takes its way. 8. Your menaces move me not. 9. We see

but dimly through the mists and vapors. 10. Man by man, and foot by foot, did the soldiers proceed over the Alps. 11. The war is already begun, and we must either conquer or perish. 12. He heaped up great riches, but passed his time miserably.

13. Night's candles are burnt out, and jocund Day
    Stands tiptoe on the misty mountain's top.—*Shakespeare.*

14.   I'll look no more,—
    Lest my brain turn, and the deficient sight
    Topple down headlong.

15. Not a word to each other; we kept the great pace—
    Neck by neck, stride by stride, never changing our place.—*Browning.*

16. Their breath is agitation, and their life
    A storm whereon they ride to sink at last.—*Byron.*

17. Who does the best his circumstance allows,
    Does well, acts nobly, angels could no more.
    Our outward act indeed admits restraint;
    'Tis not in things o'er thought to domineer.
    Guard well thy thought, our thoughts are heard in
        heaven.—*Young.*

230. PREPOSITIONS

Rule XIX—A preposition shows the relation of its object to the word upon which that object depends.

Rem. 1—The object of a preposition, as well as the preceding term, often determines what preposition should be used; as, "He read *to* me *about* the war, *with* much feeling," "He wrote *to* me *in* great haste *concerning* his losses."

EXERCISES

To be corrected, if necessary, and parsed:

1. The man is dependent on his relatives. 2. I differ with you on that point. 3. The man was killed by a sword, and died with violence. 4. The two thieves divided the money among them. 5. During his lifetime, he was twice shipwrecked.

6. Above the clouds and tempests' rage,
    Across yon blue and radiant arch,
    Upon their long, high pilgrimage,
    I watched their glittering armies march.

231. COORDINATE CONJUNCTIONS

Rule XX—Coordinate conjunctions join similar elements.

Rem. 1—Elements placed in the same relation or rank are similar; as, nouns or pronouns in the same case, verbs in the same construction, words, phrases, and clauses limiting the same term, etc.

Rem. 2—Conjunctions are sometimes omitted; as, "Had I the means, I would buy that farm" = *If* I had the means, etc. "He is rich, noble, wise, [*and*] generous."

Rem. 3—In a series of similar terms, the conjunction is usually omitted, except between the last two; as, "Henry, Horace, *and* Samuel are my pupils." When great emphasis is required, the conjunction should be supplied; as, "You have been an honest, *and* a bold, *and* a faithful hound."

Rem. 4—Dissimilar or disproportionate terms should never be joined by conjunctions; as, "I always *have* [been] and *shall be* of this opinion."

Rem. 5—Conjunctions are sometimes used as introductory words, either to awaken expectation, or to make the introduction of a sentence less abrupt; as, "*And* it came to pass in those days," etc.; "*So* you are going to New Orleans, it seems."

EXERCISES

To be corrected and parsed:

1. We moved along silently and with caution. 2. To play is more pleasant than working. 3. They either could not, nor desired to learn. 4. He can brag, but is not able to do much. 5. That lot is preferable and cheaper than yours. 6. He looks as though he was hungry. 7. He has no love nor veneration for him.

8. I cannot tell whether he has returned or not. 9. Neither James or John came home yesterday. 10. I always desire and always wished for your society. 11. The boy would and did have his own way. 12. The parliament addressed the king, and has been adjourned the same day.

232. SUBORDINATE CONJUNCTIONS

Rule XXI—Subordinate conjunctions join dissimilar elements.

Rem. 1—A clause introduced by a subordinate conjunction, conjunctive adverb, or relative pronoun, performs the office of a noun, an adjective, or an adverb. The connective unites the clause which it introduces to the word or phrase which is modified; as, "He said *that* he would come," "The man *whom* you saw is the sheriff," "Do you know *where* I live?"

Rem. 2—A subordinate connective is almost invariably placed at the beginning of the clause which it introduces. When this clause is used as the subject of a sentence, or is put in apposition with a noun in any case, the connective is a mere introductory word; as, "*That* you have deceived me doth appear from this," "The rumor *that* he is insane is unfounded."

EXERCISES

To be parsed:

1. I never thought that it could be so. 2. He locks the door after the horse is stolen. 3. I now know why you deceived me. 4. He will have friends wherever he may be.

5. However stern he may seem, he is a good man. 6. While there is life, there is hope. 7. Blessed are the merciful: for they shall obtain mercy. 8. He rushes to the fray as if he were summoned to a banquet.

9. Whether the planets are inhabited, was discussed last evening. 10. I do not know where he is. 11. There was so much noise that I could not sleep.

12. We meet in joy, though we part in sorrow;
We part tonight, but we meet tomorrow.

233. INTERJECTIONS

Rule XXII—An interjection has no dependence upon other words.

EXERCISES

To be parsed:

1. What! Might Rome have been taken? 2. Ha! Laughest thou, Lochiel, my vision to scorn? 3. Ho warden! 4. Oh, fearful woe! 5. Ah! My saying was true. 6. Ouch! That hurts.

7. Hark! Hark! To God the chorus breaks. 8. Halloo, my boys, halloo! 9. Pshaw! There's no distress in that. 10. Oh, look! 11. Aha! Is that you?

12. Alas, poor Yorick! 13. Adieu, adieu, my native land!

14. Hark! They whisper: angels say,
Sister spirit, come away.

WORDS VARIOUSLY CLASSIFIED

234. OF THE USE OF WORDS

1. The same word may belong to different parts of speech.

2. The manner in which a word is used determines its classification.

3. The **normal** use of a word is its use according to its ordinary meaning and classification.

4. The **abnormal** or *exceptional* use of a word is a variation from its usual meaning or classification.

5. The **idiomatic** use of a word or expression is a departure from the principles of universal grammar.

235. EXAMPLES

A ....(1) **Adj.**, "*A* man." "*An* ox." (2) **Prep.**, "I go *a*-fishing."

About .....(1) **Adv.**, "He wanders *about*." (2) **Prep.**, "We talked *about* the weather."

Above .....(1) **Adv.**, "He soars *above*." (2) **Prep.**, "He soars *above* the clouds."

Adieu......(1) **Noun**, "He bade me *adieu*." (2) **Interjection**, "*Adieu! Adieu!* My native land."

After ......(1) **Adv.**, "I left soon *after*." (2) **Prep.**, "He ran *after me*." (3) **Conj. adv.**, "He came *after* you left."

Again......(1) **Adv.**, "Come *again*." (2) **Conj.**, "*Again*, you have frequently seen," etc.

Alike ......(1) **Adj.**, "Those girls look *alike*." (2) **Adv.**, "I am *alike* pleased with them both."

All ....(1) **Noun**, "That is his *all*." (2) **Adj.**, "*All* men." "Goodbye to you *all*." "*All* were there." (3) **Adv.**, "He is *all* right." "We were left *all* alone."

Any ....(1) **Adj.**, "Have you *any* objections?" (2) **Adv.**, "He is not *any* better."

As.........(1) **Adv.**, "As black as night." (2) **Conj. adv.**, "Do *as* I do," (*manner*); "He is as tall *as* I am," (*comparison*); "The men cheered *as* he passed," (*time*); "I will go now, *as* [*since*] I am a little lame," (*cause* or reason). (3) **Cor. conj.**, "*As* the door turneth on its hinges, so doth the slothful man on his bed." (4) **Rel. pron.**, "They are such *as* I could find." (5) **Conj. denoting apposition**, "He shipped *as* second mate." "*As* mayor of the city, I feel much aggrieved." (6) Part of a **comp. prep.**, "*As to* that," "*As for* me," etc.

As follows may be parsed as an adverbial phrase, equivalent to *thus*, or the pronoun *it* may be supplied as the grammatical subject of "follows." Always supply *it* in parsing *as appears*, *as concerns*, and *as regards*.

Before .....(1) **Adv.**, "He went *before*." (2) **Prep.**, "The hills rise *before* him." (3) **Conj. adv.**, "He spoke *before* I did."

Below......(1) **Noun**, "I came from *below*." (2) **Adj.**, "He is in one of the offices *below*." (3) **Adv.**, "Go *below*." (4) **Prep.**, "Stand *below* me."

Best ....(1) **Noun**, "Now do your *best*." (2) **Adj.**, "Covet the *best* gifts." (3) **Adv.**, "Who can *best* work and *best* agree?" (4) **Adv. phr.**, "Tones he loved *the best*."

Better......(1) **Noun**, "They scorn their *betters*." (2) **Verb**, "Love *betters* what is best." (3) **Adj.**, "The gray mare is the *better* beast." (4) **Adv.**, "Never was monarch *better* feared."

Both.......(1) **Adj.**, "Hear *both* sides." (2) **Pron. adj.**, "*Both* of them made a covenant," "They are *both* vagabonds." (3) **Cor. conj.**, "She is *both* young and beautiful."

But........(1) **Adj.**, "If they kill us, we shall *but* die." (2) **But a, Adj.**, "He is *but* a man." (3) **Prep.**, "All *but* two were drowned," "None knew thee *but* to love thee," "Whence all *but* him had fled." (4) Part of **comp. prep.**, "He would steal *but for* the law." (5) **Conj.**, "Knowledge comes, *but* wisdom lingers," "When pride comes, then cometh shame; *but* with the lowly is wisdom." (6) Substitute for **that . . . not**, "There is no one *but* knows the truth" = "There is no one *that* does *not* know the truth."

By.........(1) **Adv.**, "He passed *by* on the other side." (2) **Prep.**, "We have come *by* the valley road."

Close ......(1) **Adj.**, "From a *close* bower this dainty music flowed," "He is a *close*, selfish man." (2) **Adv.**, "He followed *close* behind."

Each.......(1) **Pron. adj.**, "They searched *each* house," "*Each* officer," "They took one *each*," "Wandering *each* his several way," "They resemble *each* other." (See Sec. 50.)

Else ....(1) **Adj.**, "Do not call any one *else*." (2) **Adv.**, "How *else* can this be done?" (3) **Conj.**, "Thou desirest not sacrifice, *else* would I give it."

Enough ....(1) **Noun**, "He has *enough*." (2) **Adj.**, "I have trouble *enough*." (3) **Adv.**, "I know you well *enough*."

Except .....(1) **Verb**, "The teacher could not *except* John from turning in his homework since he had been present when the assignment was given." (2) **Prep.**, "I could see nothing *except* the sky," "*Except* these bonds." (3) **Conj.**, "*Except* the Lord build the house, they labor in vain that build it."

Far ....(1) **Noun**, "He came from *far*." (2) **Adj.**, "We are come from a *far* country." (3) **Adv.**, "Over the hills and *far* away," "*Far* from his home."

Farewell....(1) **Noun**, "A last *farewell*." (2) **Adj.**, "A *farewell* concert." (3) **Int.**, "*Farewell*!"

Fast . . . . (1) **Noun**, "An annual religious *fast*." (2) **Verb**, "Thou didst *fast* and weep for thy child." (3) **Adj**., "He is my *fast* friend." (4) **Adv**., "We will bind thee *fast*," "He runs *fast*."

Few . . . . (1) **Noun**, "A *few* escaped," "The *few* and the many." (2) **Adj**., "We have a *few* copies left."

For . . . . (1) **Prep**., "We waited *for* you," "He writes not *for* money nor *for* praise." (2) **Conj**., "Give thanks unto the Lord; *for* he is good: *for* his mercy endureth forever." See **As**.

Full . . . . (1) **Noun**, "The *full* of the moon." (2) **Verb**, "They *full* cloth at the woolen mill." (3) **Adj**., "The house was *full*," "A *full* supply." (4) **Adv**., "He spake *full* well."

Hard . . . . . . (1) **Adj**., "This is *hard* work." (2) **Adv**., "He works *hard*," "He lives *hard* by the river" (*Hard* modifies the phrase "by the river"); "Hold on *hard*."

However . . . (1) **Adv**., "*However* great." (2) **Conj**., "*However*, your house was not burned."

Ill . . . . (1) **Noun**, "Throw off the *ills*," "The *ills* of life." (2) **Adj**., "I was quite *ill* yesterday." (3) **Adv**., "*Ill* fares the land, to hastening ills a prey."—*Goldsmith*

Indeed . . . . . (1) **Adv**., "It is *indeed* true." (2) **Conj**., "*Indeed*, I was not aware of it."

Late . . . . (1) **Adj**., "A *late* frost destroyed the fruit." (2) **Adv**., "We studied early and *late*."

Like . . . . (1) **Noun**, "*Like* produces *like*." (2) **Verb**, "I *like* frank people." (3) **Adj**., "We have *like* chances," "The staff of his spear was *like* a weaver's beam." (4) **Prep**., "He ran *like* a deer," "The Assyrian came down *like* a wolf on the fold."

Low . . . . (1) **Adj**., "He is very *low* this evening." (2) **Adv**., "Aim *low*," "He speaks too *low*."

More . . . . . . (1) **Noun**, "Have you any *more*?" "They saved some *more*, some less." (2) **Adj**., "We want *more* men," "Let us hear no *more* complaints." (3) **Adv**., "They don't come here any *more*."

Much . . . . . . (1) **Noun**, "They made *much* of the little they had." (2) **Adj**., "He displayed *much* learning." (3) **Adv**., "I am *much* disheartened," "Think *much*."

Nay . . . . (1) **Noun**, "The *nays* have it," "I say *nay*." (2) **Adv**., "*Nay*, I said not so."

Ay, aye, yea, are similar to *nay* in use and construction; as, "The *ayes* have it," "*Yea*, verily." *Yea* and *nay* are also used as conjunctions to denote emphatic addition; as, "What carefulness it wrought in you, *yea*, what clearing of yourselves, *yea*, what indignation, *yea*, what fear, *yea*, what vehement desire, *yea*, what zeal, *yea*, what revenge!"—2 Cor. 7:11.

No . . . . (1) **Noun**, "The *noes* have it." (2) **Adj.**, "This is *no* place for mirth." (3) **Adv.**, "I can walk *no* faster."

Notwithstanding. (1) **Prep.**, "We walked *notwithstanding* the rain." (2) **Conj.**, "He is kind, *notwithstanding* he is stern."

Now . . . . (1) **Noun**, "*Now* is the accepted time," "Eternity is a never-ending *now*." (2) **Adv.**, "Come *now*." (3) **Conj.**, "*Now*, Barabbas was a robber."

Once . . . . . . (1) **Noun**, "Forgive me just this *once*." (2) **Adv.**, "He visits us *once* a year."

Only . . . . (1) **Adj.**, "Is this the *only* hotel in town?" (2) **Adv.**, "I sing *only*; I cannot play."

Over . . . . (1) **Adv.**, "They passed *over*," "Turn *over* a new leaf." (2) **Prep.**, "We drove *over* the bridge," "*Over* the hills." (3) Part of a **comp. prep.**, "*Over against* this mountain."

Right . . . . . . (1) **Noun**, "The *right* will finally triumph," "I stand here on my *right*," "Our *rights*." (2) **Adj.**, "The *right* man in the *right* place," "You are *right*." (3) **Adv.** "Do *right*," "Look *right* ahead."

Save . . . . (1) **Verb**, "*Save* a penney." (2) **Prep.**, "Of the Jews, five times received I forty stripes *save* one." (3) **Conj.**, "And that no man might buy or sell *save* he that had the mark."—Rev. 13:17.

So . . . . (1) **Adv.**, "Why are you *so* angry?" "He said *so*." (2) **Conj.**, "As in Adam all die, *so* in Christ shall all be made alive."

That . . . . (1) **Adj.**, "Watch *that* man," "*That* house is sold," "This is as good soil as *that*." (2) **Rel. pron.**, "Ye *that* fear the Lord, bless the Lord," "It was I, not he, *that* did it." (3) **Conj.**, "He heard *that* his friend was sick," "Treat it kindly, *that* it may wish to stay with us."

The . . . . (1) **Article**, "*The* stars." (2) **Adv.**, "*The* more, *the* better." (3) When *the* modifies an adverb, it forms with it an **adv. phrase**; as, "I like you *the better* for that."

Then . . . . . . (1) **Noun**, "Alas, the change twixt *now* and *then*." (2) **Adv.**, "We *then* ascended the tower." (3) **Conj.**, "If you do not want it, *then* do not buy it."

There . . . . . . (1) **Adv.**, "I live *there*," "Grass grows *there* now." (2) *As an expletive*, used to introduce a sentence in a particular way; as, "*There* were three of us."

Till . . . . (1) **Noun**, "The money was in the *till*." (2) **Verb**, "Farmers *till* the ground." (3) **Prep.**, "Stay *till* (or, *until*) next Monday." (4) **Conj. adv.**, "Stay *till* (or, *until*) I return."

Up . . . . (1) **Noun**, "The *ups* and *downs* of life are many." (2) **Adv.**, "Go *up*, baldhead." (3) **Prep.**, "They sailed *up* the river."

Well . . . . (1) **Noun**, "The *well* is sixty feet deep." (2) **Verb**, "Blood that *welled* from the wound." (3) **Adj.**, "Is it *well* with you?" (4) **Adv.**, "The work was *well* done." (5) **Ind. adv.**, "*Well*, what do you say?"

What . . . . . . (1) **Rel. Pron.**, "Pay *what* you owe." (2) **Int. pron.**, "*What* pleases you?" (3) **Adj.**, "*What* bus is that?" (4) **Adv.**, "*What* [partly] with entreaty, *what* with threatening, I succeeded," "*What* good did it do?" (5)**Interj.**, "*What*! Is it midnight?"

When . . . . . . (1) **Noun**, "Since *when* was it?" (2) **Adv.**, "*When* you were there." (3) **Conj. adv.**, "Write *when* you reach Boston."

Which . . . . . (1) **Rel. pron.**, "The house in *which* I live." (2) **Int. pron.**, "*Which* is he?" (3) **Adj.**, "*Which* road shall I take?"

While . . . . . . (1) **Noun**, "That is worth your *while*." (2) **Verb**, "We will *while* away an hour." (3) **Adv.**, "*While* waiting for the train." (4) **Conj. adv.**, "We listened *while* he played."

Worse . . . . . (1) **Noun**, "For better or *worse*." (2) **Adj.**, "He is *worse* today." (3) **Adv.**, "He might do *worse*."

Worth . . . . . (1) **Noun**, "They have lost their dignity and *worth*." (2) **Adj.**, "He is *worth* a million."

Yet . . . . (1) **Adj.**, "Our country *yet* remains." (2) **Conj.**, "I am disappointed, *yet* not discouraged."

Yonder . . . . (1) **Adj.**, "*Yonder* mountain." (2) **Adv.**, "Who beckons to us *yonder*."

Rem. 1—Nouns may perform an adjective use, and still be regarded as nouns; as, "The *sun's* rays," "*General Harrison's* residence," "Peter the *Hermit*," "Dionysius the *Tyrant*."

Rem. 2—By being placed before the words which they modify, nouns may be used as adjectives; as, "our *Indian* summer," "*Christmas* eve," "*strawberry* shortcake." Nouns thus used may be modified by adjectives; as, "the *High* Church party," "the *protective* tariff bill."

A compound adjective may be formed by uniting two nouns, or a noun and an adjective, by a hyphen; as, "*fire-clay* brick," "*air-pump* experiments," "a *white-oak* pail." In all cases, the limiting noun must be in the singular number; as, "a *four-rod* chain," "a *ten-foot* pole."

A compound adjective may be formed of an indefinite number of words, joined by hyphens, the entire phrase being used as a single word to modify the noun following; as, "the *Kansas-Nebraska* Bill," "an *out-and-out* falsehood."

Rem. 3—Nouns connected by conjunctions frequently form a compound term, which must be regarded as a *single* thing, though composed of distinct parts; as, "*Three dollars a day and board* is all I ask," "A *horse and wagon* was stolen."

Rem. 4—Phrases, inseparable in thought, may be formed by uniting prepositions with themselves or other parts of speech.

1. A *verb* and *preposition*; as, *to cast up, to buy off, to bring to, to come to, to go over*, etc. The preposition should be considered an inseparable part of the verb, but it may be parsed as an adverb.

2. A *preposition* and *adjective*; as, *on high, at large, in earnest, at most*, etc.: inseparable phrases, either adjective or adverbial.

3. *Preposition* and *preposition*; as, *over and over, by and by, out and out, through and through*, etc.: inseparable adverbial phrases.

4. *Noun, preposition*, and *noun*; as, *day by day, face to face, side by side, cheek by jowl*, etc. As the expressiveness of these phrases is destroyed by supplying any ellipsis, they should be classed among inseparable adverbial phrases. If preferred, however, each word may be parsed separately, the first noun being made the object of a preposition understood.

Rem. 5—Two prepositions frequently come together: in which case they form a complex preposition; the first in order is an adverb, or both are adverbs; as, "He comes *from over (complex preposition)* the sea," "They rode *by (adverb)* in a carriage," "The whole subject was gone *over with*" (both *adverbs*).

Rem. 6—Two or more conjunctions may come together: in which case each has its use, which should always be regarded in parsing; as, "*Now when* evening had come," "*And so* I wrote it down."

236. EXERCISES

Sentences to be used for any kind of practice deemed helpful.

1. He has been ill since November. 2. I will go, provided he sends for me. 3. Can you not still this noise? 4. The rain still continues. 5. The before-mentioned facts are before you. 6. Does he live anywhere in Ohio? 7. This boy is full ten years old. 8. I never saw a saw saw a saw as that saw saws a saw. 9. What with the bread, and what with the water, he sustained himself for several weeks. 10. Give me such as I bargained for, and as much as I bargained for.

11. What, then, could be done? 12. He has come round. 13. That man purchased a round of beef. 14. The weight of this box is forty pounds. 15. The stars are out by twos and threes. 16. Which is greater, the gold or the temple? 17. Sing unto the Lord, O ye saints of his. 18. No man can come unto me except the Father draws him. 19. He maketh me to lie down in green pastures. 20. They have promised, yet they do not perform. 21. One came, I thought, and whispered in my ear.

22. He that grasps at more than belongs to him, justly deserves to lose what he has. 23. All this, I heard as one half dead; but answer had I none to words so true, save tears for my sins. 24. Dreaming, she knew it was a dream. 25. He thought only of his subject. 26. The path of glory leads but to the grave. 27. Kings will be tyrants from policy when subjects are rebels from principle. 28. Angling is somewhat like poetry: men are apt to be born so.—*Walton*.

29. There shall nothing die of all that is the children's of Israel. 30. We have just come from Brown and Starr's. 31. Three times seven are twenty-one. 32. I paid a dollar and a half for butter this morning. 33. Wheat is two dollars a bushel. 34. He ran the train at the rate of forty miles an hour. 35. The more I see of him the better I like him.

36. Let your communication be yea, yea, and nay, nay. 37. As far as the east is from the west, so far hath He removed our transgressions from us. 38. Therefore, if thine enemy hunger, feed him; if he thirst, give him drink: for in so doing, thou shalt heap coals of fire on his head. 39. It is good for us to be here. 40. Consider the lilies of the field, how they grow; they toil not, neither do they spin. 41. If I forget thee, O Jerusalem, let my right hand forget her cunning.

42. Hitherto shalt thou come, but no further. 43. Yet man is born unto trouble, as the sparks fly upward. 44. "Madam," said I, emphatically, "you are in error." 45. This is—what shall we call it? 46. It is he, even he. 47. He was not even invited to be present. 48. Is your health good, now? Rather so. 49. The garret was filled with broken chairs, cast-off garments, and what not. 50. How long was it before the man came to? About three quarters of an hour.

51. He that will not when he may,
When he would, he shall have nay.

52. For what is worth in anything
But so much money as 'twill bring.—*Butler*.

53. The swan on still St. Mary's lake,
Float double, swan and shadow.—*Wordsworth*.

54. Think for thyself—one good idea,
But known to be thine own,
Is better than a thousand gleaned
From fields by others sown.—*Wilson*.

55. So we were left galloping, Joris and I,
Past Looz and past Tongres, no cloud in the sky;
The broad sun above laughed a pitiless laugh;
'Neath our feet broke the brittle, bright stubble like chaff;
Till over by Dalhem a dome spire sprang white,
And "Gallop," gasped Joris, "for Aix is in sight."—*Browning*.

56.   This well may be
The Day of Judgment which the world awaits;
But, be it so or not, I only know
My present duty, and my Lord's command
To occupy till he come. So at the post
Where he hath set me in his providence,
I choose for one to meet him face to face,—
No faithless servant frightened from my task,
But ready when the Lord of the harvest calls.—*Whittier.*

FIGURES OF LANGUAGE

237. DEFINITIONS

1. A **figure of speech** is a departure from the ordinary form, regular construction, or literal signification of words.

2. A **figure of etymology** is a departure from the usual *form* of a word.

3. A **figure of syntax** is a departure from the usual *construction* of words.

4. A **figure of rhetoric** is a departure from the primitive or literal *sense* of a word.

238. FIGURES OF ETYMOLOGY

1. **Apheresis** is the elision of a letter or syllable from the beginning of a word; as, *'gainst*, for *against*; *'gan*, for *began*.

2. **Prosthesis** is the prefixing of a letter or syllable to a word; as, *adown*, for *down*; *beloved*, for *loved*.

3. **Syncope** is the omission of one or more letters in the middle of a word; as, *ne'er*, for *never*; *slumb'ring*, for *slumbering*.

4. **Tmesis** is the separation of a compound word by the insertion of a word between its parts; as, *to* us *ward*, for *toward* us; *how* high *soever*, for *howsoever* high.

5. **Apocope** is the omission of the last letter or syllable of a word; as, *th'*, for *the*; *yond*, for *yonder*.

6. **Paragoge** is the addition of a letter or syllable to the end of a word; as, *bounden*, for *bound*; *withouten*, for *without*.

7. **Syneresis** is the contraction of two syllables into one; as, *don't*, for *do not*; *can't*, for *cannot*.

239. FIGURES OF SYNTAX

1. **Ellipsis** is the omission of a word, phrase, or clause necessary to complete the construction of a sentence.

Note—For examples of ellipsis, see Sec. 203.

2. **Redundancy** is the use of more words than are necessary.

Ex.—"I saw it *with these eyes.*" "All ye *inhabitants* of the world, and *dwellers on the earth.*"

Rem. 1—**Polysyndeton** is the repetition of a conjunction; as, "He is good, *and* wise, *and* generous."

Rem. 2—**Asyndeton** is the omission of connective words in a sentence; as, "We walked slowly, noiselessly, with bated breath."

Rem. 3—**Anadiplosis** is the use of the same word or expression in the termination of one clause of a sentence, and at the beginning of the next; as, "Has he a lust for *blood*? *Blood* shall fill his cup."

Rem. 4—**Epizeuxis** is the emphatic repetition of the same word or words; as, "*Alone, alone, all all alone.*"

3. **Enallage** is the use of one part of speech, or of one form, for another.

Ex.—*We*, for *I*; *you*, for *thou*; "What is *writ* is *writ.*"

4. **Hyperbaton** is the transposition of words from the plain grammatical order.

Ex.—"He wanders the *earth around.*" "From peak to peak, *the rattling crags among.*" "*Lightly* from fair to fair *he flew.*"

5. **Syllepsis** is the agreement of one word with the figurative sense of another.

Ex.—"The *Word* was made flesh, and dwelt among us: and we beheld *his* glory."—John 1:14.

6. **Parenthesis** is the insertion of a word or sentence between the parts of another sentence.

Ex.—Every planet (for God has made nothing in vain) serves a purpose.

7. **Zeugma** is a figure by which an adjective or verb, which agrees with a nearer word, is referred to one more remote.

Ex.—"Lust overcame shame; boldness, fear; and madness, reason."

240. FIGURES OF RHETORIC

1. **Simile** is an express or formal comparison.

Ex.—*Like a dog*, he hunts in dreams.—*Tennyson.*

2. **Metaphor** is the expression of similitude without the signs of comparison.

Ex.—"A *flash* of wit." "A *sea* of troubles." "The moralist is a *scout* for consequences." "The wish is *father* to the thought."

3. **Personification** consists in attributing life and mind to inanimate objects.

Ex.—"O *Winter*! Ruler of the inverted year." "The *earth* mourneth and fadeth away."

4. **Allegory** is a discourse in which one subject is described by another resembling it.

Ex.—*The Pilgrim's Progress*; Spencer's *Faerie Queene*; Swift's *Tale of a Tub*; *The Vision of Mirza.*

Rem. 1—A **fable** is a short allegory.

Ex.—Aesop's and La Fontaine's fables. Most fables are short stories about certain animals that are regarded as representatives of particular qualities; as, the fox, of cunning; the lion, of strength.

Rem. 2—A **parable** is a relation of something real in nature from which a moral is drawn.

Ex.—Parable of the Poor Man and his Lamb—2 Sam. 12:1-5; Of the Sower—Matt. 13; Of the Ten Virgins—Matt. 25.

5. **Synecdoche** is a figure by which the whole is put for a part, or a part for the whole; a species for a genus, or a genus for a species, etc.

Ex.—*Roof*, for house or dwelling; *bread*, for food generally; *cutthroat*, for assassin.

Rem. 1—**Antonomasia** is the use of a proper name for a common name, or the name of some office, rank, profession, trade, or peculiarity, instead of the true name of a people or class.

Ex.—"He is a *Buckeye*," *i.e.*, an Ohioan; "The *Crescent City*," *i.e.*, New Orleans.

Rem. 2—**Euphemism** is the substitution of a delicate word or expression for one which is harsh or offensive.

Ex.—*Departed, gone to rest, fallen asleep,* for *dead; embezzlement*, for *theft.*

6. **Metonymy** is a change of names, or a figure by which one word is put for another.

Ex.—*Gray hairs*, for *old age*; *purse*, for *money*; *fare*, for a *passenger*; *city*, for its *inhabitants*; "Ye devour widows' *inheritances*."

7. **Antithesis** is the opposition of words and sentiments contained in the same sentence.

Ex.—"*Excess* of ceremony shows *want* of breeding." "Wit laughs *at* things; humor laughs *with* them."—*Whipple*.

8. **Epigram** is a sentence in which the form of the language contradicts the meaning conveyed.

Ex.—I cannot see the city for the houses." "Summer has set in with its usual severity."—*Walpole*. "Anything awful always makes me laugh."—*Lamb*. "Nothing so fallacious as facts, except figures."—*Canning*.

Rem. 1—The epigram awakens attention by the seeming irrelevance of the assertion, or by the form given to it.

Rem. 2—The **paronomasia**, or **pun**, is a play on the various meanings of the same word.

Ex.—A friend of Curran, hearing a person near him say *curosity* instead of *curiosity*, exclaimed: "How that man murders the English language!" "Not so bad," said Curran; "he has only knocked an *i* out."

Rem. 3—The **conundrum** is a sort of riddle, in which some odd resemblance between things unlike is proposed for discovery.

9. **Hyperbole** is an exaggeration of the meaning intended to be conveyed, by magnifying objects beyond their proper bounds.

Ex.—"The land flows with milk and honey." "The English gain two hours a day by clipping words."—*Voltaire*.

10. **Interrogation** is the putting in the form of a question what is meant to be strongly affirmative.

Ex.—"Does a porcupine have quills?"

11. **Climax** is an arrangement of the parts of a sentence, by which they are made to rise step by step in interest or importance.

Ex.—"It is an outrage to *bind* a Roman citizen; to *scourge* him is an atrocious crime; to *put him to death* is almost a parricide; but to *crucify* him—what shall I call it?"—*Cicero*.

Rem.—**Anticlimax** is any great departure from the order required in climax.

Ex.—"That all-softening, overpowering knell,
        The tocsin of the soul—the dinner-bell."—*Byron*.

12. **Exclamation** is the animated or impassioned expression of sudden and intense emotion.

Ex.—"Oh, what a pity!" "A horse, a horse, my kingdom for a horse." "Blow, winds, and crack your cheeks!"

13. **Apostrophe** is the turning away from the real audience, and addressing an absent or imaginary one.

Ex.— "Ye toppling crags of ice!
Ye avalanches, whom a breath draws down,
In mountainous overwhelming, come and crush me."—*Byron*.

Rem.—**Hypotyposis**, or **vision**, is a description of things in such strong and lively colors, as to bring the absent before the mind with the force of present reality.

Ex.—"I see the rural virtues leave the land."—*Goldsmith*. "Greece cries to us by the convulsed lips of her poisoned, dying Demosthenes."—*Everett*.

14. **Innuendo** is a covert suggestion of an author's meaning, instead of an open expression of it.

Ex.—"He did his party all the harm in his power: he *spoke for it*, and *voted against it*."

15. **Irony** is a mode of expression by which what is said is contrary to what is meant.

Ex.—"No doubt but ye are the people, and wisdom will die with you." "You are a pretty fellow!"

Rem.—**Sarcasm** is a keen, reproachful, and scornful expression.

Ex.—"Who but must laugh, if such a man there be?
Who would not weep if Atticus were he?"—*Pope*.

16. **Litotes** is a mode of expressing something by denying the contrary.

Ex.—"Nor are thy lips ungrateful, sire of men.
Nor tongue inadequate: for God on thee
Abundantly his gifts hath also poured."—*Milton*.

17. **Catachresis** is wresting a word from its original signification, and making it express something at variance with its true meaning.

Ex.—"*Silver* curling *irons*." "A *glass* ink *horn*." "Her voice was but the *shadow of a sound*."—*Young*.

PUNCTUATION

241. DEFINITION

1. **Punctuation** is the art of dividing written discourse into sentences and parts of sentences, by means of points, or marks.

Rem. 1—Points are principally used for the purpose of rendering the sense more intelligible. They do not mark all the pauses made in reading, though a pause is generally made where a point is used.

Rem. 2—A change in the punctuation of a sentence generally produces a change in the meaning.

Ex.—John Keys the lawyer says he is guilty.
John, Keys the lawyer says he is guilty.
John Keys, the lawyer says he is guilty.
"John Keys the lawyer," says he, "is guilty."

2. The principal marks used in punctuation are the following:

Comma . . . . ,	Exclamation Point . . . . . .!
Semicolon . . . .;	Dash . . . . −
Colon. . . . . :	Parentheses . . . .( )
Period	Brackets . . . .[ ]
Question Mark or Interrogation Point . . .?	

242. THE COMMA

The **comma** denotes the slightest degree of separation between the elements of a sentence. It is the most frequently used mark of punctuation.

Rule I—Use commas to set off words, phrases, or clauses in a series.

Ex.—1. Mike, Dick, Eddie, and Tom went fishing, swam for an hour, and biked home. 2. We purchased five pounds of ground beef, two pounds of margarine, and a dozen eggs. 3. War, peace, darts, spears, towns, rivers—everything in his writings is alive. 4. The simplicity of his character inspired confidence, the charisma of his speaking aroused enthusiasm, and the openness of his manner invited friendship.

Rule II—Nonrestrictive clauses and other parenthetic expressions not essential to the sense of the sentence are set off by commas.

Ex.—1. Augusta, which is the capital of Maine, is on the Kennebec River.

2. Henry W. Longfellow, who wrote *Hiawatha*, was born in Maine. 3. He invented, it is said, the theory of moral science. 4. That sport, too, is very dangerous.

Rem. 1—This is difficult to apply, since the writer must determine whether or not the clause is essential. For example, in the sentence, The Thomas Wolfe who wrote *Look Homeward, Angel* was from North Carolina, the clause is essential since two Thomas Wolfes were novelists. In Ex. 2, however, there can be no question as to Longfellow's identity, since only one writer by that name is known in literature. The clause, "who wrote *Hiawatha*," only adds a nonessential fact about Longfellow.

Rem. 2—Certain other rules for using commas can be more easily understood if the words or phrases to be set off by commas are thought of as parenthetic. A noun in direct address is parenthetic; as, Well, Mike, how did school go today? So is an appositive; as, Tom Jones, the plumber, makes night house calls but charges more. A title following a name is often treated as parenthetical; as, Malcolm Collins, Ph.D., is the new principal; Max Fortier, Jr., has taken over his father's insurance business.

Rem. 3—Nouns in apposition modified by *the* only are not separated by commas; as, The Emperor Nero was a cruel tyrant; Thomson the poet was indolent.

Rem. 4—An appositive word or expression introduced by *as* or *or* should be set off by commas; as, "So that he, as God, sitteth in the temple of God," Maize, or Indian corn, is raised in Iowa.

Rem. 5—When an appositive is closely related to the noun, no comma is needed; as, William the Conqueror invaded England in 1066; Your friend Tom stopped by today.

Rem. 6—Test appositives by the same "essential" rule as restrictive or nonrestrictive clauses; as, My cousin Sandy is 23 years old; but, My cousin Sandy, the hairdresser, lives in Cleveland. In the first case, "Sandy," appositive to "cousin" is essential, since I may have more than one cousin. Hence, no commas are required. "The hairdresser," appositive to "Sandy," is not essential information.

Rule III—Use a comma after an introductory adverb clause, after an introductory participial phrase, an introductory adjective phrase, or a long introductory prepositional phrase.

Ex. 1. As you practice writing, punctuation rules become more clear. 2. Writing an essay, I consulted *Webster's New Collegiate Dictionary* and *Harvey's Grammar*. 3. Having once lost the good opinion of our friends, it is difficult for us to reclaim it. 4. Faithful to his promise, he helped me find a job. 5. Over the river and through the woods, to Grandmother's house we go.

Rem. 1—Do not confuse an introductory gerund phrase with a gerund phrase used as the subject of a sentence; as, Writing an essay is hard work.

Rem. 2—Short introductory prepositional phrases do not require a comma; as, In writing always be neat.

Rule IV—Transposed words, phrases, and clauses are usually set off by commas.

Ex.—"Whom ye ignorantly worship, Him declare I unto you."

Rem. 1—A transposed objective element is not usually set off by a comma; as, That book he has never returned.

Rem. 2—When an inverted expression begins with *it is* or *only*, it is not set off by a comma; as, Only on rare occasions they felt disposed to be merciful.

Rule V—Adverbs used independently, or modifying an entire proposition, should be set off by commas.

Ex.—1. Yea, the earth itself shall pass away. 2. Well, if that is the law, I shall obey it. 3. Indeed, you must wait awhile.

Rule VI—When a verb is omitted to avoid repetition, its place is usually supplied by a comma.

Ex.—1. One murder makes a villain; millions, a hero. 2. War is the law of violence; peace, the law of love.

Rem.—There are many exceptions to this rule. The general practice is to omit the comma unless clearness and precision demand its insertion; as, "Reading maketh a full man, conference a ready man, and writing an exact man."—*Bacon*. Punctuated thus, "Reading maketh a full man; conference, a ready man; and writing, an exact man," is acceptable but unnecessarily cluttered with semicolons and commas.

Rule VII—Contrasting words, phrases, and clauses should be separated by commas.

Ex.—1. Strong proofs, not a loud voice, produce conviction. 2. Though deep, yet clear; though gentle, yet not dull.

Rule VIII—Long independent clauses joined by the conjunctions *and*, *but*, *nor*, *for*, or *yet* require a comma; short clauses ordinarily do not.

Ex.—1. Skydiving is a hazardous sport, and auto racing often results in death. 2. Skydiving is dangerous and road racing is hazardous.

Rem.—Do not join independent clauses with a comma only; when no conjunction is present, use a semicolon; as, "To err is human; to forgive, divine."—*Pope*.

Rule IX—The clauses of complex sentences should be separated by commas, unless the dependent clauses are very short and the connection very close.

Ex.—"I took notice, in particular, of a very profligate fellow, who I did not question, came loaded with his crimes; but upon searching his bundle, I found that instead of throwing his guilt from him, he had only laid down his memory."—*Addison.*

Rule X—When words are arranged in pairs, each couplet should be set off by commas.

Ex.—Sink or swim, live or die, survive or perish, I give my hand and my heart to this responsibility.

Rem.—Do not separate the parts of a couplet with a comma. Wrong: Sink, or swim (*Sink, swim, or float*, however, is *not* a couplet—it is a series).

Rule XI—A direct quotation, separated by a principal clause, should be set off by commas.

Ex.—"Oh, Mr. Pickwick," said Mrs. Bardell, trembling with agitation, "you're very kind, sir."

Rule XII—A quoted sentence, a long infinitive phrase, or an indirect quotation introduced by *that* should usually be set off by a comma.

Ex.—1. He asked, "Why are you so melancholy?" 2. I have heard say of thee, that thou canst understand a dream to interpret it. 3. "To correct such gross vices as lead us to commit a real injury to others, is the part of morals and the object of the most ordinary education."—*Hume.*

Rem.—Note that the infinitive phrase, "To correct . . . to others," in Example 3 is the subject of the verb *is*. A comma is not ordinarily inserted between a verb and its subject, and it is necessary in this case only because of the length of the phrase. The comma could be eliminated by restructuring the sentence so that the phrase is contained in the predicate. In the case of a short opening phrase, no comma is needed; as, To study grammar improves writing skills.

Rule XIII—Words repeated for emphasis should be set off by commas.

Ex.—"Verily, verily, I say unto you."

Rule XIV—Whenever confusion would arise from its omission, a comma should be inserted.

Ex.—I have a house with nine rooms, and a shed out back. The sentence, I have a house with nine rooms and a bath, needs no comma, however.

Rule XV—Use a comma after the salutation of an informal letter. Some now also use a comma instead of a colon after the salutation of a business letter if the addressee is known to the writer; as, Dear Joe,.

Rule XVI—Few commas are preferable to too many.

EXERCISES

Insert commas wherever required in these sentences; be prepared to state in recitation why you punctuated thus.

1. Come Rover—let's take a walk. 2. We often commend as well as censure inprudently. 3. The rich and the poor the high and the low the learned and the unlearned have access alike to this fountain of peace. 4. I see then in revelation a purpose corresponding with that for which human teaching was instituted. 5. Oranges lemons and figs grow in Florida and other Southern states.

6. Do you think John Paul asked at last that the storm drove it here? 7. Yes I'm sure it's true. 8. As it was then so it is now. 9. He that seeketh findeth. 10. The idle lack steadiness of purpose; the indolent power of exertion.

243. THE SEMICOLON

The **semicolon** denotes a degree of separation greater than that denoted by the comma.

Rule I—The semicolon should be used before *as, namely, to wit, viz.*, introducing an example or an illustration.

Ex.—1. One part only of an antithesis is sometimes expressed; as, "A friendly eye would never see such faults." 2. Some men distinguish the period of the world into four ages; viz., the golden age, the silver age, the bronze age, and the iron age.

Rule II—The semicolon is used to separate the members of a compound sentence when the connective is omitted.

Ex.—Magnify the Lord with me; praise his holy name.

Rule III—The members of a compound sentence, if long or if their parts are set off by commas, should be separated by semicolons to avoid confusion, even when joined by connectives.

Ex. 1—And he gave some, apostles; and [he gave] some, prophets; and [he gave] some, evangelists; and [he gave] some, pastors and teachers.

Ex. 2—The person he chanced to see, was, to appearance, an old, sordid, blind man; but upon his following him from place to place, he at last found, by his own confession, that he was Plutus, the god of riches, and that he was just come out of the house of a miser.

Rule IV—Successive clauses or phrases having a common dependence should be separated by semicolons if some of the parts are separated by commas.

Ex.—My imagination would conjure up all that I had heard or read of the watery world beneath me; of the finny tribes that roam in the fathomless valleys; of huge octopuses, hideous sharks, or monster eels that lurk in the caverns of the deep; or those mammoth whales that swell the tales of fishermen and sailors.

Note—In the above example, *commas* would ordinarily separate the phrases, except that there is a list using commas in the phrase beginning, "of huge octopuses. . . ."

Rule V—Use a semicolon between independent clauses joined by such words as *for example, for instance, that is, besides, accordingly, moreover, nevertheless, furthermore, otherwise, therefore, however, consequently, instead, hence*.

Ex. 1—Winter in the north is an excellent time for fishing; *for instance*, even anglers who cannot afford a boat can walk on the ice to the best fishing spots in a lake.

Ex. 2—The dog warder captured the mean mongrel; *furthermore*, its owner was fined for not keeping it leashed.

Rem.—When the clauses are short, the semicolon is frequently replaced by the comma; as, "I go, but I return."

EXERCISES

Insert semicolons and commas wherever required in these sentences.

1. A Scotch mist becomes a shower and a shower a flood and a flood a storm and a storm a tempest and a tempest thunder and lightning and thunder and lightning an earthquake. 2. Wit is abrupt darting scornful and tosses its analogies in your face humor is slow and shy insinuating its fun into your heart. 3. Though it was cold the car started readily otherwise we'd have had to take the bus. 4. Mary brought sandwiches cake and cookies Tom furnished coffee and a watermelon.

244. THE COLON

The **colon** denotes a degree of separation greater than that indicated by the semicolon.

Rule I—The colon should be used after the formal introduction to a speech, a course of reasoning, a lengthy quotation, or an enumeration of particulars such as a list.

Ex. 1—Then closing the book, he proceeded in a lower tone: "The philosophers of whom you have read in the dictionary, possessed this wisdom only in part, because they were heathens."

2. Be our plain answer this: the throne we honor is the people's choice; the laws we reverence are our brave fathers' legacy; the faith we follow teaches us to live in bonds of charity with all mankind and die with hope of bliss beyond the grave.

Rule II—The colon should be used before an explanatory clause, or one which presents the meaning of the preceding independent clause in another form.

Ex.—All reasoning is retrospective: it consists in the application of facts and principles previously known. 2. By degrees he infuses into it the poison of his own ambition: he breathes into it the fire of his own courage.

Rule III—The members of a compound sentence, whose parts are phrases or clauses set off by semicolons, were formerly separated by colons.

Ex.—We do not say that his error lies in being a good member of society; this, though only a circumstance at present, is a very fortunate one: the error lies in his having discarded the authority of God, as his legislator; or, rather, in his not having admitted the influence of that authority over his mind, heart, or practice.

Today's usage, however, prefers a period and a capital letter, thus beginning a new sentence; as, " . . . a very fortunate one. The error lies in . . ."

Rule IV—Use a colon with certain numeral combinations: to separate hours from minutes; as, 6:30 P.M.; to separate Bible chapters from verses; as, John 3:16; between a volume number and a page number; as, *Harper's* 203:37 (vol. 203, page 37).

Rule V—Use a colon after the salutation of a formal letter; as, Dear Sir:

EXERCISES

Insert colons wherever required in these sentences.

1. There are five senses sight, hearing, feeling, taste, and smell. 2. The discourse consisted of two parts in the first was shown the necessity of exercise; in the second, the advantages that would result from it. 3. Men's evil manners live in brass their virtues we write in water. 4. Write on your papers the following example the lake is very deep.

245. THE PERIOD

The **period** denotes the greatest degree of separation.

Rule I—The period should be placed at the end of a declarative or imperative sentence.

Ex.—1. Contrivance proves design. 2. Study diligently.

Rem.—A period is sometimes placed at the end of the first of two or more complete sentences joined by conjunctions; as, "Seeing, then, that these things cannot be spoken against, ye ought to be quiet, and to do nothing rashly. For ye have brought hither these men, who are neither robbers of churches, nor yet blasphemers of your goddess."

Rule II—The period should be placed at the end of every abbreviated word.

Ex.—H. M. Swainson, Esq., b. Feb. 10, 1757, d. Apr. 3, 1812.

Rem. 1—The period, thus used, is a part of the abbreviation. Except at the end of a sentence, the point required by the construction should be used after it; as, "Sir Humphrey Davy, F. R. S., etc.," "Ohio is bounded N. by Mich. and Lake Erie; E. by Pa. and W. Va.; S. by W. Va. and Ky.; W. by Ind." Addresses which use zip codes require no period after the capitalized, two-letter state abbreviations; as, Albion, ME 04910.

Rem. 2—Some proper names, though shortened, should not be regarded as abbreviations; as, "Tom Moore," "Will Shakespeare," "O rare Ben Johnson."

Rem. 3—Such expressions as 4to, 8vo, 12mo, 1st, 2d, 3d, 5's, 11's, 4°, 7′, etc., are not abbreviations. The figures supply the places of the first letters of the words, and the signs or indices supply the place of words.

Rem. 4—The period should be placed before decimals, and between the denominations of American or sterling money; as, $35.75; £5. 12s. 6d.

EXERCISES

Insert periods wherever required in these sentences.

1. D K Merwin Esq was chosen chairman. 2. H C Cartwright b A D 1825, d Feb 2, 1854. 3. See Rev 12:11. 4. Chapter XXIV Part II. 5. It cost $1022 (ten dollars and 22 cents).

246. THE INTERROGATION POINT/QUESTION MARK

The **interrogation point** denotes that a question is asked.

Rule—The interrogation point, or question mark, should be used at the end of an interrogative sentence.

Ex.—1. Were you there? 2. By whom was this extraordinary work of art executed?

Rem. 1—When a question is composed of several parts, and when several questions are contained in one sentence, one answer only being required, the question mark is placed only at the end; as, "By whom is this profession praised, but by wretches who consider him as subservient to their purposes; sirens that entice him to shipwreck; and cyclops that are gaping to devour him?"

Rem. 2—The question mark should be used after each successive particular of a series of questions, related in sense, but distinct in construction; as, "Why was the French revolution so bloody and destructive? Why was the English revolution of 1641 comparatively mild? Why was the revolution of 1688 milder still? Why was the American revolution the mildest of all?"

247. THE EXCLAMATION POINT

The **exclamation point** denotes passion or emotion.

Rule—The exclamation point should be placed after expressions denoting strong emotion.

Ex.—1. Avaunt, thou witch! 2. Mercy, sir, how the folks will talk of it! 3. Alas, poor Yorick! Help!

Rem.—The exclamation point should not be used after interjections closely connected with other words, but at the end of each expression of which the interjections form a part; as, "Fie upon you!" "All hail, ye patriots brave!"

EXERCISES

Insert the punctuation required in these sentences.

1. What did my father's godson seek your life he whom my father named
2. See there look

248. THE DASH

The **dash** is a straight, horizontal line, placed between the parts of a sentence.

Rule I—The dash should be used where there is a sudden break or stop in a sentence, or a change in its meaning or construction. A dash is two hyphens in length. When typing, use two hyphens for a dash, without a space.

Ex.—1. Dim—dim—I faint—darkness comes over my eyes. 2. It glitters awhile—and then melts into tears. 3. He stamped and he stormed—then his language—oh, dear! 4. Miss frowned and blushed and then—was married.

Rule II—The dash is frequently used before words repeated in an emphatic manner.

Ex.—Why should I speak of his neglect—*neglect* did I say? Call it rather *contempt.*

Rule III—The dash is frequently placed both before and after parenthetical words instead of parentheses. Dashes indicate a less-severe grammatical break than do parentheses, but one more definite than commas.

Ex.—They see three of the cardinal virtues of dog or man—courage, endurance, and skill—in intense action.

Rule IV—Dashes can often be used instead of colons and semi-colons to produce a softer, smoother sentence.

Ex.—Special high schools have been set up in some cities—New York, Cleveland and Chicago.

249. THE MARKS OF PARENTHESIS

The **parentheses** include an expression which has no necessary con-nection, in sense or construction, with the sentence in which it is inserted.

Rem.—Such an expression is called a *parenthesis*, and the marks which surround it are called *parentheses*.

Rule—The parentheses should include those words which may be omitted without injury to the sense, or without affecting the gram-matical construction of the sentence.

Ex.—Shall we continue (alas, that I should be constrained to ask the ques-tion!) in a course so dangerous to health, so enfeebling to mind, so destruc-tive to character?

Rem. 1—When a comma is required after the word preceding a paren-thesis, it should be placed after the second parenthesis mark, as, "My gun was on my arm (as it always is in that district), but I let the weasel kill the rabbit."

Should the parenthesis be a question or an exclamatory expression, the question mark or exclamation point should go within the parentheses; as,

"She had managed this matter so well, (oh, she was the most artful of women!) that my father's heart was gone before I suspected it was in danger."

Rem. 2—The words included by the parentheses should be punctuated as an independent expression; as,

"The Frenchman, first in literary fame,
(Mention him, if you please. Voltaire?—The same).
With spirit, genius, eloquence supplied,
Lived long, wrote much, laughed heartily, and died."

Rem. 3—Final punctuation which affects the entire sentence goes outside the ending parentheses.

Rem. 4—The parentheses sometimes include letters or figures used to enumerate subjects or divisions of a subject, treated of in didactic or scientific works; as, "(a.) What it does; (b.) What it is." "The beds of the Jackson epoch, or Upper Eocene, are (1.) Lignitic clay; (2.) White and blue marls, the former often indurated." They are also used to include references; as, "(See page 21)."

EXERCISES

Insert the dash and parentheses wherever required in these sentences.

1. He had a large blunt head his muzzle black as night, his mouth blacker than any night a tooth or two, being all he had, gleaming out of his jaws of darkness. 2. The faithful man acts not from impulse but from conviction, conviction of duty the most stringent, solemn, and inspiring conviction that can sway the mind. 3. The Egyptian style of architecture see Dr. Pocock, not his discourses but his prints was apparently the mother of the Greek.

250. BRACKETS

Brackets are used to enclose words, phrases, and clauses explanatory of what precedes them, or to correct an error.

Ex.—1. They [the Indians] are fast disappearing. 2. I wish you would do like [as] I do.

251. OTHER MARKS USED IN WRITING

I. The **apostrophe** ['] is used to denote the omission of one or more letters, or to mark the possessive case.

Ex.—1. You're overwatched, my lord. 2. Variety's the very spice of life. 3. The King's English. 4. Webster's Dictionary.

Rem.—The apostrophe is also used in forming the plurals of letters, figures, marks, etc., as, "Dot your *i*'s and cross your *t*'s." "Cast out the 9's."

II. The **hyphen** [-] is used (1) to join the parts of compound words and expressions; (2) to divide words into syllables; (3) after a syllable at the end of a line when the rest of the word is carried to the next line.

Ex.—1. Heaven-born band. 2. Thou seven-headed monster thing. 3. He is my father-in-law, and always wears a pepper-and-salt suit. 4. Com-mu-ni-ca-tive-ness.

Rem.—When two or more similar adjectives precede a noun they should be hyphenated, except when the adjective ends in "y"; as, The blue-green sea. But when these adjectives are dissimilar, a comma is used; as, The cold, dark night. Use caution that you do not punctuate an adverb-adjective combination as if they were two adjectives; as, The dark [adv.] green [adj.] sea. (No hyphen, since "dark" modifies "green," not "sea.")

III. The **quotation marks** [" "] are used to show that a passage is taken *verbatim* from some author, or in dialogue to show the exact words of a speaker.

Ex.—Cowper says, "Slaves cannot breathe in England." "Dinner is ready," called Mother.

Rem. 1—A quotation included within another should be preceded by a single inverted comma, and closed by a single apostrophe; as, " 'War, war,' is still the cry, 'war even to the knife.' "

Rem. 2—When an author or speaker is paraphrased or not quoted directly, no quotation marks are used. Do not use quotes following "that."

Ex.—Mother said that dinner is ready.

Rem. 3—Do not use quotation marks merely to embellish words. It is improper to place them around slang terms, cliches, items on a restaurant menu, or slogans in an advertisement, for instance. Such sloppy use of quotation marks merely calls attention to indecisive, imprecise writing.

Rem. 4—Quotation marks may be used to enclose words, phrases, or sentences under discussion when they are run into the text.

Ex.—The verb "to be" is irregular. "Never did no" is a double negative construction once used for emphasis by good writers, though currently held to be incorrect.

Rem. 5—Quotation marks with other punctuation: Periods and commas always go inside quotation marks; semicolons and colons always stand outside. Question marks go within the quotes if the entire clause is a question;

outside if only the quoted material is a question. Exclamation points follow the rule for question marks.

Ex.—Did the salesman say, "I'll give you a year's free repair service"? Did the salesman say, "Will you accept a year's free repair service"?

Rem. 6—Quotation marks should be placed around titles of magazine articles and short stories.

Ex.—"The Man Behind the Manifesto," by McCandlish Phillips, appears on pages 10-12 of the January 1982 issue of *Moody Monthly*.

IV. The **asterisk** [*] refers to notes in the margin or at the bottom of the page.

V. A row of three spaced periods [. . .] indicates words omitted from a quoted sentence. Four spaced periods [. . . .] indicates one or more sentences omitted from a quoted paragraph, as in a research assignment.

VI. The **brace** [{ }] connects a number of words with a common term.

VII. The **tilde** [ñ]—a Spanish mark placed over *n*—annexes to it the sound of *y*; as, *cañon*, pronounced *can-yon*.

VIII. The **cedilla** [ç],—a French mark, joined to *c*,—gives to this letter the sound of *s*; as, *façade*.

Note to Teachers—Exercises in punctuation may be selected from the Readers in general use. Require pupils to give rules or cite remarks for the use of all the points they may find. Select, also, passages from good contemporary authors, and pronounce the words in consecutive order, slowly and distinctly, as in a spelling lesson, without indicating the grammatical construction by tone or inflection. Require pupils to write these as pronounced, and to separate them into sentences and parts of sentences by the proper points.

Punctuate properly the following examples, dividing into paragraphs as needed, and observe the rules for the use of capitals.

What tubero did that naked sword of yours mean in the battle of pharsalia at whose breast was its point aimed what was then the meaning of your arms your spirit your eyes your hands your ardor of soul what did you desire what wish for I press the youth too much he seems disturbed let me return to myself I too bore arms on the same side *cicero*

presently my soul grew stronger hesitating then no longer
sir said I or madam truly your forgiveness I implore
but the fact is I was napping and so gently you came rapping
and so faintly you came tapping tapping at my chamber door
that I scarce was sure I heard you here I opened wide the
    door darkness there and nothing more *poe*

PART IV

PROSODY

252. DEFINITIONS

1. **Prosody** deals with the quantity of syllables, of accent, and of the laws of versification.

2. A **verse** is a line of poetry consisting of a certain number of accented and unaccented syllables, arranged according to metrical rules.

3. **Versification** is the art of metrical composition.

4. **Discourse** is written either in *prose* or *verse*.

5. **Prose** is discourse written in language as ordinarily used, having reference, mainly, to a clear and distinct statement of the author's meaning.

6. **Poetry** is discourse written in metrical language. Its aim is to please, by addressing the imagination and the sensibilities.

7. Poetry is written either in *rhyme* or *blank verse*.

8. **Rhyme** is a correspondence of sound in the last syllables of two or more lines, succeeding each other immediately or at no great distance.

> **Ex.**—"Onward its course the present *keeps*;
> Onward the constant current *sweeps*."

Rem. 1—*Perfect rhymes* require: (1) that the syllables be accented and that the vowel sounds be the same; (2) that the sounds following the vowels be the same; (3) that the sounds preceding the vowels be different.

The student who wishes to write poetry should consult the vocabulary of rhymes found in the appendixes of many unabridged and collegiate dictionaries. To trust one's own ear in rhyme will inevitably result in imperfect rhymes.

> **Ex.**—*Talk* and *walk*, *town* and *crown*, are perfect rhymes. *Breathe* and *teeth*, *home* and *come*, are imperfect rhymes.

Rem. 2—A *single rhyme* is an accented syllable standing alone at the end of a line; as, *mind, refined*. A *double rhyme* consists of an accented syllable, followed by an unaccented one; as, *dreaming*, seeming. A *triple rhyme* consists of an accented syllable, followed by two unaccented ones; as, *fearfully, cheerfully*.

Rem. 3—A **couplet**, or *distich*, consists of two lines rhyming together. A **triplet** consists of three lines rhyming together.

Rem. 4—*Middle rhyme* is that which exists between the last accented syllables of the two sections of a verse or line.

Ex.—"We were the *first* that ever *burst*
Into that silent sea."—*Coleridge*.

9. **Blank verse** is verse without rhyme.

10. A **stanza** is a group of lines forming a division of a poem.

253. POETIC FEET

1. A **foot** is a certain portion of a line in poetry, combined according to *accent*.

2. **Accent** is a stress of voice on a certain syllable of a word or foot.

Rem. 1—In Greek and Latin, verse is made according to the *quantity* of syllables; *i.e.*, the relative time employed in pronouncing them. A *long* syllable requires twice the time in uttering it that a *short* one requires.

In English, verse is composed wholly according to accent. An accented syllable is considered *long*; an unaccented syllable, *short*.

Rem. 2—In poetry, monosyllables receive accent.

Ex.—And *to'* | and *fro'*, | and *in'* | and *out'*.

3. The principal feet used in English verse, are the *iambus*, the *trochee*, the *spondee*, the *pyrrhic*, the *anapest*, the *dactyl*, and the *amphibrach*.

Rem.—In the formulas, an accented, or long syllable, is represented by *a*; an unaccented, or short syllable, by *u*.

4. The **iambus** consists of an unaccented and an accented syllable. Its formula is *u a*. The iambus is the most common metrical measure in English verse.

Ex.—"A mind' | not to' | be changed' | by place' | or time'."

5. The **trochee** consists of an accented and an unaccented syllable. Its formula is *a u*.

Ex.—"Ru 'in | seize ' thee, | ruth 'less | king '."

6. The **spondee** consists of two accented syllables. Its formula is *a a*.

Ex.—"Rocks ', caves ', | lakes ', fens ', | bogs ', dens ', | and shades ' | of death '."

7. The **pyrrhic** consists of two unaccented syllables. Its formula is *u u*.

Rem.—The pyrrhic is sometimes used in iambic verse, to avoid accenting an unimportant word.

Ex.—"What could ' | be less ' | *than to* | afford ' | him praise '?"

8. The **anapest** consists of two unaccented and an accented syllable. Its formula is *u u a*.

Ex.—"All at once ' | and all o'er ' | with a might '- | y uproar '."

9. The **dactyl** consists of one accented and two unaccented syllables. Its formula is *a u u*.

Ex.—"Heed ' not the | corpse ', though a | king's ' in your | path '."

10. The **amphibrach** consists of one unaccented, one accented, and one unaccented syllable. Its formula is *u a u*.

Ex.—"A pret 'ti- | er din 'ner | I nev 'er | set eyes ' on."

11. A long or accented syllable used as one foot, is called a **caesura**.

Ex.—Gold ', | gold ', | gold ', | gold '!

12. A foot of three unaccented syllables is called a **tribrach**. It is rarely found in English poetry.

Rem. 1—The iambus and the anapest are interchangeable.

Ex.—"There were grace '-|ful heads ', | with their ring '-|lets bright '."

Rem. 2—The trochee and the dactyl are also interchangeable.

Ex.—   "Joy ' to the | spir 'it ' | came ',
Through ' the wide | rent ' in | Time's e- | ter 'nal | veil '."

Rem. 3—The following lines, by Samuel Taylor Coleridge, will assist in remembering the character of the different kinds of feet:

"**Tro'chees** | trip ' from | long ' to | short '.
From long ' | to long ', | in sol '- | emn sort, '
Slow ' **Spon'** | **dee'** stalks '; | strong ' foot ', yet | ill ' able
Ev 'er to | come ' up with | **Dac'tyl** tri- | syl 'lable.
Iam' | **bics** march ' | from short ' | to long '.
With a leap ' | and a bound ', | the swift **An'** | **apests** throng '.
One syl 'la | ble long ', with | one short ' at | each side ',
Anphi'brach- | **ys** hastes ' with | a state 'ly | stride.'"

254. KINDS OF VERSE

1. Verse is named from the kind of foot which predominates in a line; as, the *iambic*, from the iambus; the *trochaic*, from the trochee; the *anapestic*, from the anapest; the *dactylic*, from the dactyl.

2. A verse containing one foot is called a *monometer*; one containing two, a *dimeter*; one containing three, a *trimeter*; one containing four, a *tetrameter*; one containing five, a *pentameter*; one containing six, a *hexameter*; one containing seven, a *heptameter*; and one containing eight, an *octometer*.

3. Verse, therefore, may be *iambic monometer, iambic dimeter,* etc., *trochaic monometer, trochaic dimeter,* etc.; *anapestic monometer, anapestic dimeter,* etc.; *dactylic monometer, dactylic dimeter,* etc.

4. A verse or foot in which a syllable is wanting at the end is called *catalectic*; a full verse or foot is called *acatalectic*; a verse or foot in which a syllable is wanting at the beginning is called *acephalous*; a line which has a redundant syllable at the end is called *hypermeter* or *hypercatalectic*.

255. POETIC PAUSES

1. There are two pauses in every verse: a *final* and a *caesural*.

2. The **final pause** is a pause made at the end of a line, in reading.

3. The **caesural pause** is a pause in a verse.

Rem.—The caesural pause is a natural suspension of the voice in reading. The shorter kinds of verse are without it. Its natural place is near the middle of the line; but the sense often requires that it be placed elsewhere.

Ex.—"Warms in the sun, || refreshes in the breeze,
　　　Glows in the stars, || and blossoms in the trees."—*Pope.*

　　　"And on the sightless eyeballs || pour the day."

256. IAMBIC MEASURES

1. *Iambic monometer. . . u a*
　　Invite '
　　Delight '

2. *Iambic dimeter . .u a* × 2.
　　And called ' | the brave '
　　To blood '- | y grave '.

3. *Iambic trimeter . . . . u a* × 3.
　　What sought ' | they thus ' | afar '?
　　Bright jew '- | els of ' | the mind '?

4. *Iambic tetrameter . . . u a* × 4.
　　Majes ' | tic mon '- | arch of ' | the cloud '!
　　Who rear'st ' | aloft ' | thy re '- | gal form '.

5. *Iambic pentameter . . . u a × 5.*

> O then ', | methought ', | what pain ' | it was ' | to drown '!
> What dread '- | ful noise ' | of wa '- | ters in ' | my ears '!

Rem.—This is often called **heroic measure**, because *epic* or *heroic* poetry is written in it. Rhymed iambic pentameter is sometimes called **heroic couplet**. Heroic verse was used by such important poets as Chaucer, Dryden, Byron, and Alexander Pope. Pope's heroic couplets set a pattern which dominated English verse in the 18th century.

Ex.—But when ' | to mis ' | chief mor ' | tals bend ' | their will ',
> How soon ' | they find ' | fit in ' | struments ' | of ill '!

6. *Iambic hexameter . . . u a × 6.*

> Our sweet ' | est songs ' | are those ' | which tell ' | of sad '-
> | dest thought '.

Rem.—This verse is called **alexandrine**.

7. *Iambic heptameter . . . u a × 7.*

> How hard ' | when those ' | who do ' | not wish ' | to lend ', |
>   thus lose ', | their books ',
> Are snared ' | by an '- | glers,—folks ' | that fish ' | with lit '- |
>   era '- | ry hooks '!

8. **Long meter** is iambic tetrameter, arranged in stanzas of four lines, rhyming in couplets or alternately.

Ex.—Praise God ' | from whom ' | all bless '- | ings flow ':
> Praise him ' | all creat '- | ures here ' | below ';
> Praise him ' | above ', | ye heaven '- | ly host ';
> Praise Fath '- | er, Son ', | and Ho '- | ly Ghost '.

9. **Common meter** is a stanza of four iambic lines, the first and third being tetrameter; the second and fourth, trimeter.

Ex.—Come let ' | us join ' | our cheer '- | ful songs ',
> With an ' | gels round ' | the throne ':
> Ten thou '- | sand thou '- | sand are ' | their tongues ',
> But all ' | their joys ' | are one '.

10. **Short meter** is a stanza of four iambic lines, the first, second, and fourth being trimeter; the third, tetrameter.

Ex.—There sin ' | and sor '- | row cease ',
> And ev '- | ery con '- | flict's o'er ';
> There we ' | shall dwell ' | in end '- | less peace,
> Nor thirst ' | nor hun '- | ger more '.

11. **Hallelujah meter** is a stanza of six iamibc lines, the first four being trimeter; the last two, tetrameter.

> **Ex.**—Now may ' | the king ' | descend ',
>   And fill ' | his throne ' | of grace ';
> Thy scep '- | ter, Lord '! | extend ',
>   While saints ' | address ' | thy face ':
> Let sin '- | ners feel ' | thy quick '- | 'ning word ',
> And learn ' | to know ' | and fear ' | the Lord '.

Rem.—The last two lines are frequently separated into four, containing two iambics each.

12. The **elegiac stanza** consists of four iambic lines, rhyming alternately, with the formula *u a* × 5. (See Gray's *Elegy*.)

13. The **Spenserian stanza** consists of nine iambic lines, the first eight having the formula *u a* × 5, the last, *u a* × 6; the first and third rhyming; the second, fourth, fifth, and seventh; and the sixth, eighth, and ninth. (See Spenser's *Faerie Queene*.)

14. A **sonnet** is a poem complete in fourteen iambic lines. Its formula is *u a* × 5.

15. **Iambic hypermeters.**

u a + ... Relent '- | ing.
u a × 2 + . . . Thine eye '- | lids quiv '- |er.
u a × 3 + . . . 'Tis sweet ' | to love ' | in child '- | hood.
u a × 4 + . . . What seek ' | ye from ' | the fields ' | of heav '- | en?
u a × 5 + . . . The air ' | is full ' | of fare '- | wells to ' | the dy '- | ing.
u a × 6 + . . . Thine eye ' | Jove's light '- | ning seems ', | thy voice ' |
            his dread '- | ful thun '- | der.
u a × 7 + . . . I think ' | I will ' | not go ' | with you ' | to hear ' |
            the toasts ' | and speech '- |es.

257. TROCHAIC MEASURES

1. *Trochaic monometer . a u*
    Chang 'ing,
    Rang 'ing

2. *Trochaic dimeter. . .a u* × 2.
    Hope ' is | van 'ished,
    Joys ' are | ban 'ished

3. *Trochaic trimeter . . . a u* × 3.
    Then ' let | mem'ry | bring ' thee
    Strains ' I | used ' to | sing ' thee.

4. *Trochaic tetrameter . . . a u* × 4.

    Tell ' me | not ' in | mourn 'ful | num 'bers,
    Life ' is | but ' an | emp 'ty | dream '.

5. *Trochaic pentameter* . . . . *a u* × 5.

> Nar 'rowing | in 'to | where ' they | sat·' as- | sem 'bled,
> Low 'vo- | lup 'tuous | mu 'sic | wind 'ing | trem 'bled.

6. *Trochaic hexameter* . . . . . *a u* × 6.

> On ' a | mount 'ain | stretched ' be- | neath ' a | hoar 'y | wil 'low,
> Lay ' a | shep 'herd | swain ', and | viewed ' the | roll 'ing | bil 'low.

7. *Trochaic heptameter* . . . . *a u* × 7.

> In ' the | spring ' a | fee 'ble | crim 'son | comes ' up- | on ' the |
> rob 'in's | breast '.

8. *Trochaic hypermeters.*

a u + ... Mer 'ry | May '.
a u × 2 + . . . All ' that's | bright ' must | fade '.
a u × 3 + . . . Chill 'y | win 'ter's | gone ' a- | way '.
a u × 4 + . . . I 'dle | af 'ter | din 'ner | in ' his | chair '.
a u × 5 + . . . Hail ' to | thee ', blithe | spir 'it! | bird ', thou |
nev 'er | wert '.
a u × 6 + . . . Half ' the | charms ' to | me ' it | yield 'eth, | mon 'ey |
can 'not | buy '.
a u × 7 + . . . Bet 'ter | fif 'ty | years ' of | Eu 'rope | than ' a | cy 'cle |
of ' Cath- | ay '.

258. ANAPESTIC MEASURES

1. *Anapestic monometer* . . . . *u u a.*

Move your feet '
To our sound '.

2. *Anapestic dimeter* . . . . . *u u a* × 2.

In my rage ', | shall be seen '
The revenge ' | of a queen '.

3. *Anapestic trimeter* . . . . . *u u a* × 3.

I have found ' | out a gift ' | for my fair ';
I have found ' | where the wood '- | pigeons breed '.

4. *Anapestic tetrameter* . . . . . *u u a* × 4.

Through the ranks ' | of the Sax '- | ons he hew'd ' | his red way '.

Rem.—The first foot of an anapestic verse may be an iambus.

Ex.—Our life ' | is a dream '.

5. *Anapestic hypermeters.*

u u a × 2 + . . . Like the dew ' | on the moun '- | tain.

u u a × 3 + . . . Give their roof ' | to the flame ', | and their flesh ' |
to the ea '- | gles.

259. DACTYLIC MEASURES

1. *Dactylic monometer a u u.*
    Fear 'fully
    Tear 'fully

2. *Dactylic dimeter a u u* × 2.
    Cor 'al reefs | un 'der her,
    Read 'y to | sun 'der her

3. *Dactylic trimeter* . . . . .*a u u* × 3.

    Wear 'ing a- | way ' in his | use 'fulness,
    Love 'liness, | beau 'ty, and | truth 'fulness

4. *Dactylic tetrameter* . . . . . *a u u* × 4.

    Boy ' will an- | tic 'ipate, | lav 'ish, and | dis 'sipate
    All ' that your | bu 'sy pate | hoard 'ed with | care.

5. *Dactylic hexameter* . . . . . *a u u* × 5 + *a u.*

    List ' to the | mourn 'ful tra- | di 'tion still | sung ' by the |
    pines ' of the | for 'est.

Rem.—A dactylic verse rarely ends with a dactyl. It is sometimes catalectic, or ends with a trochee; sometimes hypermeter, or ends with a long syllable.

Ex.—Bright 'est and | best ' of the | sons ' of the | morn 'ing,
    Dawn ' on our | dark 'ness, and | lend ' us thine | aid '.

260. AMPHIBRACH MEASURES

1. *Amphibrach monometer* . . . *u a u.*

    Hearts beat 'ing
    At meet 'ing
    Tears start 'ing
    At part 'ing

2. *Amphibrach dimeter* . . . . *u a u* × 2.

    O would ' I | were dead ' now,
    Or up ' in | my bed ' now.

3. *Amphibrach trimeter* . . . . *u a u* × 3.

    A breath ' of | submis 'sion | we breathe ' not;
    The sword ' we | have drawn ', we | will sheathe ' not

4. *Amphibrach trimeter catalectic* . . . . *u a u* × 3.

>   Ye shep 'herds | so cheer 'ful | and gay ',
>   Whose flocks ' nev- | er care 'less- | ly roam '

5. *Amphibrach tetrameter* . . . . . *u a u* × 4.

>   The flesh ' was | a pict 'ure | for paint 'ers | to stud 'y,
>   The fat ' was | so white ', and | the lean ' was | so rud 'dy.

6. *Amphibrach tetrameter catalectic* . . . . . *u a u* × 4.

>   But hang ' it,— | to po 'ets | who sel 'dom | can eat ',
>   Your ver 'y | good mut 'ton's | a ver 'y | good treat '.

261. MIXED VERSE

Different measures are frequently used in the same poem.

Tell what feet compose each line of the following example.

>   Merrily swinging on briar and weed,
>   Near to the nest of his little dame,
>   Over the mountain side or mead,
>   Robert of Lincoln is telling his name,
>   Bob-o-link, Bob-o-link;
>   Spink, spank, spink;
>   Snug and safe is that nest of ours,
>   Hidden among the summer flowers.
>   Chee, chee, chee.—*Bryant.*

262. POETIC LICENSE

Poetic license is an indulgence in the use of peculiar words, forms, and expressions, allowed to poets by common consent.

Rem. 1—Poetic license permits the use of antiquated words and phrases, foreign words and idioms, common words shortened, lengthened, or changed in pronunciation, and any ellipsis that will not destroy the sense.

Ex.—*Eke* (also), *erst, eyne, eve, beweep, evanish, albeit, fount, trow, hight* (called), *vastly, wis, ween, wight* (person), etc. "A train-band captain *eke* was he." "His timeless death *beweeping*." "[He] Who steals my purse, steals trash." "Like [a] shipwrecked mariner on [a] desert coast."

Rem. 2—It permits a transitive use of intransitive verbs.

Ex.—They *lived* the rural *day*, and *talked* the flowing *heart*.

Rem. 3—Poets make use of an inverted order of arrangement more frequently than prose writers.

Ex. — "*Sunk* was the *sun*." "The rattling *crags among*."

263. SCANNING

Scanning is an analysis of versification. To *scan* a line is to divide it into the feet of which it is composed.

EXERCISES

1. Sweet day! so cool, so calm, so bright,
   The bridal of the earth and sky;
   The dews shall weep thy fall tonight;
   For thou must die.—*Herbert*.

2.   Under the greenwood tree
   Who loves to lie with me
   And tune his merry note
   Unto the sweet bird's throat
   Come hither, come hither, come hither!
      Here shall he see no enemy
   But winter and rough weather.—*Shakespeare*.

3. Nature, attend! join, every living soul,
   Beneath the spacious temple of the sky;
   In adoration join; and, ardent, raise
   One general song! To Him, ye vocal gales,
   Breathe soft, whose Spirit in your freshness breathes;
   Oh, talk of Him in solitary glooms,
   Where, o'er the rock, the scarcely waving pine
   Fills the brown shade with a religious awe.—*Thomson*.

4. With fruitless labor, Clara bound
   And strove to stanch the gushing wound:
   The Monk, with unavailing cares,
   Exhausted all the church's prayers:
   Ever, he said, that, close and near,
   A lady's voice was in his ear,
   And that the priest he could not hear,
      For that she ever sung,
   "In the lost battle, borne down by the flying,
   Where mingles war's rattle with groans of the
      dying!"
      So the notes rung.—*Scott*.

5.   Bird of the wilderness,
       Blithesome and cumberless,
  Sweet be thy matin o'er moorland and lea!
       Emblem of happiness,
       Blest is thy dwelling place—
  Oh to abide in the desert with thee!—*Hogg.*

6. Full many a gem of purest ray serene,
     The dark, unfathomed caves of ocean bear;
  Full many a flower is born to blush unseen,
     And waste its sweetness on the desert air.—*Gray.*

7. Thou art—directing, guiding all—Thou art!
     Direct my understanding, then, to Thee;
  Control my spirit, guide my wandering heart,
     Though but an atom midst immensity,
  Still I am something fashioned by thy hand!
     I hold a middle rank 'twixt heaven and earth,
  On the last verge of mortal being stand,
     Close to the realms where angels have their birth,
  Just on the boundaries of the spirit land.—*Derzhaven.*

DIAGRAMS

264. EXPLANATION

1. In the following diagrams, the subject, the predicate, and the copula of each principal proposition are placed above a horizontal baseline.

2. The subject is separated from the predicate or the copula by a vertical line drawn across this baseline. (See Diagrams I and II.)

3. The copula is separated from the predicate by a colon. (See Diagrams I and II.)

4. The objective element and the term which it modifies are separated by a vertical line drawn to the horizontal line below them. (See Diagrams IV, XXIX, and XXXIV.)

5. An indirect object is placed on a horizontal line above a direct object. (See Diagram IX.)

6. An object denoting a person or thing is placed above one denoting the rank, office, or character of the person or the species of the thing. (See Diagram XI.)

7. A noun or an adjective following the infinitive or participle of a copulative verb is separated from it by a dash. (See Diagrams XXXIV and XLVII.)

8. An adjective or adverbial element is placed below the term which it modifies, and in the angle formed by a vertical and a horizontal line. Several elements of the same kind may sometimes be placed in the same angle. (See Diagrams XIII and XIV.)

9. Coordinate conjunctions are printed in italics. They should be underscored in written diagrams. (See Diagrams XX, XXIV, and XLI.)

10. Subordinate conjunctions, when not used as conjunctive adverbs, are enclosed by parentheses. (See Diagrams XXXV and XXXVI.)

11. Conjunctive adverbs are printed in italics and enclosed by parentheses. (See Diagram XXXIX.)

12. Expletives and other attendant elements are placed on horizontal lines not connected with lines in the diagrams. (See Diagrams IX and XVIII.)

13. Words supplied are enclosed by brackets. (See Diagrams XXX and XXVI.)

SIMPLE SENTENCES

I. Glass is transparent.   II. John looks cold.

Glass | is : transparent   John | looks : cold

III. Birds sing.   IV. Farmers sow grain.

Birds | sing   Farmers | sow | grain

V. The steamship Hibernia has arrived.
VI. My brother broke Eli's skate.

VII. The sun shines brightly.
VIII. He is not handsome.

```
sun    |    shines              He  | is : handsome
  | The  |       brightly             |  | not
```

IX. King Agrippa, believest thou the prophets?
X. My father gave me a good book.

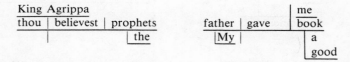

```
King Agrippa                                          me
thou | believest | prophets      father | gave     book
       |          | the            | My  |         a
                                                   good
```

Note—The places which direct and indirect objects should occupy in diagrams are indicated in Diagram X. The indirect object "me" is placed above the direct object "book," and a line is drawn between them.

XI. They have chosen Mr. Ames speaker.
XII. He was elected president.

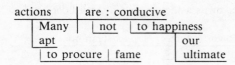

```
They | have chosen /Mr. Ames      He | was elected : president
   |              \speaker           |
```

XIII. A life of prayer is a life of heaven.

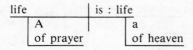

```
life              | is : life
      A           |     a
      of prayer   |     of heaven
```

XIV. Many actions apt to procure fame are not conducive to our ultimate happiness.

```
actions    | are : conducive
    Many   |  | not  | to happiness
    apt    |              our
      | to procure | fame    ultimate
```

XV. I will go tomorrow.   XVI. That is worthwhile.

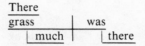   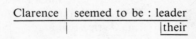

XVII. There was much grass there.
XVIII. Clarence seemed to be their leader.

```
There                                 Clarence │ seemed to be : leader
grass          │   was                         │              │their
    │ much     │       │ there
```

Note—"Seemed to be" is a complex or strengthened copula. "To be" is an adverbial element modifying "seemed." (See Section 186, Model XXIII.)

XIX. Industry, honesty, and economy generally insure success.
XX. I alone was solitary and idle.

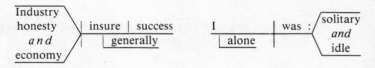

XXI. He came and went like a pleasant thought.

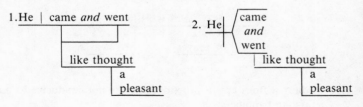

XXII. My father owns a factory and a steamboat.

```
father │ owns │ factory │ and steamboat
   │My │          │ a          │ a
```

XXIII. I want to be loved and to be lovely.
XXIV. Give me neither poverty nor riches.

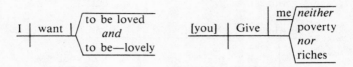

Note—"Neither" introduces the compound direct objective element; "nor" connects the two nouns "poverty" and "riches."

XXV. The soldiers fought bravely and successfully.

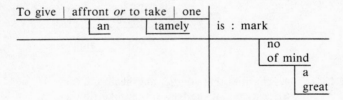

XXVI. To give an affront or to take one tamely is no mark of a great mind.

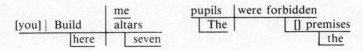

XXVII. Build me here seven altars.
XXVIII. The pupils were forbidden the premises.

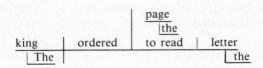

XXIX. The king ordered the page to read the letter.

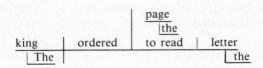

COMPLEX SENTENCES

XXX. The credulity which has faith in goodness is a sign of goodness.

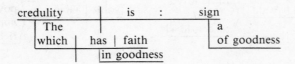

XXXI. That the earth is round was not then believed.

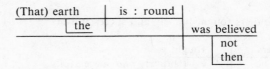

XXXII. Except ye repent, ye shall all likewise perish.

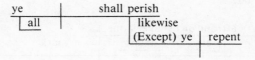

XXXIII. The charities that soothe, and heal, and bless
Are scattered at the feet of men like flowers.

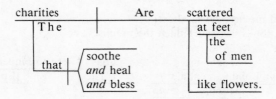

Rem.—Diagram XXXIII, and several others, are poetry. For this reason each line begins with a capital letter, though it may not always begin a new sentence.

XXXIV. The gentleman who was dressed in brown-once-black, had a sort of medico-theological exterior, which we afterwards found to be representative of the inward man.

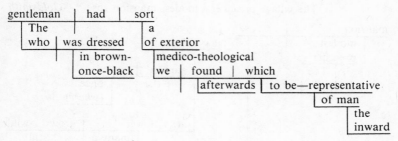

XXXV.   He spake as one having authority.

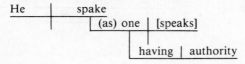

XXXVI.   He is worth more than you.

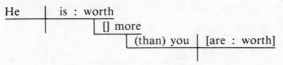

Note—In this sentence "more" is an adjective used as a noun. As an adjective, it can be modified by the adverbial element introduced by "than."

XXXVII.   He who does as he lists, without regard to the wishes of others, will soon cease to do well.

XXXVIII. The more I see him, the better I like him.

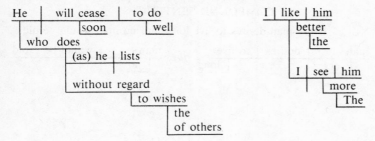

XXXIX.　"Near yonder copse, where once the garden smiled,
　　　　　And still where many a garden flower grows wild,
　　　　　There, where a few torn shrubs the place disclose,
　　　　　The village preacher's modest mansion rose."—*Goldsmith*

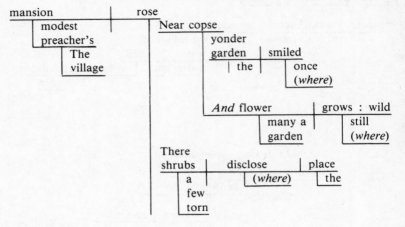

XL.　He was a man to all the country dear,
　　　And passing rich with forty pounds a year.

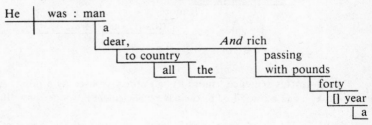

COMPOUND SENTENCES

XLI.　Every man desires to live long; but no man would be old.

man	desires	to live		man	would be : old
Every		long	*but*	no	

XLII.   Night's candles are burnt out, and jocund Day
         Stands tiptoe on the misty mountain's top.

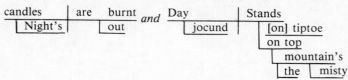

XLIII.   Talent is power; tact is skill.

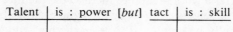

ABRIDGED PROPOSITIONS

XLIV.   I know him to be a sailor.

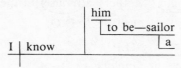

Note—The abridged proposition, "him to be a sailor," is the object of "know." Instead of a rule, apply the first part of Rem. 1, Section 206, in parsing "him" and "sailor."

XLV.   I was aware of his being my enemy.

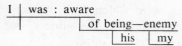

XLVI.   The shower having passed, we pursued our journey.

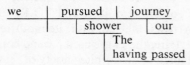

Note—"The shower having passed" is an abridged proposition modifying "pursued." It is equivalent to "when the shower had passed," (See Section 207, Model XXXVIII.)

XLVII.   His being an outlaw was not known to his companions.

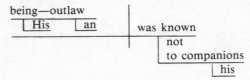

265. DIAGRAMS — ANOTHER METHOD

Those who prefer a whole-sentence method of teaching word relationships within the sentence can study the sample shown below. This method can usefully be employed to test whether students understand the relationships of the sentence's parts.

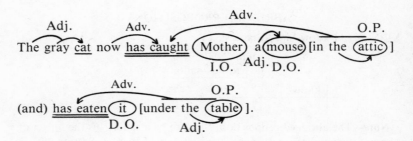

Notice that verbs and their helpers are underlined twice. This should be done before the nouns are identified, since the verb determines the subject; i.e. the noun which does the action of "has caught/has eaten" must be seen to be the subject, *not* any other noun. The subject is then underlined once.

Prepositional and verbal phrases are enclosed in brackets; the pupil who does so thereby shows that he understands where the phrase begins and terminates. Objects are circled and labeled, "I.O." for indirect object, "D.O." for direct object, and "O.P." for object of the preposition, etc. Arrows, labeled, indicate modifiers and the words which they modify. Parentheses are used around conjunctions.

This method can be adapted to an infinite variety of sentences and modified to suit the teacher. In practice, it has been shown to be an effective means of teaching grammar. Some teachers may wish to begin with this whole-sentence method, then introduce diagramming at a later date.